FIFTH CANADIAN EDITI

SIMON & SCHUSTER WORKBOOK FOR WRITERS

Lynn Quitman Troyka
Douglas Hesse

Updated by
Cy Strom

Peggy Jolly
University of Alabama at Birmingham

Dorothy Minor
Tulsa Community College

Leslie Leach
College of the Redwoods

Pearson Canada
Toronto

ISBN-13: 978-0-13-607270-6
ISBN-10: 0-13-607270-4

Acquisitions Editor: David S. Le Gallais
Sponsoring Editor: Carolin Sweig
Supervising Developmental Editor: Suzanne Schaan
Managing Editor: Söğüt Y. Güleç
Production Manager: Peggy Brown
Page Layout: Deanne Walle
Permissions Research: Amanda McCormick

1 2 3 4 5 13 12 11 10 09

Printed and bound in the United States of America.

CONTENTS

***Please note:** There are no *Workbook* exercises that correspond to Chapters 7, 8, and 10–12 of the *Simon & Schuster Handbook for Writers*, Fifth Canadian Edition.

***Please note:** There are no *Workbook* exercises that correspond to Chapters 45 and 46 of the *Simon & Schuster Handbook for Writers*, Fifth Canadian Edition.

Preface

The *Simon & Schuster Workbook for Writers*, Fifth Canadian Edition, contains exercises and writing activities that parallel its parent, the *Simon & Schuster Handbook for Writers*. The workbook offers numerous opportunities for practice, including

- Thorough coverage of all basic topics—grammar, punctuation, mechanics, the writing process, and critical thinking.
- Exercises on specific ESL concerns.
- Exercises on integrating quotations and writing paraphrases and summaries—topics not usually included in writing workbooks.
- Sequenced exercises that lead students to independent work so that students progress from simple tasks (such as identifying sentence elements) to guided writing (such as sentence combining) to original sentences, paragraphs, and essays.
- Exercise content in connected discourse to replicate more closely the activities of revising and editing real writing. The topics from across the curriculum engage interest.

PART ONE: THE WRITING PROCESS

Adapting to Your Audience and Purpose

EXERCISE 1-1
(1b–c)

Look at this picture of an earthquake. Describe the scene as part of your response to each of the four different audiences described below. Use your own paper.

1. You have just seen a news report of a serious earthquake in South America. Some people are still trapped in the wreckage, while thousands are in need of shelter, food, and medical help. You work for a charity that offers rapid response volunteers in situations like this. Prepare a statement to be read out on local TV and radio that explains the services your organization offers and why people should donate money for an immediate relief mission to the area.
2. You recently moved to Victoria, British Columbia. Your grandmother is concerned about earthquake activity in the Pacific Rim and is worried about you. She doesn't know how you can live in a place where disaster might strike at any time. Write back explaining your attitude to this risk. Reassure her that you are taking what precautions you can and that, in the event of any tremors, you would know what to do.
3. While on a Study Abroad program recently, you were caught up in an earthquake that totalled the school building yet, miraculously, cost no lives. Write a short piece for your school's newspaper detailing this experience.

4. Your business is opening a branch in a region that is prone to earthquakes. The photograph shows an earthquake that struck several years ago in the city that your new office building will locate in. Write a letter to the contractor that is responsible for the construction of your office building, outlining your concerns and requesting detailed information on local construction codes and the specific enhancements planned for your building to make it earthquake-resistant.

Using Idea-Gathering Techniques

EXERCISE 2-1
(2d–n)

Select four topics from this list, and prepare to write by narrowing each one. Use a different idea-gathering technique for each: freewriting, brainstorming, the journalist's questions, and mapping. Use your own paper, but record your narrowed topic on the line next to each subject you use.

1. celebrity ______________________________
2. someone I can count on ______________________________
3. travelling alone ______________________________
4. fitness ______________________________
5. online social networking sites ______________________________
6. breakfast ______________________________
7. the city ______________________________
8. my grandparents ______________________________
9. a personal loss ______________________________
10. choosing a computer ______________________________

Grouping and Ordering Ideas

EXERCISE 2-2
(2o–p)

Select two of the topics you explored in Exercise 2-2. For each, group ideas in clusters of related material and then order the clusters. Remember that not every item in an idea-generating exercise has to appear in the final essay. Feel free to omit items that do not fit your pattern. If there are gaps, return to idea-gathering techniques to get more material. Your end products will be informal outlines.

Writing Thesis Statements

EXERCISE 2-3

(2q)

A: Most of the following thesis statements are unacceptable because they are too broad or too narrow. Label each thesis *acceptable* or *unacceptable*. Then revise each unacceptable thesis to make it suitable for an essay of about 500 words.

EXAMPLE The United States is a nice place to visit.
Its nearness to Canada, its important cities and distinctive landscapes, and its cultural variety make the United States an attractive choice for a family vacation.

1. Planned budget cuts will do terrible damage to the university.

   ____

2. Many students do not study as much as they should.

   ____

3. My parents blame today's violence on movies, but I blame it on society.

   ____

4. I saw an interesting hockey game last week.

   ____

5. I fell in love when I was seventeen.

   ____

6. In interviews a job applicant should not beat around the bush.

   ____

7. The local mall is the focal point of many suburbs.

   ____

8. Remodelling an older home involves three major steps.

   ____

9. In May I visited Turkey.

   ____

10. The Battle of Vimy Ridge took place in 1917.

    ____

B: Write thesis statements for the four topics you narrowed in Exercise 2-1 and for six original topics. Be sure that each topic is suitably narrow for an essay of about 500 words and that the thesis statement shows a purpose and a point of view.

EXAMPLE Topic: *how shopping has been changed by the development of closed malls*

Thesis Statement: *The development of closed malls has led to a revolution in the way Canadians shop: We can shop easily at night and in rough weather; we see a greater variety of goods than in any single store, and we are encouraged to think of shopping as fun rather than as a chore.*

1. Topic ______________________________

   Thesis Statement ______________________________

2. Topic ______________________________

   Thesis Statement ______________________________

3. Topic ______________________________

   Thesis Statement ______________________________

4. Topic ______________________________

   Thesis Statement ______________________________

5. Topic ______________________________

   Thesis Statement ______________________________

6. Topic ______________________________

   Thesis Statement ______________________________

7. Topic ______________________________

   Thesis Statement ______________________________

8. Topic ______________________________

   Thesis Statement ______________________________

9. Topic ______________________________

   Thesis Statement ______________________________

10. Topic ______________________________

    Thesis Statement ______________________________

Planning a Formal Outline

EXERCISE 2-4
(2r)

The following topic outline contains twelve errors in form and logic. Revise the outline, using the guidelines listed in 2r. Draw a single line through each error and write your revision beside it.

Thesis Statement: Leaving a roommate for a single apartment can have definite drawbacks.

1. Unsatisfactory Furnishings
    A. Appliances
        1. Major
            a. Stove
            b. Refrigerator
        2. Minor
            a. Microwave
            b. Blender
            c. Toaster
            d. Mixer
        3. Washer
    B. Furniture
        1. Futon
        2. Living room
            a. Sofa
            b. Chairs
            c. Tables
        3. Kitchen
            a. Table
            b. Chairs
    C. Equipment
        1. For entertainment
            a. VCR
        2. Exercise

II. Not enough money to pay the bills
    A. Rent
    B. Utilities
        1. ISP
        2. Electricity
        3. Phone

C. Food
    1. Groceries
D. Entertainment

III. Inadequate companionship
    A. Loneliness is a frequent problem
    B. Occasional fear
    C. Friendly neighbours

Making a Formal Outline

EXERCISE 2-5

(2r)

Convert one of the informal outlines you developed in Exercise 2-2 into a formal outline. Write a sentence outline or a topic outline, but be sure not to mix the two types. Begin by placing the thesis statement you developed in Exercise 2-3B at the top of your page. Use the list of conventions in 2r for guidance and as a checklist when you are done.

Revising, Editing, and Proofreading Essays

EXERCISE 2-6

(2u–w)

A: Here is a middle draft of a short essay. It has already been revised, but it has not yet been edited. Edit the essay, using the editing checklist in 2v. If you like, you may also make additional revisions. When you are done, submit a carefully proofread copy of the completed essay to your instructor.

Forks, knives, and spoons seam so natural to most of us that its hard to imagine eaten dinner with out them. Yet many people, such as the chinese, use chopsticks instead, and other's use their hands to eat.

Knives are the oldest western utensils. The first ones were made of stone 1.5 million years ago. It was originally use to cut up dead animals after a hunt. The same knife were used to: butcher game slice cooked food, and kill enemies. Even later in History, nobles was the only ones who could afford separate knives for different uses. People use all-purpose knives, pointed like todays steak knives. The round-tipped dinner knife is a modern invention. It became popular in 17th cen. France because hosteses want to stop guests from picking they're teeth with the points of there dinner knives.

The spoon is also an anceint tool. Wooden spoons twenty thousand years old have been found in Asia; spoons of stone, wood, ivory, and even gold have been found in Egyptian tombs. Spoons scoop up foods that were to thick to sip from a bowl.

The fork is a newcomer. Forks did not become widely accepted until the eighteenth century; when the French nobility adopted the fork as a status symbol, and eating with ones hands became unfashionable. At about the same time, individual place settings became the rule to. Previous, even rich people had shared plates and glasses at meals, but know the rich demanded individual plates, glasses, forks, spoons, and knives. Today in North America, a full set of utensils is considered a necessity. We forget that as recently as the american revolution some people still considered anyone who use a fork to be a fussy showoff.

B: Here is the first draft of an essay. It needs a great deal of work, as most first drafts do. Revise the essay, using the revision checklist in 2u. Then edit your work, using the editing checklist in 2v. Finally, submit a carefully proofread copy of the completed essay.

A Canoe Trip

Last year I had an adventure of the sort that many people never experience in their lives, even though you may call it a typical Canadian experience, or at least a part of Canadian folklore. I went on a solo canoe trip to Northern Ontarios Temagami region. In this essay I will tell you my thoughts about going on a solo canoe trip and the benefits it had for both body and spirit.

I've been a pretty good canoeist since I was young. Nevertheless, when I told my friends of my intention to do solo trip, they replied that "Isn't that a dangerous thing your planning to do?" Admittedly, a solo trip may be dangerous. But many other sports and activites — including rock climbing, which has become hugely popular, is dangerous as well. A solo canoe trip need no be a cause for concern. As long as the canoeist is more experienced and takes the proper precautions. It is essential for you to be in good phsyical condition, of course, it is essential to wear at all times a life jacket in the canoe, and to come prepared with extra food and warm clothing. To have learned and able to apply techniques of woodcraft, etc. Having met all these conditions, the final preparation was to inform my friends and local folks of my route and the expected day of my return.

I choose a route that I knew I could do, a solo trip is no time to show foolish bravado. Then off I went. For six days I was alone beneath the vast sky, paddling hard against the waves and winds of Temagami. All the while, my senses were hieghtened, for my safety was in own hands. My eyes, ears, and nose were alert to smells, signs of wild animals, and changes in the weather. I listened to the wind roaring at night. One day I sat out a really awesome storm in my tent, perched on the shore of a tiny island. Late that afternoon, I watched with mounting excitement as a strong west wind gradually drove off the storm clouds and freed me from the storm, I could continue my travels. Every night I crawled into my tent exhausted but pleased with what I had accomplished.

On the last day, I rode the high waves of Ferguson Bay to my final destination, pitching up on the sandy shore with a breath of relief. As I mentioned earlier, a solo canoe trip has benefits fro the body, because it gives you exercise in the outdoors. Spiritually, I felt the deep, meditative calm of being alone with myself and my thoughts. I was reminded how small and vulnerable one single person is faced with the might of nature. At the same time, I had the satisfaction of depending only on myself and overcoming the challenges that confront me.

Identifying Sentences That Do Not Fit the Topic Sentence

EXERCISE 3-1

(3e)

Identify the topic sentence in each paragraph, and write its number in the first column. Then, identify any irrelevant sentences (ones that do not fit the topic sentences), and write their numbers in the second column.

	TOPIC SENTENCE	IRRELEVANT SENTENCES
EXAMPLE [1]The flute is a very old instrument.[2]It existed as long ago as 3500 B.C.[3]My brother plays the flute. [4]Archaeologists digging in the cities of ancient Sumeria and Egypt have found well-preserved flutes.[5]When these flutes were tested, they sounded much like modern flutes.[6]However, they look different. [7]My brother's flute is silver. [8]Ancient flutes were played vertically, and they were 45 centimetres long but only a centimetre wide.	1	3, 7
1. [1]Many people associate the clarinet with jazz or the Big Bands of the forties. [2]However, the clarinet has been around since ancient times. [3]The clarinet can be hard to play. [4]The first clarinet appeared in Egypt before 2700 B.C. [5]The double clarinet appeared about eight hundred years later. [6]The first modern Westerner to compose for the clarinet was a sixteenth-century German, Johann Christoph Denner. [7]He improved the clarinet by making it of wood, using a single rather than a double reed, and increasing its length from 30 centimetres to 60 centimetres.	______	______
2. [1]The lute is the ancestor of many modern stringed instruments. [2]There is even a mural, dating from 2500 B.C., that shows a Babylonian shepherd playing a lute. [3]The guitar, the ukulele, and the sitar are descendents of the lute. [4]The sitar became popular in the West after the Beatles' George Harrison studied with Indian musician Ravi Shankar. [5]The violin, fiddle, and cello also are descended from the lute.	______	______

[6]The bows used to play these instruments are an eighth-century Islamic addition to the tradition of stringed instruments.

3. [1]The trumpet is another instrument with a long history. [2]The first trumpets were made of bamboo cane or eucalyptus branches. [3]The eucalyptus tree is found in Australia and is the chief food source for koalas. [4]The first metal trumpets, made of silver, were found in the tomb of King Tutankhamen of Egypt, who died about 1350 B.C.[5]The Greek trumpets of the fifth century B.C. were made of carved ivory. [6]Like us, the Romans had both straight and J-shaped trumpets.[7]The Romans are often depicted in paintings as enjoying music.

   ______________ ______________

4. [1]The first bagpipes were very unusual instruments.[2]They were made from the complete hide of a sheep or goat.[3]The chanter, a pipe with finger holes, was set in a wooden plug placed in the animal's neck. [4]The drones, the pipes that produced the bagpipe's droning sound, were set in wooden plugs placed in the forelegs. [5]Then as now, a blowpipe was used to fill the bag with air. [6]The player pressed the bag under one arm, forcing air out the drones, and fingered the chanter, making the bagpipe's amous sound. [7]The bagpipe originally came from Asia.

   ______________ ______________

5. [1]Many people assume that the piano is an improved version of some older keyboard instrument, such as the harpsichord. [2]Actually, the harpsichord, the clavichord, and the piano are widely different.[3]In a harpsichord, the strings are plucked. [4]This plucking enables the instrument to sustain a note.[5]In the clavichord, the strings are struck by blades of metal.[6]Once a blade moves off a string, the note stops.[7]The first clavichord dates back to about 1385.[8]In the piano, the strings are struck by small hammers that rebound immediately.[9]The piano did not become popular until the eighteenth century.

   ______________ ______________

Identifying Transitions

EXERCISE 3-2

(3g)

Underline all the transitional words and expressions in these paragraphs. Then list the transitions on the lines provided.

1. Canada may be the "true north," but it also extends well to the south. Point Pelee, Canada's southernmost point, is further south than the northern tip of California. Similarly, Montreal is on the same parallel as the southern French city Bordeaux, and Toronto is on a line with Florence in Italy.

   ____

2. Most people think the boomerang is found only in Australia; however, this is not so. People use curved hunting sticks in four other parts of the world: Indonesia, eastern Africa, the Indian subcontinent, and the southwestern United States. In the United States, the Hopi, Acoma, and Zuni Indians use such sticks to hunt small animals. Few boomerangs are designed to return to their owners, but the Australian aborigines have perfected a kind that does return. In fact, the word "boomerang" comes from the aborigines' name for such a hunting stick.

   ____

3. Shorty after 2005, rising energy prices and international demand created yet another oil boom in Alberta. As soon as the price of oil reached about $50 a barrel, it became economical to develop the province's vast tar sands deposits. The multinationals poured billions into the province, because tar sands, unlike oil wells, are a guaranteed payoff and also because Canada, unlike many other oil-producing nations, is a stable country and a safe haven for investors. Yet the boom led to problems with inflation as well as an overvalued Canadian dollar, and it caused a local housing crisis and a labour shortage. Further, it brought a huge increase in pollution and degradation of the northern landscape. Early in 2008, Alberta proposed a green plan to mitigate some of the effects of the oil industry on the enviornment.

   ____

4. Everyone knows the story of Cinderella. She was treated as a servant by her step-mother and stepsisters, helped by a fairy godmother, and finally rescued by a prince who identified her because her small foot fit the glass slipper that his "mystery woman" had left behind at the ball. Were glass slippers fashionable centuries ago, or did someone make a mistake? Someone certainly made a mistake. In 1697, Charles Perrault translated Cinderella from Old French into modern French. Unfortunately, he rendered *vair* as *verre*, meaning "glass." Actually, *vair* means "white squirrel fur." So, Cinderella's shoes were much more comfortable than we had been told.

   ____

5. Unlike most other circuses, Quebec's *Cirque du Soleil* has no animal acts. Nor does it boast of the size or number of its rings. In fact, all its acts take place in one ring—and sometimes the acts intentionally spill over into the audience, who sit right up close to the action. Since its beginnings in the 1980s, this unique circus has emphasized breath-taking acrobatics in addition to anarchic clowning that verges on theatre of the absurd. Finally, the theatrical staging and powerful music establish an unforgettable, magical mood.

   ____

Identifying Devices That Provide Coherence

EXERCISE 3-3

(3g)

Read this paragraph carefully, and then answer the questions that follow.

[1]Have you ever wondered how the painted lines in the road are made straight? [2]No one painting freehand could consistently keep lines straight, so machines are used. [3]Before a small road or street is painted, a highway crew marks it at 6-metre intervals, following an engineer's plan. [4]Then a gasoline-powered machine, about the size of a large lawnmower, is pushed along by one person. [5]The operator follows the marks on the road, while air pressure forces out a stream of paint or hot plastic.[6]Hot plastic lasts from eighteen months to three years; paint lasts from three to six months.[7]Of course, this machine is too slow for use on highways. [8]Instead, four-person crews use a large truck equipped with a pointer that can be used to follow the median strip, so there is no need to mark the road before painting.[9]The truck is faster than the one-person machine for other reasons as well: it has two adjustable sprayguns that paint lines at the required distances apart, and it moves at 8 kilometres an hour. [10]Crew members must have great skill. [11]In fact, they receive up to a year of training.

1. Which words and phrases serve as transitional devices?

2. What key words are repeated (include all forms of the words)?

3. How does parallelism function in sentences 6 and 9?

4. What key words are later replaced by pronouns? List the nouns and the pronouns that substitute for them.

Organizing Sentences to Create a Coherent Paragraph

EXERCISE 3-4
(3d–g)

Rearrange the sentences in each set to create a coherent paragraph. Write the letters of the sentences in their new order. Then write out the paragraph.

1. a. First, look at the source of the Web site and its author or authors.
   b. Always investigate sources carefully before citing them in a paper.
   c. Finally, read it through critically, and discover if the information is well supported with evidence.
   d. This kind of investigation is especially important for sources you locate on the World Wide Web.
   e. Next, evaluate the site for evidence of bias and see if its information is up-to-date.

2. a. It is known as the earliest permanent European settlement in Canada, and it remains the only city north of Mexico City to have kept its fortified stone walls.
   b. St. John's, Newfoundland, is even older than Tadoussac, although the claim that St. John's was a permanent settlement so early has not been accepted by all historians.
   c. Quebec City was founded in 1608 by Samuel de Champlain on the site of an old Iroquois settlement.
   d. Other temporary European settlements preceded Quebec City, however.
   e. These include Port Royal and the trading post of Tadoussac, which was established in 1599.

3. a. Sir Alexander Fleming discovered the penicillin mould, the first modern antibiotic, by accident in 1928.
   b. For the next 2000 years, scientists sought a cure for infection.
   c. The Chinese used this soybean mould to treat skin infections.
   d. The first antibiotic was made from mouldy soybeans around 500 B.C.
   e. Soon after, other cultures began using mouldy bread and cobwebs to treat infected wounds.
   f. Strangely, modern scientists never looked into these folk remedies.

4. a. The government abolished such racial discrimination as an immigration criterion in 1962.
   b. Until the 1960s, Canada limited immigration mostly to people of European descent.
   c. The legal measure that completed this trio of immigration reforms was Canada's ratification of the Geneva Convention provisions on refugees two years later.
   d. Thus, by the early 1970s, Canada had begun accepting tens of thousands of immigrants from Hong Kong and South Asia, including Asian refugees from Idi Amin's Uganda.
   e. Then, in 1967, the rule that favoured migrants from Europe and the United States was changed.
   f. Other refugees who swelled Canada's population of immigrants included Chileans fleeing their country's violent military regime, Americans escaping the military draft, and Vietnamese Boat People fleeing communism.

Supporting the Topic Sentence

EXERCISE 3-5
(3d–g)

For each topic sentence below, supply three to five relevant details. Then, using your own paper, write a unified and coherent paragraph using the topic sentence and your supporting details.

1. Topic Sentence: A foreign language credit should (should not) be required for high school graduation.

   Details:

2. Topic Sentence: Cell phone plans are a complicated choice.

   Details:

3. Topic Sentence: The ______________________ have contributed many things (members of an ethnic group) to Canadian culture.

   Details:

4. Topic Sentence: Computer games are not a waste of time.

   Details:

5. Topic Sentence: The laws regarding _______________ should be changed.

   Details:

6. Topic Sentence: Choosing a college or university can be difficult.

   Details:

Organizing Details within Paragraphs

EXERCISE 3-6

(3h–i)

Details in a paragraph are often organized in one of four patterns: chronological order (time), spatial order (location), general to specific, or climactic order (least important to most important). For each pattern, select a subject from the ones given, construct a topic sentence, and list three to five supporting details. Then, on your own paper, use the topic sentence and details to write a unified and coherent paragraph of at least four sentences. It may be possible to combine two closely related details in one sentence.

1. CHRONOLOGICAL ORDER: the steps in applying to college or university; preparing for vacation; setting up a peripheral

   Topic Sentence:

   Details:

2. SPATIAL ORDER: the view from the classroom window; the floor plan of the local video rental store; the layout of a curling rink

   Topic Sentence:

   Details:

3. GENERAL TO SPECIFIC: the advantages (disadvantages) of working while attending school full time; the mood on New Year's Eve; the reasons _______________ is my favourite meal

   Topic Sentence:

   Details:

4. CLIMACTIC ORDER: why I've chosen my career; how I control anger; how I would raise responsible children

   Topic Sentence:

   Details:

Using Examples in Paragraphs

EXERCISE 3-7

(3i)

Write two paragraphs in which examples are used to support your topic sentence. In the first paragraph, use three to five short examples; in the second, use one extended example. First compose a topic sentence. Next, list the supporting example(s) you will use. After that, write your paragraph, using your own paper.

Select your topics from this list: the risks of walking alone at night; my favourite actor/actress; the advantages (disadvantages) of living on campus; how peer pressure can be hard to resist; professional athletes are overpaid (underpaid); the difficulty of adjusting to a new neighbourhood, school, or job.

1. Multiple Examples

Topic Sentence: ______________________________

Examples: a. ______________________________

b. ______________________________

c. ______________________________

d. ______________________________

e. ______________________________

2. Extended Example

Topic Sentence: ______________________________

Example: ______________________________

Using Paragraph Development Strategies

EXERCISE 3-8

(3f)

Most paragraphs are developed through a combination of several of the strategies discussed in this chapter. Usually one strategy predominates, however. For each development strategy listed below, select a topic from the list; compose a topic sentence; list three to five details, examples, or other pieces of support; and then, using your own paper, write the paragraph.

1. NARRATIVE

   Topics: a time I surprised myself; a success story; meeting someone special; recovering from a tragedy

   Topic Sentence: ______________________________

   Events: a. ______________________________

   b. ______________________________

   c. ______________________________

   d. ______________________________

   e. ______________________________

2. DESCRIPTION

   Topics: a secluded study location; a weekend evening at a local dance club; Silken Laumann or Terry Fox; an odd person in my neighbourhood

   Topic Sentence: ______________________________

   Details: a. ______________________________

   b. ______________________________

   c. ______________________________

   d. ______________________________

   e. ______________________________

3. PROCESS

   Topics: how to study for a test; how to plan a Halloween party; how to furnish a small room; how to read a map

   Topic Sentence: ______________________________

   Steps: a. ______________________________

   b. ______________________________

   c. ______________________________

   d. ______________________________

   e. ______________________________

4. DEFINITION

Topics: my ideal job; a perfect day; fear; science fiction

Topic Sentence: ______________________________

Qualities: a. ______________________________

b. ______________________________

c. ______________________________

d. ______________________________

e. ______________________________

5. ANALYSIS AND CLASSIFICATION (pick one)

Topics for Analysis: types of sports shoes; types of bicycles; types of fear; types of dreams

Topic Sentence: ______________________________

Subgroups: a. ______________________________

b. ______________________________

c. ______________________________

d. ______________________________

e. ______________________________

Topics for Classification: movies; desserts; younger brothers (sisters); bosses

Topic Sentence: ______________________________

Individual
Components: a. ______________________________

b. ______________________________

c. ______________________________

d. ______________________________

e. ______________________________

6. COMPARISON AND CONTRAST

Topics: my brother (sister) and I; being a commerce major and being a sciences major; team sports and individual competition; Avril Lavigne's stage personality and that of another performer

Topic Sentence:

Points of Comparison
and Contrast: a. ______________________________

b. ______________________________

c. ______________________________

d. ______________________________

e. ______________________________

7. ANALOGY

Topics: a possessive person and a spider in its web; starting a new job (attending a new school) and jumping into a cold pool; a lie and a forest fire; daydreaming and surfing the Web

Topic Sentence: ____________________

Similarities: a. ____________________

b. ____________________

c. ____________________

d. ____________________

e. ____________________

8. CAUSE AND EFFECT

Topics: why I chose the school I am now attending; why I dropped an old friend; how a breakup affects a student's study habits; why I (my parents) came to Canada.

Topic Sentence: ____________________

Causes or Effects: a. ____________________

b. ____________________

c. ____________________

d. ____________________

e. ____________________

Revising Introductions and Conclusions

EXERCISE 3-9

(3b, k)

Each of these introductions and conclusions is inadequate as part of a 500-word essay. Determine what is wrong with each. Then, using your own paper, revise each paragraph. Some may need to be completely rewritten.

1. **THE BUILDING OF THE CANADIAN PACIFIC RAILWAY**

Introduction: The Canadian Pacific Railway was built to persuade British Columbia to enter Confederation, and for a century this railway symbolized Canadian unity. It also was known for political scandals, financial manipulations, and the backbreaking labour of thousands of European and Chinese immigrant workers, but this essay will not be able to treat these other things in enough detail.

Conclusion: In this paper I have tried to show how the Canadian Pacific Railway, the transcontinental railway completed in 1885, became an important Canadian symbol. By the way, it is not the same as the Canadian *National* Railway, which came into use in the 1920s.

2. **THE CAUSES OF VOLCANIC ERUPTIONS**

Introduction: There are 850 active volcanoes in the world. More than 75 percent of them are located in the "Ring of Fire," an area that goes from the west coasts of North and South America to the east coast of Asia, all the way down to New Zealand. Twenty percent of these volcanoes are in Indonesia. Many are also in Japan, the Aleutian Islands (off Alaska), and Central America. Other big groups of volcanoes are in the Mediterranean Sea and Iceland. In contrast, there are only six volcanoes in Africa and three in Antarctica.

Conclusion: So this is why volcanoes erupt.

3. **SHOULD SO-CALLED VICTIMLESS CRIMES BE LEGALIZED?**

Introduction: The answer is clear: Offences such as speeding on an empty highway and consumption of illegal substances create no victims. Where there is no victim, no one complains to the police and therefore no criminal charges are laid.

Conclusion: In this essay I have proved that so-called victimless crimes never do any harm, that the law has a place only where a victim can be pointed out, and that we should revise our idea of the purpose of the criminal justice system.

4. **THE FEDERAL APPOINTMENT OF SUPREME COURT JUSTICES**

Introduction: The constitutional provision that allows the federal government to appoint Supreme Court Justices should be amended.

Conclusion: Fourth, the original BNA Act did not contemplate an activist role for Supreme Court justices in interpreting the Constitution in a quasi-legislative fashion. Since 1982, however, we have had the Charter of Rights and Freedoms. When the Court uses the Charter to decide a case, its members are often making new laws, not just interpreting existing law.

5. **LEARNING A SECOND LANGUAGE**

Introduction: In this essay I will discuss why it is important for English-speaking Canadians to speak and read more than one language. Knowing a second language helps people to explore another culture, keeps them in touch with their roots, and can make travelling abroad much easier and more interesting. Therefore, all English-speaking Canadians should learn a second language.

Conclusion: There are, then, three good reasons to learn a second language. First, knowing a language such as French or German enables a person to read some of the world's most important literature, philosophy, and science. Second, learning the language of our ancestors may help us to learn about our families and ourselves and may help us to preserve vanishing ways. Third, travel in Europe, Asia, or South America is easier when the traveller is able to speak to the inhabitants in their own language. Finally, once we have struggled to learn a new language we can understand how newcomers struggle to learn English. This can make us more patient and understanding, leading to better relations with our neighbours and co-workers.

Writing Introductions and Conclusions

EXERCISE 3-10

(3b, k)

Write introductory and concluding paragraphs for three of the topics listed here. Refer to the chapter for suggested strategies. Before writing, list your thesis statement and strategies on the lines below. Use a different strategy for each paragraph. Use your own paper.

Topics: selecting a sensible diet for life; violence in the stands at sports events; applying for a student loan; dealing with difficult neighbours; noise pollution; motorcycles; old movies; talking to your doctor; adoption of children from foreign countries; urban transit systems; science fiction monsters

ESSAY 1

Thesis Statement: ______________________________

Strategy for Introduction: ______________________________

Strategy for Conclusion: ______________________________

ESSAY 2

Thesis Statement: ______________________________

Strategy for Introduction: ______________________________

Strategy for Conclusion: ______________________________

ESSAY 3

Thesis Statement: ______________________________

Strategy for Introduction: ______________________________

Strategy for Conclusion: ______________________________

Distinguishing Fact from Opinion

EXERCISE 4-1
(4c)

Identify each passage as fact or opinion. Be prepared to explain your answers.

EXAMPLES	Once people had little choice in what they ate.	*fact*
	They would have preferred our food.	*opinion*
A.	1. The diet of prehistoric people was confined to what they could gather or catch.	________
	2. Control of fire enabled people to cook their food.	________
	3. Cooking undoubtedly improved the taste.	________
	4. Gradually people learned to plant seeds and tame animals.	________
	5. Planting and herding allowed people to settle in one place.	________
	6. Some people must have longed for their former nomadic life.	________
	7. Early civilizations sprang up in areas that could produce bountiful crops.	________
	8. The fact that some could produce more than they needed freed others for nonagricultural chores.	________
	9. Farming cannot have been very difficult if one person could produce so much food.	________
	10. With such abundance I imagine many became wasteful.	________
	11. People gradually learned to preserve food by curing, drying, and pickling.	________
	12. My favourite pickle is the sweet gherkin.	________
	13. Bacon is a form of cured meat still popular today.	________
	14. Dried fruit does not taste as good as fresh fruit.	________
	15. Some dehydration machines on today's market are great.	________
B.	1. An international survey puts Canada in tenth place worldwide in the number of foreign tourists who visit.	________
	2. Nine other countries are more interesting places to visit than Canada.	________

3. Fluctuations in the value of the dollar are more important than our scenery in attracting foreign visitors. ________________

4. The Rocky Mountains attract crowds of tourists every year. ________________

5. Banff, Alberta, is probably the most scenic spot in Canada. ________________

6. Tourists from Japan can find salespeople in Banff who are able to serve them in their own language. ________________

7. Banff National Park was Canada's first national park. ________________

8. No other national park in Canada receives more visitors each year than Banff National Park. ________________

9. With its galleries and museums, Ottawa is as worthwhile a place to visit as Montreal or Toronto. ________________

10. Métis architect Douglas Cardinal designed the Canadian Museum of Civilization in Gatineau, Quebec. ________________

11. Cardinal's masterpiece is superior to architect Moshe Safdie's National Gallery of Art in Ottawa. ________________

12. No other building in the National Capital Region has attracted as much controversy as Safdie's. ________________

13. The Peace Tower rises high above the Parliament Buildings. ________________

14. With the Peace Tower, the Parliament Buildings form the most beautiful architectural ensemble in Ottawa. ________________

Developing Claims and Thesis Statements

EXERCISE 5-1

(5c)

Develop a claim and a thesis statement for each of the topics in the following list.

1. **Topic:** Violence in hockey

   Claim: ____________________

   Thesis statement: ____________________

   ____

2. **Topic:** The purpose of the Canadian military

   Claim: ____________________

   Thesis statement: ____________________

   ____

3. **Topic:** The value of studying Canadian literature

   Claim: ____________________

   Thesis statement: ____________________

   ____

4. **Topic:** Genetic modification of organisms

   Claim: ____________________

   Thesis statement: ____________________

   ____

Supporting Your Arguments

EXERCISE 5-2

(5a–l)

Choose one of the thesis statements that you developed in Exercise 5-1 and plan an oral presentation that argues that thesis. (As an alternative, plan an essay that argues the thesis.) Support your argument with evidence, reasons, and examples, and develop responses to potential objections.

Analyzing Images

EXERCISE 6-1

(6a–c)

Choose one image without words and another that contains a small amount of written text (such as a public service announcement or an advertisement, or perhaps an illustration from one of your textbooks). In no more than three brief paragraphs for each, write a summary, analysis, synthesis, and evaluation of each of the images. Refer to the questions in the summary box in section 6a, and use any other suggestions that come to you from reading sections 6a–c. If the image that contains the written text makes a visual argument, be sure to discuss that argument.

Using Images

EXERCISE 6-2

(6b–d)

Select a piece of writing that you have submitted for one of your classes, or any other brief written passage that you know well, and choose an image to illustrate it. You may find the image in another source, use a photo that you took, or do a simple sketch that gives a general indication of what the final image would look like. (If you plan to use an image from another source, ask your instructor for advice on the kinds of images you are allowed to copy and how you may use them.) Compose a brief, informative caption for the image. Then explain why that image is appropriate and exactly what it contributes to the piece of writing.

PART TWO: WRITING RESEARCH

*7 Research Writing as a Process

*8 Finding and Evaluating Sources

9 Using Sources and Avoiding Plagiarism

*10 MLA Documentation with Case Study

*11 APA Documentation with Case Study

*12 CM and CSE Documentation

***Please note:** There are no *Workbook* exercises that correspond to Chapters 7, 8, and 10–12 of the *Simon & Schuster Handbook for Writers*, Fifth Canadian Edition.

EXERCISE 9-1

(9g–h)

A. Select the portions of this passage that could be usefully quoted in an essay on marketing. Carefully and accurately incorporate those portions of the passage into your writing.

Then came the brand equity mania of the eighties, the defining moment of which arrived in 1988 when Philip Morris purchased Kraft for $12.6 billion—six times what the company was worth on paper. The price difference, apparently, was the cost of the word "Kraft." Of course Wall Street was aware that decades of marketing and brand bolstering added value to a company over and above its assets and total annual sales. But with the Kraft purchase, a huge dollar value had been assigned to something that had previously been abstract and unquantifiable—a brand name. This was spectacular news for the ad world, which was now able to make the claim that advertising spending was more than just a sales strategy: it was an investment in cold hard equity. The more you spend, the more your company is worth. Not surprisingly, this led to a considerable increase in spending on advertising. More important, it sparked a renewed interest in puffing up brand identities, a project that involved far more than a few billboards and TV spots. It was about pushing the envelope in sponsorship deals, dreaming up new areas in which to "extend" the brand, as well as perpetually probing the zeitgeist to ensure that the "essence" selected for one's brand would resonate karmically with its target market. For reasons that will be explored in the rest of this chapter, this radical shift in corporate philosophy has sent manufacturers on a cultural feeding frenzy as they seize upon every corner of unmarketed landscape in search of the oxygen needed to inflate their brands. In the process, virtually nothing has been left unbranded. That's quite an impressive feat, considering that as recently as 1993 Wall Street had pronounced the brand dead, or as good as dead.

—NAOMI KLEIN, *No Logo*

B. Select any sample paragraph in Chapter 3 of the handbook and write a paraphrase that includes the most important passages as quotations.

C. Select a paragraph from one of your textbooks or any other nonfiction work, and take notes that combine paraphrase with careful, selective quotation.

Paraphrasing

EXERCISE 9-2
(9i)

A. Paraphrase the following selection.

Though the words are often used interchangeably, branding and advertising are not the same process. Advertising any given product is only one part of branding's grand plan, as are sponsorship and logo licensing. Think of the brand as the core meaning of the modern corporation, and of the advertisement as one vehicle used to convey that meaning to the world.

The first mass-marketing campaigns, starting in the second half of the nineteenth century, had more to do with advertising than with branding as we understand it today. Faced with a range of recently invented products—the radio, phonograph, car, light bulb and so on—advertisers had more pressing tasks than creating a brand identity for any given corporation; first, they had to change the way people lived their lives. Ads had to inform consumers about the existence of some new invention, then convince them that their lives would be better if they used, for example, cars instead of wagons, telephones instead of mail and electric light instead of oil lamps. Many of these new products bore brand names—some of which are still around today—but these were almost incidental. These products were themselves news; that was almost advertisement enough.

—NAOMI KLEIN, *No Logo*

B. Select any sample paragraph in Chapter 3 in the handbook and paraphrase it.

C. Select a paragraph from one of your textbooks or any other nonfiction work and paraphrase it.

Summarizing

EXERCISE 9-3
(9j)

A. Summarize the following passage.

The astronomical growth in the wealth and cultural influence of multi-national corporations over the last fifteen years can arguably be traced back to a single, seemingly innocuous idea developed by management theorists in the mid-1980s: that successful corporations must primarily produce brands, as opposed to products.

Until that time, although it was understood in the corporate world that bolstering one's brand name was important, the primary concern of every solid manufacturer was the production of goods. This idea was the very gospel of the machine age. An editorial that appeared in *Fortune* magazine in 1938, for instance, argued that the reason the American economy had yet to recover from the Depression was that America had lost sight of the importance of making *things*:

> This is the proposition that the basic and irreversible function of an industrial economy is the *making of things*; that the more things it makes the bigger will be the income, whether dollar or real; and hence that the key to those lost recuperative powers lies ... in the factory where the lathes and the drills and the fires and the hammers are. It is in the factory and on the land and under the land that purchasing power *originates*.[1]

And for the longest time, the making of things remained, at least in principle, the heart of all industrialized economies. But by the eighties, pushed along by that decade's recession, some of the most powerful manufacturers in the world had begun to falter. A consensus emerged that corporations were bloated, oversized; they owned too much, employed too many people, and were weighed down with *too many things*. The very process of producing—running one's own factories, being responsible for tens of thousands of full-time, permanent employees—began to look less like the route to success and more like a clunky liability.

At around this same time a new kind of corporation began to rival the traditional all-American manufacturers for market share; these were the Nikes and Microsofts, and later, the Tommy Hilfigers and Intels. These pioneers made the bold claim that producing goods was only an incidental part of their operations, and that thanks to recent victories in trade liberalization and labor-law reform, they were able to have their products made for them by contractors, many of them overseas. What these companies produced primarily were not things, they said, but *images* of their brands. Their real work lay not in manufacturing but in marketing. This formula, needless to say, has proved enormously profitable, and its success has companies competing in a race toward weightlessness: whoever owns the least, has the fewest employees on the payroll and produces the most powerful images, as opposed to products, wins the race.

—NAOMI KLEIN, *No Logo*

1. "Government Spending Is No Substitute for the Exercise of Capitalist Imagination," *Fortunes* September 1938, 63–64.

B. Select any sample paragraph in Chapter 3 of the handbook and summarize it.

C. Select a paragraph from one of your textbooks or any other nonfiction work and summarize it.

PART THREE: WRITING ACROSS THE CURRICULUM—AND BEYOND

EXERCISE 13-1

(13b–d)

A. Look at the Works Cited list for one of the secondary sources you are using. Underline those you feel might help you understand the secondary source—and hence the primary source—better. Locate and read at least one additional secondary source.

B. Find out the correct method of documentation for the types of secondary sources used most often in your discipline.

Verb Tenses and Analysis

EXERCISE 14-1
(14i)

A. Look at a draft paper you are writing. Check that present and past tenses have been used correctly and consistently.

B. Consider a literary work you have been asked to analyze. What aspects of the work seem most accessible to you as you try to interpret it?

Interviewing and Citation

EXERCISE 15-1

(15b, h)

A. Consider any research you have carried out involving interviews. Did you learn anything new about the interviewing process? What is most important for you to remember next time?

B. Identify a *type* of secondary source that you have not used before in writing a science report. Locate an example of this type of source and cite it, using the documentation style your instructor requires.

Cue Words and Key Terms

EXERCISE 16-1

(16b)

A. Draft two questions which you think might come up in your next exam, paying particular attention to cue words. Then write a rough plan showing how you would organize your answers.

B. Look at a sample exam paper and underline the key terms in each question.

EXERCISE 17-1

(17b–d, g–h)

A. Find examples of business letters you have received (e.g., unsolicited mail, letters from the government, replies from companies, colleges, or universities). Have the senders followed all the guidelines given in 17b and c? If not, has this affected the impact of the letters?

B. Locate advertisements for two different jobs which interest you. Adapt your résumé to each one and draft suitable covering letters.

C. Compare the e-mails you write to friends with those you write to strangers. Which conventions do you ignore when you are writing to friends? Which conventions are you particularly careful to observe when writing to strangers?

EXERCISE 17-2

(17l–o)

A. Identify a problem in your home or school community to which you believe you have a solution. Draft a letter addressing community leaders in which you explain the problem and put forward your solution.

B. Choose any local organization that serves the public (for example, a political group or charity) and prepare a report detailing the organization's goals for the upcoming year and the strategy it plans to use to achieve those goals.

Oral Presentations

EXERCISE 18-1
(18b–d, h–l)

A. Imagine that you have been asked to speak to a group of high schoolers on an issue you know well. The talk should last 20 minutes. Formulate a working thesis and prepare an organizational outline. Consider what traditional presentation aids would help you to get your message across.

B. Write a ten-minute speech on a topic of your choice to deliver in class. Highlight the key elements that you used to both capture and hold your audience's attention.

Multimedia

EXERCISE 18-2
(18f–g)

A. Consider what multimedia aids would help you get your message across in Exercise 18-1(A). Outline the particular advantages of each.

B. Design and present four PowerPoint® slides or a two-minute video or audio presentation to accompany the speech in Exercise 18-1(B).

Analyzing Visual Design

EXERCISE 19-1
(19b–g)

Select a document of your choice. It can be an advertisement, a magazine article, a public service announcement, a poster, an illustrated book, or any other document that emphasizes visual design. Consider the effectiveness of the design as a whole and the contribution that visual elements make to the document. Pay special attention to the relationship between words and design. Outline your conclusions in two or three short paragraphs totalling about 250 words.

Analyzing Web Sites

EXERCISE 20-1

(20c–e)

A. Choose a Web site belonging to a public organization, a government department, a business, a university, or a college. Or choose a Web site that deals mostly with current events, sports, politics, cultural activities, or any other subject that interests you. Consider the site's strengths and weaknesses in contents, design, user-friendliness, and ease of navigation, or any other categories that seem relevant. Write out your conclusions in a point-form outline.

B. Briefly demonstrate the Web site to your class as a means of presenting your conclusions.

PART FOUR: UNDERSTANDING GRAMMAR AND WRITING CORRECT SENTENCES

Identifying Nouns

EXERCISE 21-1

(21b)

Underline all the nouns. Write them on the lines to the right.

1. Many people have now seen, or at least heard about, "e-books." ____________
2. They may replace traditional, manuscript-based books. ____________
3. It is essential, however, to distinguish between a digital book and a book-reading appliance. ____________
4. At its simplest, a digital book is a literal translation of a printed work. ____________
5. It is created by scanning or generating a PDF file. ____________
6. Book-reading appliances are devices resembling small laptops. ____________
7. They enable you to read digital books. ____________
8. Costing a few hundred dollars, the appliances feature high-quality screens but no keyboards. ____________
9. They run for a long time on batteries and can store several books. ____________
10. Some book-reading appliances are designed to work with your own library of downloaded digital books. ____________
11. Without the appliance, you would be unable to read the books, which are encrypted and stored on your computer. ____________
12. Other book-reading appliances use modems to download works directly from library services over phone lines. ____________
13. Some companies are working on software that will enable digital books to be displayed on general-purpose computers. ____________
14. Even so, digital books may never be as popular as their traditional counterparts. ____________
15. Screens do not offer a pleasant environment for reading very long texts. ____________
16. In addition, highlighting or making notes in a digital book is awkward. ____________
17. Certain types of books, however, are very popular in electronic form. ____________
18. They include dictionaries, encyclopedias, directories, product catalogues, and maintenance manuals. ____________

19. Readers of this type of book are generally in search of a small amount of specific information.
20. When doing lengthy reading, however, people seem to prefer to print on-screen text.
21. They are using paper—a simple but effective viewing technology—as their preferred user interface.

Identifying Pronouns

EXERCISE 21-2

(21c)

Underline all the pronouns. Write them on the lines to the right. If a sentence contains no pronouns, write *none* on the line.

EXAMPLE Since the 1930s, scientists have been trying to get chimpanzees to communicate with them. *them*

1. In the 1940s, one couple raised a chimpanzee named Vickie in their home.
2. They treated her as if she were a human child.
3. They tried to teach Vickie to say English words by shaping her mouth as she made sounds.
4. She learned to say only three words: *Mama*, *Papa*, and *cup*.
5. Even that was amazing because chimpanzees do not have the right vocal structures to produce human sounds.
6. Realizing this, scientists in the 1960s began teaching sign language to chimpanzees.
7. Chimpanzees have their own ways of communicating among themselves.
8. One chimpanzee was taught over a hundred words in American Sign Language.
9. She also formed her own original sentences.

10. She would even hold simple conversations with anyone who knew sign language. __________ __________

11. Other chimpanzees were trained to ask for what they wanted by pressing a series of symbols on a computer keyboard. __________ __________

12. Chimpanzees are not the only animals whose trainers "talk" with them. __________ __________

13. Gorillas, dolphins, and even parrots supposedly can communicate with us. __________ __________

14. Not everyone believes this is possible. __________ __________

15. Some say members of different species can have only limited communication with one another. __________ __________

16. What do you think about animal speech? __________ __________

17. Would you want to have conversations with your pets? __________ __________

Identifying Verbs

EXERCISE 21-3
(21d)

Underline all the verbs, including complete verb phrases. Write them on the lines to the right.

EXAMPLE Everyone desires a happy life. ____*Desires*____ ________

1. These tips can lead to such a life.
2. Always recognize your good qualities.
3. Everyone has positive traits, such as sympathy or generosity.
4. You should think of these qualities often.
5. Sometimes, another person may cause us problems.
6. Discuss that problem with a friend or a loved one.
7. You might also ask yourself several questions.
8. Who is at fault, and why is that person at fault?
9. Always take responsibility for your part of the problem.
10. A solution to the problem may require a joint effort.
11. What else might lead to a happy life?
12. Tolerate other people's behaviours.
13. Accept their differences.
14. Also, do not dwell upon the past mistakes of your own life.
15. Mistakes are part of a continuous learning process.
16. Without mistakes, you might not learn the right way.
17. Look back at all your successes, not your failures.
18. Be available to assist others.
19. They would do the same for you in most cases.
20. Above all, always find time for relaxation, and enjoy everything around you.

Identifying Forms of Verbs

EXERCISE 21-4

(21d–e)

Decide if each italicized word or phrase is a verb, an infinitive, a past participle, a present participle, or a gerund. Write your answers on the lines to the right.

EXAMPLE Perfume *refers* to a fragrant fluid preparation with an appealing scent. *verb*

1. The word "perfume" *originates* from the Latin "per fumum," which can be translated as "through smoke." ______
2. *Scenting* the body is a custom that dates back to the ancient Egyptians. ______
3. Once the Egyptians had learned how *to extract* the scent from flower petals, they then burned natural oils to scent temples, private homes, and royal palaces. ______
4. There *is* evidence that even Egyptian tombs were scented with fragrant ointments and oils. ______
5. The Egyptian discovery eventually *spread* to all parts of Europe. ______
6. An Arab physician discovered a way to produce a *distilled* fluid that could be used in the perfume-making process. ______
7. This process greatly *reduced* the cost of making the essential oils that went into perfume. ______
8. The first modern perfume to combine *scented* oils that were blended into alcohol was made in 1370. ______
9. Europeans *called* it "Hungary Water," since the perfume was created by order of Queen Elizabeth of Hungary. ______
10. Some records *suggest* that the perfume industry prospered in Renaissance Italy. ______
11. *To improve* the industry, Catherine de Medici's personal perfumer searched for a way to refine perfume in the sixteenth century. ______
12. During the 1500s, many *considered* France to be the perfume centre of Europe. ______
13. Louis XIV, who was dubbed the "perfumed king," was responsible for the industry's *increasing* popularity. ______
14. Much later, fragrance makers in Paris, like Chanel, contributed their names to the *growing* industry. ______
15. France still *produces* some of the most expensive fragrances in the world. ______
16. To *increase* the size of the market, manufacturers have extended the industry to men. ______
17. There *are* many different categories of perfume, including floral blends, which are the most popular. ______
18. *Gaining* popularity is the spice-blends category, which consists of aromas like clove, cinnamon, and nutmeg. ______
19. Men's perfume *derives* from fragrances such as citrus, spice, and lavender. ______
20. Perfumes are also cleverly used to *hide* undesirable smells common to paints and cleaners. ______

Identifying Adjectives

EXERCISE 21-5

(21f)

Underline all adjectives, except the articles *a*, *an*, and *the*. Write them on the lines to the right.

EXAMPLE Who wants to be the patient of an <u>irascible</u> doctor? *irascible* ______

1. Viewers of an acclaimed television series must ask themselves that question regularly. ______ ______
2. The popular series *House* stars Hugh Laurie as a brilliant medical investigator. ______ ______
3. Dr. Gregory House may be brilliant, but he is eccentric and highly irritable. ______ ______
4. David Shore, the Canadian writer who created the series, modelled his character on the fictional detective Sherlock Holmes. ______ ______
5. Shore explains—in case anyone misses the sly reference—that the name "House" puns on the pronunciation of the famous name "Holmes." ______ ______
6. Shore, who was raised in London, Ontario, attended law school in Toronto. ______ ______
7. He quickly abandoned this lucrative profession for the more risky one of comedy writer. ______ ______
8. His new ambition of writing comedy took Shore to Los Angeles. ______ ______
9. Comedy soon gave way to another specialty: television drama. ______ ______
10. The move to dramatic writing let Shore use the knowledge he had gained from his first career, the law. ______ ______
11. Crime shows and others set in the legal world dominate the evening TV schedule. ______ ______
12. Shore imagined Gregory House as a kind of medical detective. ______ ______
13. House accepts only cases that involve particular difficulty, especially cases that other hospitals have failed to diagnose properly. ______ ______
14. Methodical deductions combined with surprising intuitions mark House's style of investigation. ______ ______

15. In this, he resembles Sherlock Holmes, but unlike Holmes, House shows hardly any patience with his less intelligent colleagues. ______________ ______________
16. House's grey eyes strike each one of them with a piercing glare. ______________ ______________
17. The unkind and even offensive remarks that he makes are a favourite with the show's fans. ______________ ______________
18. Shore created House as a man who limps from the constant pain of a leg injury. ______________ ______________
19. Careful viewers may notice that House holds his cane in the wrong hand. ______________ ______________
20. This, Hugh Laurie says, was an intentional choice to establish the character he plays as a contrarian. ______________ ______________

Identifying Adverbs

EXERCISE 21-6
(21g)

Underline all the adverbs and circle all the conjunctive adverbs. Remember that some phrases or clauses can function as adverbs. Write your answers on the lines to the right. If there are no adverbs, write *none* on the line.

EXAMPLE Chimpanzees, commonly called chimps, belong to the ape family; however, they form the single species *Pan troglodytes*.	*commonly* *adverb*	*however* *conj. adverb*
1. Chimps inhabit only the tropical rain forests of central Africa.	______	______
2. They are the most intelligent of all apes.	______	______
3. Chimps are also the most easily taught.	______	______
4. Typically, except for a white patch near its rump, the chimp's coat of fur is black; however, its face is mostly bareskinned and either black, spotted, or pale.	______	______
5. Chimpanzee hands, feet, and ears have a more pinkish tone.	______	______
6. In the forest, chimps are extremely noisy; indeed, they will often shriek, scream, and slap the ground.	______	______
7. However, when humans enter their territory, the chimps usually quiet down.	______	______
8. While living in the forest, chimps do not just swing from branch to branch to get around.	______	______
9. They are also quite skilled in the ability to walk on the ground.	______	______
10. Generally, chimps walk on all fours; still, they do sometimes walk and run in an upright position, much like a human.	______	______
11. In fact, when standing erect, a chimp stands anywhere from 1.25 to 1.75 metres tall.	______	______

Identifying Prepositions

EXERCISE 21-7
(21h)

Underline all prepositions and circle their objects. Write them on the lines to the right.

	PREPOSITIONS	OBJECTS
EXAMPLE The bicycle has been a form of *local transportation* for years.	*of*	*local transportation*
	for	*years*
1. In China, there are more than 300 million bicycles on the road.	______	______
	______	______
2. The bicycle began to develop after a French model, the *célérifère*, was created.	______	______
	______	______
3. The *célérifère*, a type of foot-powered scooter, had a stationary front wheel, unlike those that followed.	______	______
4. Until an invention by a German baron solved the problem of the stationary front wheel, the *célérifère* could not be steered.	______	______
5. Karl von Drais developed the first steerable wheel for this bicycle, called *the draisienne*.	______	______
6. Several years later, in a Scottish workshop, blacksmith Kirkpatrick Macmillan created the first bicycle with pedals.	______	______
	______	______
7. The pedals were attached to the rear wheels and were controlled by means of cranks.	______	______
	______	______
8. During the 1860s, the French *vélocipède,* which had pedals attached to the front wheels, was introduced.	______	______
	______	______
9. In England in 1879, H. J. Lawson developed a bicycle made with a chain and sprocket that controlled the huge front wheel.	______	______

10. Just six years later, J. K. Stanley developed a safety bicycle, which became the prototype for today's bicycle. __________ __________ __________ __________

11. Instead of a larger front wheel, Stanley's bicycle had wheels that were equal in size. __________ __________

12. During the 1880s, pneumatic tires, rubber tires filled with compressed air, were introduced. __________ __________ __________ __________

13. The two- and three-speed hub gears, along with the *derailleur* gear, were developed in the 1890s. __________ __________ __________ __________

14. Later developments of the bicycle led to attempts to motorize it. __________ __________

Identifying Conjunctions

EXERCISE 21-8
(21i)

Underline all coordinating and subordinating conjunctions. Write them in column 1. Then indicate the type of conjunctions by writing *CC* or *SC* in column 2.

EXAMPLE Roméo Dallaire is haunted by by memories <u>and</u> fears.	*and*	*CC*
1. When he was sent to Rwanda in 1993, General Roméo Dallaire was hopeful.	________	________
2. The United Nations mission to Rwanda was the Canadian general's first experience in the field.	________	________
3. For several decades, the Hutu and Tutsi populations of Rwanda had been caught up in violent confrontations.	________	________
4. However, in 1993 peace became possible, since leaders of both sides had agreed to a power-sharing agreement.	________	________
5. Lingering tensions still had to be resolved before the peace accord could succeed.	________	________
6. A militia composed of Hutus was mobilizing against the minority Tutsis, while armed Tutsi exiles were active across the border in Uganda.	________	________
7. The 2500 UN troops that Dallaire led were told to monitor the situation but not to intervene in internal Rwandan affairs.	________	________
8. Nor did they expect to do any fighting—the soldiers, drawn from several countries, were only lightly armed.	________	________
9. Violence broke out suddenly after the Rwandan president's airplane was brought down by a missile in April 1994.	________	________

10. The extremist Hutu militia began to organize massacres of Tutsis and Hutu moderates; the government collapsed. ____________ ____________

11. Dallaire appealed for reinforcements to help rescue civilians, yet all but 450 of his troops were sent home to safety. ____________ ____________

12. As the number of dead approached 800 000, the world's major powers still refused to admit that the killings amounted to genocide. ____________ ____________

13. Although international treaties require United Nations members to prevent genocide, the major powers were anxious not to risk their soldiers in a small African country. ____________ ____________

14. The slaughter continued for a hundred days until the Tutsi army from Uganda defeated the Hutu forces. ____________ ____________

15. Roméo Dallaire, a nearly helpless witness to mass murder, now warns the nations of the world that they must never let such a thing happen again. ____________ ____________

Identifying the Parts of Speech: Review

EXERCISE 21-9
(21a–j)

Write the part of speech of each underlined word on the corresponding numbered line.

Chewing[1] gum was discovered[2] in the 1860s during[3] a search for rubber materials.[4] Gum is very much a North American product[5] and[6] it is rarely[7] found anywhere outside Canada and the United States. The recipe for[8] chewing gum received[9] its[10] first patent in 1869. The basic raw material used[11] for all gum is the natural gum known as chicle. Since[12] it is very expensive and hard to obtain, synthetic[13] materials and other natural gums are often used in place of[14] chicle. Bubble gum differs[15] from regular gum because it is made[16] with[17] rubber latex, a compound that provides[18] the gum with the strength to make a bubble. Sugarless gum is made[19] from[20] sugar alcohols,[21] such as xylitol and mannitol, not[22] from regular sugar. North American wholesale[23] factory sales of chewing gum have often[24] approached one billion[25] dollars.

1. ______________	9. ______________	17. ______________
2. ______________	10. ______________	18. ______________
3. ______________	11. ______________	19. ______________
4. ______________	12. ______________	20. ______________
5. ______________	13. ______________	21. ______________
6. ______________	14. ______________	22. ______________
7. ______________	15. ______________	23. ______________
8. ______________	16. ______________	24. ______________
		25. ______________

Identifying Subjects and Predicates

EXERCISE 21-10
(21l)

A: Draw a line in each of these sentences to separate the complete subject from the complete predicate.

EXAMPLE The ice in a skating rink / does not melt.

1. Warm air cannot melt the ice.
2. The temperature beneath the ice is kept very low.
3. This keeps the ice from melting even in the sun.
4. The ice at a figure-skating rink is 5 centimetres thick.
5. Ice hockey rinks have slightly thicker layers of ice.
6. The ice is on a concrete floor.
7. The concrete contains 2.5-centimetre pipes located no more than 5 centimetres apart.
8. An Olympic-sized rink has about 16 kilometres of piping.
9. A very cold liquid, like the antifreeze in cars, circulates through the pipes.
10. The liquid absorbs heat from the concrete.
11. Machinery keeps the liquid at –3° to –8°C.
12. More and more people are enjoying an afternoon of skating at an ice rink.

B: Draw a single line under the simple subject and a double line under the verb. Be sure to underline the complete verb and all parts of compound subjects and verbs. Write them on the lines to the right.

	SUBJECT	VERB
EXAMPLE Most Canadians brush their teeth daily.	*Canadians*	*brush*
1. The original toothbrushes were simply twigs with one soft, shredded end.	______	______
2. People rubbed these "chew sticks" against their teeth.	______	______
3. The first genuine toothbrushes originated in China 500 years ago.	______	______
4. The bristles came from hogs.	______	______
5. Hogs living in the cold regions of China grew stiff bristles.	______	______
6. During this time, few Europeans brushed their teeth regularly.	______	______

7. Horsehair toothbrushes and small sponges were used by some Europeans. ______ ______

8. Many men and women picked their teeth clean after meals. ______ ______

9. The stems of feathers or special toothpicks were employed for this. ______ ______

10. Brass or silver toothpicks were safer than animal-hair toothbrushes. ______ ______

11. Germs developed on animal bristles, leading to frequent infections. ______ ______

12. There was no solution to this problem until the 1930s. ______ ______

13. The discovery of nylon led to a big change in the toothbrush industry and made tooth care easier. ______ ______

14. Nylon was tough and resisted the growth of germs. ______ ______

15. The first nylon-bristle brushes were sold in the North America in 1938. ______ ______

16. Unfortunately, they were very hard on gums. ______ ______

17. Soft gum tissue scratched and bled easily. ______ ______

18. In the 1950s, a new, softer version of the nylon toothbrush was developed. ______ ______

19. It cost five times as much as the old, harder brushes. ______ ______

20. With this development, national dental care improved. ______ ______

21. Dentists and oral surgeons have made some suggestions for dental health. ______ ______

22. Toothbrushes should be used regularly and should be replaced every few months. ______ ______

23. Bent bristles are useless in cleaning teeth and can cut gums. ______ ______

Identifying Objects

EXERCISE 21-11
(21m)

Draw a single line under all direct objects and a double line under all indirect objects. Not all sentences have both. Write your answers on the lines to the right.

	Sentence	Direct Object	Indirect Object
Example	It's never too late to send your friends a Facebook invitation.	*invitation*	*friends*
1.	Do you want to show the whole world your private life?		
2.	Or do you prefer to give only your closest friends a glimpse?		
3.	Social networking sites connect people with friends as well as strangers.		
4.	Sites like Facebook don't charge you any money to join.		
5.	However, indiscreet postings on these sites have cost people their pride.		
6.	A breach of your privacy can also cause you serious trouble.		
7.	You don't want to give yourself a serious shock some day.		
8.	But you just might, if your postings give your employer reason to think you are an irresponsible party animal.		
9.	Pose yourself this question: Are you prepared for the consequences?		
10.	What social networking sites are especially good for is bringing people with similar interests together with one another.		
11.	They are also good at bringing friends updates on one another.		
12.	People use Facebook, for instance, to meet for impromptu activities.		
13.	You may be doing someone a favour with an invitation to become one of your Facebook friends.		
14.	That is, as long as you give that person credit for knowing how to post responsibly on the site.		

Identifying Complements

EXERCISE 21-12 (21n)

Decide if each italicized word is a subject complement or an object complement. Indicate your answer by writing *SC* or *OC* in column 1. Then indicate if it is a noun or an adjective by writing *N* or *Adj* in column 2.

	1	2
EXAMPLE Chocolate is *delicious.*	*SC*	*Adj*
1. Strawberries are not true *berries.*		
2. They are an *offshoot* of the rose plant family.		
3. Strawberries taste *sweet.*		
4. Harpo Marx was not a *mute.*		
5. Many considered his silence *charming.*		
6. In fact, friends have called him *talkative.*		
7. Many people consider elephants *fearless.*		
8. However, mice can make them *frantic* with fright.		
9. Carrots are not a *remedy* for poor eyesight.		
10. This belief is a *myth.*		
11. Only for improving night vision are they *helpful.*		
12. India ink is not *Indian.*		
13. It is *Chinese.*		
14. Lions are *cats*, or felids.		
15. Many people mistakenly call them *the largest cats* in the cat family.		
16. Yet the largest cat is the *tiger.*		
17. The Siberian tiger is the *king* of all felids.		
18. A rabbit is a *lagomorph.*		
19. It is not a *rodent.*		
20. Its distinguishing feature is its *digestive system.*		
21. People mistakenly consider pigs *dirty.*		
22. Yet pigs are very *clean.*		
23. Often, their owners leave pig sties *unclean.*		

Identifying and Using Adjectives and Adverbs

EXERCISE 21-13
(21f–g)

A: Decide if each italicized word is an adjective or an adverb. Write your identification on the lines to the right.

EXAMPLE Bingo is one of the *most*[a] *frequently*[b] played games in *several*[c] countries around the world.

a. *adverb*
b. *adverb*
c. *adjective*

1. *Each*[d] player's chances of winning depend *entirely*[e] on the numbers that are drawn.
2. Because it is so *easily*[f] mastered, the game attracts *many*[g] players.
3. Bingo cards are *universally*[h] designed; they have *five*[i] rows of five squares each.
4. The letters B-I-N-G-O are *clearly*[j] printed on the top of each card; each letter heads a *vertical*[k] row.
5. *Any*[l] number from one to seventy-five is placed in a box on the card, except for the centre square, which is *always*[m] a free square.
6. There are seventy-five *corresponding*[n] balls, each with a letter and a number that is drawn *randomly*[o] from a bowl or box by the caller.
7. The *bingo*[p] caller chooses a ball and *quickly*[q] announces its letter and number.
8. *Those*[r] players who have a square with a number matching the one that was called must *carefully*[s] place a marker over the square.
9. The *first*[t], player to cover five boxes *vertically*[u] or horizontally yells, "Bingo!" and wins the game.
10. *Usually*,[v] the winner receives a prize: *typically*,[w] a *grand*[x] prize is given to the player who can cover the entire card.

d. ______________
e. ______________
f. ______________
g. ______________
h. ______________
i. ______________
j. ______________
k. ______________
l. ______________
m. ______________
n. ______________
o. ______________
p. ______________
q. ______________
r. ______________
s. ______________
t. ______________
u. ______________
v. ______________
w. ______________
x. ______________

B: Fill in the blanks in each sentence with adjectives or adverbs as needed. Write your answers in column 1, and in column 2 identify each as an adjective or an adverb.

	1	2
EXAMPLE I had had a ____________ day with my sister.	*terrific*	*adjective*
1. We left very _________ this morning.	____________	____________
2. The highway was _________, so we hit no traffic.	____________	____________
3. Since the sun was _________ shining we kept the sunroof open.	____________	____________
4. Her _________ car is fun to drive.	____________	____________
5. We arrived at the musuem _________ earlier than we thought we would.	____________	____________
6. We _________ found a _________ parking spot right near the main entrance.	____________	____________
7. _________, since we were both so hungry, there was a _________ cafe right next to the museum that was serving breakfast.	____________	____________
8. After strolling around the museum, we both knew what we _________ wanted to do next: visit the _________ museum gift shop.	____________	____________
9. We bought a _________ vase for our mother's birthday next week; _________, it was on sale.	____________	____________
10. _________, we headed for home, because both of us were _________ exhausted from a great day out together.	____________	____________

Identifying Appositives

EXERCISE 21-14

(21n)

Appositives in these sentences have been italicized. On the lines to the right, write the words or phrases modified by the appositives.

EXAMPLE Foster Hewitt, *a young journalist,* became an early sports broadcaster. ___Foster Hewitt___

1 Hewitt made his first radio broadcast of a hockey game, a *minor-league* contest, on March 22, 1923. ____________

2. Some people say that this match, *an otherwise forgotten game between Kitchener and Toronto Parkdale*, was the occasion of the world's first hockey broadcast. ____________

3. At the rink, Hewitt spoke through a telephone, *itself a fairly recent invention.* ____________

4. His telephoned commentary was received by a radio transmitter, *the means by which his words reached the radio audience.* ____________

5. Later, Hewitt was given his own broadcasting studio, *a small glass booth at the rink*, equipped with a radio set. ____________

6. Hewitt also broadcast the first game played at Maple Leaf Gardens, *the new home of Toronto's NHL team*, in 1931. ____________

7. His broadcasts, a *Saturday night tradition for decades*, helped create the legend of the great Maple Leaf teams of long ago. ____________

8. Hewitt invented the famous shout *"He shoots, he scores!"* ____________

9. If he could have collected royalties on this phrase, *a favourite cry of generations of Canadian children*, he would have become a very wealthy man. ____________

10. Over the years, countless French-speakers listened in amusement to Hewitt's attempts to pronounce the names *Léo Boivin and Yvan Cournoyer.* ____________

11. In the 1950s, the "*Age of Television,*" Hewitt began broadcasting televised hockey games. _______________

12. Hewitt's son *Bill* began to take over the television work in the 1960s. _______________

13. Still, it was Foster Hewitt, *the veteran play-caller,* who was chosen to announce the 1972 series between Canada and the Soviet Union. _______________

14. Hewitt later said that this series, *the one featuring Paul Henderson's winning goal*, was the highlight of his long career. _______________

Identifying Phrases

EXERCISE 21-15
(21o)

A: Identify the underlined phrases, and write on the lines to the right *NP* for a noun phrase, *VP* for a verb phrase, *PP* for a prepositional phrase, and *AP* for an absolute phrase.

EXAMPLE Each year, lives are lost when inexperienced swimmers are caught in rip tides. ______*NP*______

1. A rip tide is a dangerous current. ____________
2. It sucks water away from the shore. ____________
3. Rips are formed when waves break rapidly in shallow water. ____________
4. Having accumulated near the shore, the water cannot easily return. ____________
5. It seeks out underwater troughs through which to escape. ____________
6. If there are none, the water will erode a channel for itself. ____________
7. The effect is similar to bathwater escaping down a drain. ____________
8. Rip tides should not be confused with undertows. ____________
9. Undertows are associated with larger surf. ____________
10. Once caught in a rip tide, remain calm. ____________
11. Do not tire yourself by attempting to swim against it. ____________
12. Instead, swim parallel to the shore until you are past the current. ____________
13. Alternatively, you should tread water until help arrives. ____________

B: Identify the italicized verbal phases and write on the lines to the right *in* for an infinitive phrase, *part* for a participial phrase, and *ger* for a gerund phrase.

EXAMPLE *To ensure harmony in the home or office*, consider applying the principles of Feng Shui. ___*inf*___

1. *Practised in China for more than 4000 years*, Feng Shui, or the ancient art of placement, is now becoming popular in the West. ________

2. *Literally translated*, Feng Shui means "wind and water." ________

3. *Believing that everything in the world constitutes an interwoven field of energy or "chi,"* devotees of Feng Shui pay close attention to their surroundings. ________

4. *Derived from Daoist philosophy*, Feng Shui has three basic schools: the Land School, the Compass School, and the Black Sect Tantric Buddhist School. ________

5. *To harmonize their lives with the forces of nature*, the farmers of the Land School evaluated a landscape and its natural features—trees, rivers, mountains—to determine the best placement for buildings and crops. ________

6. *Utilizing compass points, astrology, and mathematics* rather than landscape features, the practitioners of the Compass School developed the ba-gua, an eight-sided chart that is still used today. ________

7. *Founded by Chinese-American master Thomas Lin Yun around fifty years ago*, the BTB school of Feng Shui uses the door of a room or building as the main point of reference. ________

8. *Using the ba-gua chart*, modern practitioners of Feng Shui select and arrange objects in a room to create harmony. ________

9. *To achieve a positive flow of chi,* they follow principles which may at first seem superstitious. ________

10. For example, *hanging wind chimes* near the front door is said to keep money in the house. ________

11. *Having smooth, round objects* in the home rather than sharp, pointed ones, is also considered beneficial. ________

12. *Sleeping with your feet facing the door*, however, is thought to cause sleepless nights. ________

13. *To maximize chi*, a person should consider not only how a building is furnished but where it is situated. ________

14. *Living too close to jagged rocks*, for example, is not advisable. ________

15. If you are unable to move, however, *setting a large round rock in the yard* will help restore harmony. ________

Identifying Dependent Clauses

EXERCISE 21-16
(21p)

Underline all dependent clauses. Write the first and last words of each dependent clause on the lines to the right.

EXAMPLE When you visit London, be sure to take a ride on the London Eye. *when* ____ *visit London* ____

1. The London Eye Ferris wheel, which was designed as part of London's Millennium celebrations, was built as the largest attraction of its kind in the world. ____ ____
2. The structure, which stands 135 metres high, was built by British Airways at a cost of 35 million pounds. ____ ____
3. There was disappointment, however, on New Year's Eve 1999, when technical problems delayed the opening of the wheel. ____ ____
4. A fault was discovered in the clutch mechanism of one of its 32 glass pods, which meant the wheel had to be shut down. ____ ____
5. Rather than close just one pod, BA decided on a complete overhaul. ____ ____
6. The 250 people who had been invited to ride the wheel that night were given a rain cheque. ____ ____
7. Although each pod can carry 25 people, fewer people are admitted in hot weather. ____ ____
8. The wheel does not cause motion sickness, as it travels extremely slowly. ____ ____
9. However, when one passenger suffered vertigo, the wheel had to be reversed to let her off. ____ ____
10. One thing that most people enjoy about the wheel is that it is noiseless. ____ ____

11 The wheel sold its millionth ticket in April 2000, which was well ahead of schedule. _______________ _______________

12. Because of the success of the wheel, other cities—including Boston and Toronto—have asked if they can copy it. _______________ _______________

Using Subordination

EXERCISE 21-17
(21p)

Using the subordinating conjunction or relative pronoun given in parentheses, join each of these pairs of sentences. You may sometimes need to omit a word, but no major rewordings are required.

EXAMPLE Eight different species of potatoes are grown.
Most North Americans know only one kind of potato. (although)
Although most North Americans know only one kind of potato, eight different species are grown.

1. Potatoes grown from seed may not inherit the parent plant's characteristics. Potatoes are usually grown from the eye of a planted piece of potato. (since)

   ____

2. Potato blossoms look like those of the poisonous nightshade plant. Centuries ago, Europeans were afraid to eat potatoes. (because)

   ____

3. Tomatoes, tobacco, and eggplant are all relatives of the potato. They do not look alike. (although)

   ____

4. The sweet potato is not related to the potato. Its Indian name, *batata*, was mistakenly taken to mean "potato" by its European "discoverers." (even though)

   ____

5. The potato skin is a good source of dietary fibre. Most people throw it away. (which)

   ____

6. About 25 percent of Canada's potato-farming land is located in Prince Edward Island. This province has only 0.1 percent of Canada's total land area. (while)

   ____

7. Would you believe something? Twelve percent of the U.S. potato crop is made into potato chips. (that)

   ____

8. There are misinformed people. They believe the potato is only a poor person's food. (who)

   ____

9. They overlook something.
   Potatoes have nourished the people of Europe since the eighteenth century. (that)

   ___

10. Nutritious potatoes allowed the population to expand until 1845.
    Parts of Europe—especially Ireland—were almost destroyed by a disease that killed the potato crop. (when)

    ___

11. Potato chips were created in New England.
    A hotel chef became angry with a fussy customer. (because)

    ___

12. The customer sent back his french fries twice, saying they were not crisp enough.
    No one else had ever complained. (although)

    ___

13. The chef apparently had a bad temper.
    He decided to teach the man a lesson. (who)

    ___

14. He cut the potatoes paper-thin and fried them.
    They were too crispy to pick up with a fork. (until)

    ___

15. The customer tasted these potatoes.
    He was delighted. (once)

    ___

16. The chef never got his revenge, but he did get his own restaurant.
    These "chips" became very popular. (so that)

    ___

Identifying Different Types of Sentences

EXERCISE 21-18
(21)

Underline all subjects once and all verbs twice. Then circle and label all coordinating conjunctions (*CC*), subordinating conjunctions (*SC*), relative pronouns (*RP*), and conjunctive adverbs (*CA*). Finally, on the lines to the right, label each sentence as simple, compound, complex, or compound-complex.

EXAMPLE Forgetting is the loss of information previously stored in the memory, (and) [cc] all of us have experienced it. *compound*

1. Forgetting is not always permanent. ______
2. Interference sometimes keeps us from remembering. ______
3. When this happens, we may not be able to stop thinking about something else even though we know it is wrong. ______
4. For example, we may not recall a friend's name, and we may even want to call her by someone else's name. ______
5. Other times, we try hard to remember, but our memories may not work at all. ______
6. The information seems lost until we receive a clue that helps us remember. ______
7. Some scientists believe that memories may completely fade away, and then we can never get them back. ______
8. Recent studies show that storing memory changes the brain tissue. ______
9. However, no one has shown that these changes can be erased, so the "fading-away" theory of forgetting remains unproven. ______
10. Scientists who believe in the interference theory of forgetting identify different kinds of interference. ______
11. Sometimes learning new material is made difficult by conflicting old material. ______
12. Confusion between the old material and the new makes it hard to remember either one. ______
13. Coming upon similar material soon after learning something can also interfere. ______
14. Scientists have shown this in experiments, but everyday experience can convince us too. ______
15. Anyone trying to learn two similar languages, such as French and Spanish, at the same time knows the feeling of confusion. ______

Writing Different Types of Sentences

EXERCISE 21-19
(21q)

A: Combine these groups of simple sentences according to the directions in parentheses. It will be necessary to add coordinating conjunctions, subordinating conjunctions, or relative pronouns. Sometimes it will be necessary to drop or change a few words. Since most passages can be combined in several ways, take the time to draft a few alternatives and then select the version you like best. Try to use at least one elliptical clause in this exercise.

EXAMPLE Sometimes people repress their memories. They cannot recall anything about an event. (compound)
Sometimes people repress memories, so they cannot recall anything about an event.

1. Psychoanalysis helps people deal with these forgotten memories.
   Psychoanalysis works at exploring them consciously. (compound)

   ____

   ____

2. Repression can make life difficult.
   Repression is the burying in the unconscious of fearful experiences. (complex)

   ____

   ____

3. People repress frightening thoughts and experiences.
   Then they try to go on living normally. (compound)

   ____

   ____

4. People repress experiences.
   They avoid having to relive them.
   They feel better for a time. (compound-complex)

   ____

   ____

5. Experiments show something.
   People forget bad experiences quickly.
   People forget good experiences less quickly. (complex)

   ____

   ____

6. Repression occurs in the mentally ill.
   It occurs also in mentally healthy people. (compound)

   ____

   ____

7. A certain kind of learning atmosphere leads to better memory.
   This kind of learning atmosphere is the kind where people can relax. (complex)

   ____

   ____

8. Any student knows this.
   So does any teacher. (compound)

   ____

   ____

9. People are often distracted in stressful situations.
   They simply do not see everything.
   Therefore, they cannot remember everything. (compound-complex)

   ____

   ____

10. This may explain something.
    Accident victims often do not recall details of their experiences. (complex)

    ____

    ____

11. Many people do not remember much from their childhoods.
    This does not mean that they are repressing bad memories. (compound)

    ____

    ____

12. They may have been too interested in some events to notice any others.
    These other events were happening at the same time.
    Maybe their childhoods were simply too boring to remember. (compound-complex)

    ____

    ____

B: Using independent and dependent clauses, expand each of these simple sentences, making a compound, then a complex, and finally a compound-complex sentence.

EXAMPLE He is always late.
(compound) *He is always late, and his brother is always early.*
(complex) *He is always late because he oversleeps.*
(compound-complex) *He is always late when there is a test, so the teacher is moving him to a later class.*

1. Fast food is not cheap.
(compound) ______________________________
(complex) ______________________________
(compound-complex) ______________________________

2. The lecture hall was packed.
(compound) ______________________________
(complex) ______________________________
(compound-complex) ______________________________

3. Read contracts before you sign them.
(compound) ______________________________
(complex) ______________________________
(compound-complex) ______________________________

4. Thai restaurants are increasingly common.
(compound) ______________________________
(complex) ______________________________
(compound-complex) ______________________________

5. Grocery stores should be open twenty-four hours a day.
(compound) ______________________________
(complex) ______________________________
(compound-complex) ______________________________

C: Write complete sentences by adding one or more independent clauses to each of these subordinate clauses.

EXAMPLE if I have a chance

If I have a chance, I'll learn to draw. ______________________

1. because she has a pet snake

____

2. whoever has the flu

____

3. before the union votes on the contract

____

4. even though they paid the electric bill

____

5. where the keys are

____

6. that fit in your pocket

____

7. who has the prize-winning ticket

____

8. since she learned to drive

____

9. whether the bus stops on that corner

____

10. if it has only one moving part

____

Writing Present-Tense Verbs

EXERCISE 22-1

(22c)

Fill in the blanks with the third person singular, present tense of the verbs in parentheses.

EXAMPLE Every driver (to hope) *hopes* to avoid an accident.

1. However, sometimes a cautious driver (to rush) _______________ to cross railway tracks but doesn't make it.
2. Even if the driver (to tie) _______________ in the race with the train, he or she loses.
3. A standard diesel locomotive (to weigh) _______________ 135 tonnes.
4. The train engineer (to need) _______________ almost 2 kilometres to stop a train that is going 100 km/h.
5. Often, a driver (to attempt) _______________ to go around lowered gates at the crossing.
6. A person who (to fail) _______________ to obey warning signs, gates, and signals is in great danger.
7. Similarly, a driver who (to start) _______________ across the tracks before the gates have been lifted puts all the people in the car in danger.
8. The safety gate (to open) _______________ only when both directions of the train's path are clear.
9. If a driver (to wait) _______________ for only one train to pass, he or she may not realize that another train may be coming from the opposite direction.
10. Another dangerous situation (to occur) _______________ when slick pavement and excessive speeds cause a driver to skid onto the tracks.
11. A police officer (to report) _______________ that many train-related accidents are caused by drivers whose abilities have been impaired by alcohol or drugs.
12. Adverse weather (to affect) _______________ driving conditions as well.
13. A safety bulletin (to recommend) _______________ that drivers watch carefully for the yellow and black warning signs.
14. Such a sign (to warn) _______________ drivers to slow down for an oncoming train.
15. A nearby sign (to post) _______________ the appropriate speed limit, which should always be observed near a railway crossing.
16. Because of traffic laws, a school bus (to stop) _______________ completely at railway crossings—even when the gates are not lowered.

17. The law (to require) _______________ the same safety procedure for trucks carrying combustible or hazardous materials.

18. When behind a vehicle of this sort, a driver (to know) _______________ not to follow too closely or to become impatient.

19. When a driver (to hear) _______________ a bell suddenly activate while passing over the tracks, he or she should not panic.

20. The device (to allow) _______________ enough time for the driver to cross the tracks before the train arrives.

21. The gate (to remain) _______________ raised until the car gets over to the other side.

22. If a driver (to brake) _______________ and reverses, he or she may be blocked by a car in the rear.

23. A train (to cause) _______________ an accident only when drivers are careless or impatient.

24. A driver (to face) _______________ severe penalties in most jurisdictions for not obeying the warning gates and lights.

25. If a driver (to practise) _______________ safety and caution, others will follow, making railway crossings safer for all other drivers.

Writing Past-Tense Verbs

EXERCISE 22-2
(22d)

Fill in the blanks with the past-tense forms of the verbs in parentheses.

EXAMPLE Have you ever (to wonder) *wondered* why people fly kites?

1. Malayans (to start) _______________ to use kites for ceremonial purposes at least 3000 years ago.
2. In ancient hieroglyphics, Egyptians (to record) _______________ legends about kites.
3. Yet kites probably (to develop) _______________ first in China.
4. In the Han Dynasty, the emperor (to use) _______________ kites to intimidate invaders.
5. He (to insert) _______________ bamboo pipes into the kites.
6. When flown above the invaders' camp, the kites (to issue) _______________ moaning sounds that (to startle) the men below.
7. Because the night was dark, the men (to perceive) _______________ nothing in the sky above them.
8. It is not surprising that they (to jerk) _______________ up their tents and immediately (to head) _______________ for home.
9. More recently, Benjamin Franklin (to employ) _______________ a kite for his experiments with electricity.
10. An Englishman, George Pocock, (to pull) _______________ a carriage and passengers with two eight-foot kites.
11. The Wright brothers (to experiment) _______________ with kites even after their success with the airplane.
12. And you (to imagine) _______________ that people flew kites just for fun!

Writing Irregular Past-Tense Verbs

EXERCISE 22-3

(22d)

Fill in the blanks with the correct past-tense forms of the irregular verbs in parenthesis.

EXAMPLE We (to swear) *swore* we would never leave the door unlocked again.

1. The woman (to wake) _______________ early and looked at the clock. It was 5:00 a.m.
2. Sensing something was wrong, she (to get) _______________ up and opened the door to the utility room, where her dog normally (to sleep)
3. She (to freeze) _______________ at what she saw: the room was empty and the door (to stand) _______________ open.
4. The woman (to shake) _______________ her husband awake and (to tell) him that the dog was missing.
5. Then she (to throw) _______________ on some clothes and jumped in the car.
6. She (to drive) _______________up and down nearby streets looking for her pet.
7. She even (to swing) _______________ by her friend's house two miles away to see if he was there.
8. However, she (to draw) _______________ a blank. Finally she admitted defeat and (to come) _______________ home.
9. When she (to see) _______________ her husband, she (to burst) _______________ into tears.
10. They both (to think) _______________ they would never see their dog again.
11. The woman (to go) _______________ to work and (to spend) _______________ the entire day wondering if her dog was safe.
12. When she (to get) _______________ home, she (to speak) _______________ to her neighbour and asked if he had seen the animal.
13. Then she (to hear) _______________ a rustling behind her.
14. She (to spin) _______________ around, and (to see) _______________ the dog cowering in the bushes.
15. At the sound of his name, however, he (to spring) _______________ out.
16. He (to shake) _______________ his coat, which was muddy and matted.
17. She immediately (to sweep) _______________ him up in her arms and (to take) _______________him inside.
18. He (to cling) _______________ to her as if traumatized.
19. However, she (to feel) _______________ no broken bones, and he (to eat) _______________ and (to drink) _______________ normally.
20. When her husband (to ring) _______________ to say he was on his way home, she (to tell) him the good news.

Conjugating be

EXERCISE 22-4
(22e)

The verb *be* has many irregular forms. Fill in the chart with all of its forms. Then check your work by looking at the chart in 22e.

	Person	Present Tense	Past Tense
Singular			
	First	__________	__________
	Second	__________	__________
	Third	__________	__________
Plural			
	First	__________	__________
	Second	__________	__________
	Third	__________	__________

Present Participle __________

Past Participle __________

Using the Verb be

EXERCISE 22-5

(22e)

Fill in the blanks with appropriate forms of the verb *be*.

As Earth's climate warms, the people who live in the far north _______ looking for ways to cope. Even their housing may _______ affected. Some houses in Nunavut whose foundations stand on the permafrost have _______ undermined as the permafrost begins to melt. Buildings today _______ sinking and are even _______ torn apart as they tilt and buckle on the softening earth.

Richard Carbonnier, an architect who works for the government of Nunavut, ______ developing a new kind of house for the far north. His prototype _______ called the Inuksuk Residence, and its supporters think that it should _______ adopted widely. It _______ a strange looking structure, Carbonnier admits, but it _______ meant _______ above all else a practical structure.

Instead of _______ supported by a regular foundation, the house stands well above the ground on a tripod made of three stilts. Each stilt _______ able to shift if the earth underneath it moves. Supported by this tripod system, the house will _______ able to withstand the melting permafrost safely.

Carbonnier always has _______ eager to borrow those features of the traditional igloo that could make the Inuksuk Residence a practical dwelling for the north. As well, because Carbonnier _______ concerned from the very start about the environment, he made sure that a number of ecological advances _______ incorporated in its design.

The prototype house as it can be seen today _______ a modular building formed from three large cylinders. These _______ joined together and they all lie flat, so that from the air the whole structure looks like a large Y. If you _______ ever lucky enough _______ flying over Pond Inlet in Nunavut, _______ sure to look out for Carbonnier's house on the hill overlooking the town.

Using Helping Verbs

EXERCISE 22-6
(22e)

Fill in the blanks with the helping verbs from this list. Some sentences have several possible answers, but be sure to use each helping verb at least once.

are	do	is	was
be	does	may	were
can	has	seem	will
could	have	should	would

EXAMPLE In order for a child to develop into a helpful member of society, the family unit *should* act as a mini-society.

1. Children who volunteer time, first in the home and then in society, _______________ destined to develop qualities like self-sacrifice and a strong commitment to the community.
2. The year 2001 _______________ declared the International Year of Volunteers, a project supported by the federal government.
3. Volunteerism _______________ be defined as the willingness to go beyond self-interest.
4. People who volunteer in their communities _______________ contribute freely toward the common good.
5. Without doubt, volunteering _______________ require giving more than spare change: it requires energy, time, and commitment.
6. Adults who _______________ raised in homes with limits on their behaviour have learned that they were not the centre of attention.
7. A family _______________ act as a mini-society by demanding of the child what society eventually will.
8. Society _______________ eventually expect an honest, responsible, and respectful individual to develop.
9. Society _______________ most benefit from a member who is willing to share, to help others, and to encourage the growth of the community.
10. The family _______________ responsible for instilling in a child these important values at an early age.
11. Parents _______________ begin teaching a child about volunteerism as early as the age of three by assigning routine household chores.
12. At first, children _______________ merely be expected to pick up after themselves and keep their rooms in order.

13. A few years later, the child _______________ be responsible for chores that involve the home, such as mopping and vacuuming the floor or helping with the dishes.

14. Children who _______________ participate in family chores learn that family is not only about fun; it is also about cooperation.

15. Giving children money for doing chores _______________ be an obstacle in the learning process because money teaches them that they should expect something in return for their efforts.

16. A child can _______________ taught the three Rs of good citizenship at an early age: respect, responsibility, and resourcefulness.

17. Volunteering _______________ become an important part of family values in Canada, both for parents and children.

18. In fact, over 7.5 million Canadians _______________ participated actively in community service at one time or another, thus making each community a better place.

Identifying Transitive, Intransitive, and Linking Verbs

EXERCISE 22-7
(22f)

Identify each italicized verb by writing *transitive*, *intransitive*, or *linking* on the lines to the right.

EXAMPLE The platypus of Australia *is* an unusual animal. *linking*

1. Europeans first *saw* the platypus in 1796. ____________
2. The platypus *is* nocturnal. ____________
3. Usually it *stays* out of sight. ____________
4. The Europeans *could* hardly believe their eyes. ____________
5. The platypus *has* a bizarre appearance. ____________
6. Its bill *resembles* that of a duck. ____________
7. However, the bill *is* really a soft snout. ____________
8. With the bill the platypus *probes* in the mud for food. ____________
9. The platypus *has* a tail and fur like a beaver. ____________
10. With its webbed feet it *swims* well. ____________
11. Nevertheless, the feet *have* claws for digging in river banks. ____________
12. The platypus *is* a mammal. ____________
13. Yet it *lays* eggs. ____________
14. After hatching, the young *nurse*. ____________
15. No wonder one scientist *named* the platypus paradoxus. ____________
16. It *is* indeed a paradox. ____________

Writing Sentences with Transitive and Intransitive Verbs

EXERCISE 22-8
(22f)

Write two sentences for each of the following verbs, one in which it is transitive and one in which it is intransitive.

EXAMPLE open
Bilad's garage door opens easily.
Bilad opens his garage door easily when he uses a crowbar.

1. answer

   intransitive: ______________________________

   transitive: ______________________________

2. walk

   intransitive: ______________________________

   transitive: ______________________________

3. prepare

   intransitive: ______________________________

   transitive: ______________________________

4. drive

   intransitive: ______________________________

   transitive: ______________________________

5. paint

   intransitive: ______________________________

   transitive: ______________________________

Distinguishing the Forms of lie/lay, sit/set, and rise/raise

EXERCISE 22-9
(22f)

Fill in the blanks with the verb in parentheses that best suits the meaning of each sentence.

EXAMPLE The morning sun (raised, rose) *rose* over the Prairie landscape.

1. Dawn revealed a small number of grain elevators (setting, sitting) __________ by the railway line.

2. The railway, which (laid, lay) __________ across the Prairie, stretched eastward to Lake Superior, where the city of Thunder Bay (lays, lies) __________.

3. In Thunder Bay, more grain elevators (raised, rose) __________ their profiles against the dawn sky.

4. The wheat (laying, lying) __________ in the Prairie elevators was newly harvested.

5. In Thunder Bay, however, much of the wheat had (laid, lain) __________ in the elevators for days.

6. Some wheat already (sat, set) __________ in the holds of oceangoing ships, ready for export.

7. The first grain elevators (raised, rose) __________ above the Prairie landscape soon after the first rail lines were (laid, lain) __________.

8. Farmers' cooperatives often (raised, rose) __________ the funds to erect the wooden, box-like structures.

9. Huge concrete grain elevators, like those in Thunder Bay, were usually (sat, set) __________ up by private companies.

10. The grain elevator got its name from the conveyor belt used to (raise, rise) __________ buckets of grain up into the storage compartment.

Using the Perfect and Progressive Tenses

EXERCISE 22-10
(22i–j)

Fill in the blanks with the verb forms described in parentheses. Be prepared to discuss why each verb is appropriate in its sentence.

EXAMPLE The aftereffects of kisses (to cause: present perfect) _have caused_ researchers to recommend a daily dose of this sign of affection.

1. German physicians and psychologists (to discover: present perfect) __________ that a kiss can improve a person's health.

2. Spouses who (to kiss: present perfect progressive) __________ their partner each day before work since the beginning of their marriages tend to live healthier, happier, and longer lives than those who don't.

3. Researchers (to begin: present progressive) __________ to understand why.

4. One researcher, Dr. Arthur Szabo, (to study: present perfect progressive) __________ those who kiss and those who don't.

5. He (to find: present perfect) __________ that those who kiss their spouses in the morning miss fewer workdays because of illness than those who don't.

6. Furthermore, it turns out that those who kiss (to involve: past perfect progressive passive) __________ in fewer automobile accidents while on the way to work than those who didn't.

7. It also seems that spouses who start the day with a kiss (to earn: present progressive) __________30 percent more than those who do not.

8. Dr. Szabo (to say: past perfect) __________ that the difference is that spouses who kiss start their day with a more positive attitude, one which allows them to get through their day a bit easier.

9. In fact, kissing (to link: present perfect progressive passive) __________ to living longer; on average, those who kiss (to live: present progressive) __________ five years longer than those who don't.

10. Why is it that kisses (to have: present perfect progressive) __________ such huge effects on people?

11. Dr. Szabo (to suggest: present perfect) __________ that since a kiss is a form of approval, those who don't experience one in the morning do not have the same positive feelings and confidence as those who do kiss.

12. With this report, new superstitions (to start: present progressive) __________to develop already.

13. Perhaps, people all along (to know: present perfect) __________ that a morning kiss is the right way to start the day.

14. But they could not (to understand: present perfect) __________ why this is true until very recently.

15. Certainly, the physicians and psychologists who (to study: present perfect progressive) __________ kisses strongly recommend them for a boost in spirit, health, and happiness.

Identifying Active and Passive Verbs

EXERCISE 22-11
(22n)

Underline the entire main verb in each sentence, and then identify it as active or passive on the lines to the right.

EXAMPLE The Louvre *contains* some of the world's most famous art work. *active*

1. The Louvre in Paris was not built as an art museum. ____________
2. The original Louvre was constructed in the twelfth century as a fortress. ____________
3. Francis I began the present building as a residence. ____________
4. A gallery connecting it with the Tuileries Palace was started by Henry IV and completed by Louis XIV. ____________
5. A second gallery, begun by Napoleon, would have enclosed a great square. ____________
6. However, it was not finished until after his abdication. ____________
7. Revolutionaries overthrew the Bastille on July 14, 1789. ____________
8. Just four years later, the art collection of the Louvre was opened to the public. ____________
9. The collection can be traced back to Francis I. ____________
10. Francis, an ardent collector, invited Leonardo da Vinci to France in 1515. ____________
11. Leonardo brought the *Mona Lisa* with him from Italy. ____________
12. Nevertheless, the royal art collection may have been expanded more by ministers than by kings. ____________
13. Cardinals Richelieu and Mazarin can take credit for many important acquisitions. ____________
14. Today the Louvre has a new entrance. ____________
15. A glass pyramid in the courtyard was designed by I. M. Pei. ____________
16. Pei's name can be added to a distinguished list of Louvre architects. ____________

Revising for the Active Voice

EXERCISE 22-12

(22o)

A: Change each of the passive sentences you identified in Exercise 22-11 into the active voice. You may need to add words to act as subjects of your new sentences. Use your own paper.

B: On the lines to the right, identify each sentence as active or passive. Then rewrite each passive sentence into the active voice. However, if you think a sentence is better left passive, write your reason on the line instead.

EXAMPLE Today's country of Zimbabwe was named after important ruins. *passive*
Patriots named today's country of Zimbabwe after important ruins.

1. The ruins were not known by people outside Africa until 1868. ______________

____

2. The largest of the ruins, Great Zimbabwe, has two main structures. ______________

____

3. The building on the hill was constructed primarily for defence. ______________

____

4. Its stones are fitted together without mortar. ______________

____

5. A lower, elliptical building is encircled by a nine-metre wall. ______________

____

6. An inner wall forms a passage to a sacred enclosure. ______________

____

7. Majestic soapstone sculptures were discovered there. ______________

____

8. The enclosure contains towers twelve metres high. ______________

____

9. Ancestors of the Shona-speaking people maintained Great Zimbabwe as a trade centre from the twelfth through the fifteenth centuries. ______________

____

10. Tools for working with gold have been found in the ruins. ______________

____

11. The Shona traded gold and ivory with Arab merchants. ______________

____

Knowing the Personal Pronouns

EXERCISE 23-1

(23b)

The personal pronouns change form to show whether they are being used as subjects, objects, or possessives and to match the person and number of their antecedents. Fill in this chart with the appropriate forms of the personal pronouns. Then check yourself by looking at the chart at the beginning of Chapter 23.

Person	Subjective Case	Objective Case	Possessive Case
Singular	________	________	________
First	________	________	________
Second	________	________	________
Third	________	________	________
Plural	________	________	________
First	________	________	________
Second	________	________	________
Third	________	________	________

Identifying Pronoun Case

EXERCISE 23-2
(23b)

Underline the personal pronouns. Then on the lines to the right indicate their cases.

EXAMPLE I am thinking of revising my travel plans. ______*subjective*______ ______*possessive*______

1. Friends recommended Newfoundland to me for a vacation. ______________ ______________
2. They said that the people there are the friendliest in all of Canada. ______________ ______________
3. No visitor among the Newfoundlanders can escape their hospitable attentions, apparently. ______________ ______________
4. "Your hosts will insist on showing you the island's magnificent sights," was the unanimous refrain. ______________ ______________
5. Among these are its granite shores and the grey ocean that beats upon them. ______________ ______________
6. Tiny wooden fishing villages still cling to their rocky perches. ______________ ______________
7. The mountains of the interior rise above dark forests like those we read of in the tales of the early Canadian explorers. ______________ ______________
8. I was told, though, that St. John's is now a cosmopolitan city, like many of our other favourite destinations. ______________ ______________
9. But these friends say that my hosts will definitely have other plans for me as well. ______________ ______________
10. Your cousin Stephen and his sister Laura have carefully corroborated this information. ______________ ______________
11. The people who befriend me there will try to make me kiss a codfish on the lips—an old ritual for welcoming newcomers to the island. ______________ ______________
12. That explains why I am asking you today about flights to Saskatchewan. ______________ ______________

Using Personal Pronouns

EXERCISE 23-3
(23b)

Select the correct pronoun from the choice in parentheses. Write your answers on the lines to the right. If two or more choices are needed, use a comma to separate them on the answer line.

EXAMPLE My family and (I, me) visited Ottawa last spring. ____*I*____

1. Other tourists and (we, us) were delighted by what (we, us) saw. ________
2. (It, Its) is a beautiful city. ________
3. By the end of the week, each of (us, ours) had a favourite place. ________
4. My little brother was impressed by what (he, his) saw at the Royal Canadian Mint. ________
5. (He, Him) and (I, me) took a tour of the Mint. ________
6. We could not believe (our, ours) eyes when we saw people actually making money. ________
7. As (he, him) and (I, me) watched people minting coins, my brother said it was a great job because the people could keep some money for (them, themselves). ________
8. I told (he, him) that he was kidding (him, himself) if he really believed that. ________
9. Employees have security people watching (them, themselves) and the money (it, itself) is counted and recounted to prevent theft. ________
10. I wondered if (them, their) working around money all day might make money less exciting to these people after a while. ________
11. Still, it was fascinating for (we, us) to watch all that money being coined. ________
12. The Parliament Buildings were (me, my) favourite place. ________
13. Near the Parliament Buildings stands a statue of John A. Macdonald (hisself, himself), looking out over the capital. ________

14. Standing near that statue made my sister and (I, me) feel very calm, as if Macdonald were watching out for (us, ourselves). ________________

15. My sister said that the most exciting place for (she, her) was the Canadian Museum of Civilization, in Gatineau. ________________

16. This is probably because of (her, hers) desire to be an anthropologist. ________________

17. If (you, yous) go to Ottawa, make a trip to Gatineau to visit the Museum of Civilization even if (you, your) are not planning to be an anthropologist or archaeologist. ________________

18. Children will especially enjoy the chance the museum gives (they, them) to see old films of First Nations ceremonies and practices. ________________

19. While there, they can also see for (theirselfs, themselves) towering totem poles. ________________

20. Now that I have told you about my family's favourite places in the National Capital Region, will you tell me about (your, yours)? ________________

Identifying and Using Personal Pronouns as Appositives and Complements

EXERCISE 23-4

(23e–f)

A: Underline all personal pronouns used as appositives or complements. Then draw an arrow connecting each to its antecedent. Be prepared to explain why each pronoun takes the case it does.

EXAMPLE The winner is I.

1. The composers, he and she, have won many awards for their music.
2. A merry old king was he.
3. The raccoons moved into the only furnished attic on the block, ours.
4. The latest composers to have their hit song chosen as a cell phone ring tone are they.
5. I cleared up my last large debt, my telephone bill, thirteen months later.

B: Select the correct pronoun for formal situations from the choices in parentheses. Write your answers on the lines to the right.

EXAMPLE The smartest couple, you and (I, me) ________ will be on the cover of the yearbook. ________*I*________

1. If anyone deserves a medal, it is (she, her) ______. ______________
2. Our travel agent has booked a vacation tour for us, just you and (I, me) _______. ______________
3. The recipient of the donated heart was (he, him) ______. ______________
4. I saw the thieves, (he, him) ________ and his brother. ______________
5. Altos, (I, me) ________ for one, don't get to sing any of the great opera roles. ______________

Using who, whoever, whom, *and* whomever

EXERCISE 23-5

(23g)

Select the correct relative or interrogative pronoun (*who, whom, whoever,* or *whomever*) from the choices in parentheses. Write your answers on the lines to the right.

EXAMPLE The number of children (who, whom) are in a family may affect the intelligence of all the children. ______ *who* ______

1. Researchers (who, whom) studied over 350 000 men in the 1940s found that IQ fell as family size increased. ____________
2. Children (who, whom) were born into a family later tended to have lower IQs. ____________
3. Recent research supports the theory that (whoever, whomever) is born first has an advantage. ____________
4. Children (who, whom) researchers checked for IQ and school performance did better if they were the oldest in small families. ____________
5. (Whoever, Whomever) was an only child, however, scored like a younger child. ____________
6. (Who, Whom) can be sure why these trends occur? ____________
7. It may be that younger children receive less mental stimulation because their brothers and sisters (who, whom) teach them are immature. ____________
8. Only children, (who, whom) are usually considered lucky, may miss out because they never have a chance to grow by teaching their own younger brothers and sisters. ____________
9. Perhaps parents' attention, no matter to (who, whom) it is given, is limited, so there is simply more of it per child in smaller families. ____________
10. Of course, there are highly intelligent and successful people (who, whom) are born into large families. ____________
11. Teachers and parents of young children should be careful about (who, whom) they make judgments. ____________
12. We cannot use these studies to predict the future of (whoever, whomever) we please, because in the end success depends on a lot more than birth order and family size. ____________
13. Few successful people (who, whom) have been asked the secret of their success talk about birth order. ____________

14. Often, successful people give credit to their drive to achieve something and to the people (who, whom) supported them. ______________

15. For example, listen to the speeches at any awards ceremony and you will hear people thanking the parents, teachers, and friends without (who, whom) they could not have succeeded. ______________

16. (Who, Whom) would you thank if you were giving such a speech? ______________

Choosing Pronoun Cases Carefully

EXERCISE 23-6

(23h–k)

Select the correct pronoun from the choices in parentheses. Write your answers on the lines to the right.

EXAMPLE The National Film Board has trained Canadian filmmakers and funded (they, them) since 1939. *them*

1. After he had proved (him, himself) as an innovative filmmaker in England, Scottish-born John Grierson was invited to come to Canada in 1938. ______________
2. Canadian authorities wanted (he, him) to give advice on a government-run film agency. ______________
3. (His, Him) studying the question led Grierson to recommend setting up the National Film Board. ______________
4. Grierson became the first commissioner of the new agency, known as the NFB; no other commissioner has been as influential as (he, him). ______________
5. It was (he, him) who invented the term documentary and who inspired the NFB to become a world leader in documentary filmmaking. ______________
6. A highly creative man, Grierson hired many other talented people and inspired (they, them) to do some of their best work. ______________
7. During the Second World War, the NFB played an important role through (it, its) informing and encouraging soldiers and civilians. ______________
8. The NFB also publicized the aims and efforts of the Allies to US audiences before the United States (it, itself) entered the war in late 1941. ______________

9. By 1945, the agency was fighting with the government to keep the independence that allowed (it, itself) to explore social problems and advocate workers' rights. ______________
10. That year, Grierson resigned his position; many people believe (he, him) to have been forced out. ______________
11. The NFB renewed (it, itself) in the 1950s, when directors such as Norman McLaren began to win awards for innovative work in animation. ______________
12. In the 1970s, under Kathleen Shannon, the NFB's Studio D produced films by women, dealing with women's work and (their, they) position in society. ______________
13. By the 1990s, however, much of the NFB's funding had been cut, Studio D was closed down, and filmmakers were questioning the NFB's importance to their profession and (them, themselves). ______________

Using Pronouns to Refer to a Single Nearby Antecedent

EXERCISE 23-7

(23l–n)

Underline the pronouns in these passages. Then, if the antecedents are clear and close enough to their pronouns, copy the sentences onto the lines. If the antecedents are unclear or too far away, use the lines to revise the sentences.

EXAMPLE Henry C. Wallace and his son Henry A. Wallace held the same cabinet post. He was the Secretary of Agriculture under US Presidents Harding and Coolidge, and he was Secretary of Agriculture under Franklin Roosevelt.

Henry C. Wallace and his son Henry A. Wallace held the same cabinet post. The elder Henry C. Wallace was the Secretary of Agriculture under US Presidents Harding and Coolidge, and the younger Henry A. Wallace was the Secretary of Ag iculture under F anklin Roosevelt.

1. Unlike most recent Canadian prime ministers, three out of the first five Canadian prime ministers were born in Scotland or England. Most of them were born in Canada.

2. The first Canadian-born prime minister, Sir John Abbott, held office in 1891 and 1892; the last British-born prime minister was John Turner. He led the government for a few weeks in 1984.

3. For religious reasons, US president-elect Zachary Taylor refused to take the oath of office on a Sunday, so David Rice Atchison (president of the Senate) was president for a day. He spent the day appointing his temporary cabinet.

4. Jean Chrétien did not want to be succeeded in office by his old rival Paul Martin.

5. An American Indian, Charles Curtis, became vice-president when Herbert Hoover was elected president in 1928. He was one-half Kaw.

6. William DeVance King, vice-president under Franklin Pierce, was in Cuba during the election and had to be sworn in by an act of Congress, never bothering to return to Washington. A month later, never having carried out any official duties, he died.

____

____

7. The Republicans got their elephant and the Democrats got their donkey as symbols from political cartoonist Thomas Nast.

____

____

8. Like their British counterparts, Conservatives in Canada were nicknamed "Tories," but unlike theirs, Liberals in Canada were called "Grits," not "Whigs."

____

____

9. The first woman presidential candidate was Victoria Woodhull. Years before Geraldine Ferraro ran for vice-president, she was on the Equal Rights Party ticket—in 1872.

____

____

10. The first woman to lead a major party in the Canadian House of Commons was Audrey McLaughlin, and the second was Kim Campbell. She became the first woman prime minister.

____

____

11. As a child, president-to-be Andrew Johnson was sold as an indentured servant to a tailor. He was supposed to work for seven years, but he ran away.

____

____

Using Pronouns to Refer to Definite Antecedents

EXERCISE 23-8
(23o–p)

Revise these vague passages so that all pronouns have definite antecedents. Be alert for implied antecedents and the misuse of *it, they,* and *you.*

EXAMPLE Ordinary people could soon be living and working aboard space stations. They are unusual but quite safe. *Ordinary people could soon be living and working aboard space stations. The stations are unusual but quite safe.*

1. A California company called the Space Island Group is planning to recycle one of the shortest-lived components of the space shuttle. It is ingenious.

 ____

 ____

2. Engineers at SIG plan to construct dozens of wheel-shaped space stations using empty shuttle fuel tanks. They are eminently suited to the task.

 ____

 ____

3. A shuttle's fuel tanks are huge. Each one is 8.5 metres in diameter and nearly 50 metres long—approximately the size of a jumbo jet. It jettisons them just before it reaches orbit, leaving them to burn up and crash into the ocean.

 ____

 ____

4. Over 100 of these tanks, known as ETs, have been used and destroyed since the first shuttle launch in 1981. So you can see how much hardware has gone to waste.

 ____

 ____

5. Using ETs to form manned space stations—and developing passenger shuttles to take people to them—was originally NASA's idea. At first, they were enthusiastic about this possibility.

 ____

 ____

6. However, it would have taken too long for NASA to develop and test passenger shuttles, so it was dropped.

____

____

7. SIG's plan is to build the passenger shuttles and lease them to commercial airlines. They believe that this is the fastest way to get ordinary people into space.

____

____

8. The space stations will also be leased—at a rate of $10 to $20 per cubic foot per day—to anyone wishing to run a business in space. You simply take the shuttle, transfer to the space station, and set up your office.

____

____

9. While the space stations have a projected life of 30 years, they claim that tenants would fully pay for them within 2 to 3 years. This means that the passenger shuttle program could actually operate at a profit.

____

____

Revising to Eliminate Misuse of you

EXERCISE 23-9

(23r)

Revise this paragraph to eliminate the inappropriate use of *you*, Begin by changing "You have to be careful" to "Everyone has to be careful." Then change further uses of *you* to suitable nouns or pronouns. It may be necessary to change some verbs in order to have them agree with new subjects.

You have to be careful when buying on credit. Otherwise, you may wind up so heavily in debt that it will take years to straighten out your life. Credit cards are easy for you to get if you are working, and many finance companies are eager to give you instalment loans at high interest rates. Once you are hooked, you may find yourself taking out loans to pay your loans. When this happens, you are doomed to being forever in debt.

There are, of course, times when using credit makes sense. If you have the money (or will have it when the bill comes), a credit card can enable you to shop without carrying cash. You may also want to keep a few gasoline credit cards with you in case your car breaks down on the road. Using credit will allow you to deal with other emergencies (tuition, a broken water heater) when you lack the cash. You can also use credit to take advantage of sales. However, you need to recognize the difference between a sale item you need and one you want. If you cannot do this, you may find yourself dealing with collection agents, car repossessors, or even bankruptcy lawyers.

Subject–Verb Agreement

EXERCISE 24-1
(24a–n)

A: Fill in the blanks on the right with the present-tense forms of the verbs in parentheses. Be sure each verb agrees in person and number with the subject of the sentence. (24c)

EXAMPLE The Cuna Indians (to produce) an unusual kind of art. ___*produce*___

1. Cuna Indians (to occupy) the San Blas Islands off the coast of Panama. __________
2. The outside world (to associate) them with distinctive women's clothing. __________
3. Cuna women (to wear) blouses containing two panels of appliquéd cloth. __________
4. The Cuna word *mola* (to refer) to either a blouse or one of its panels. __________
5. The Cuna (to work) their molas in reverse appliqué. __________
6. Traditional appliqué (to consist) of turning under edges of a piece of fabric and sewing it onto a larger piece. __________
7. Molas (to use) a different technique. __________
8. A Cuna woman (to baste) together several layers of cloth of different colours. __________
9. She then (to cut) through all but the bottom layer. __________
10. When turned under, the upper layers (to reveal) contrasting colours. __________

B: Fill in the blanks on the right with the appropriate present-tense forms of the verbs in parentheses. (24d–f)

EXAMPLE Most resources of the earth (to be) not renewable. ___*are*___

1. Neither coffee grounds nor an apple core (to need) to be thrown out. __________
2. Food waste, along with grass clippings, (to make) good compost. __________
3. Many items from your garbage (to be) recyclable. __________
4. Aluminum cans, plastic jugs, and glass bottles (to deserve) a second life. __________
5. One of the most tedious jobs (to seem) to be sorting garbage. __________
6. Yet rewards from such work (to be) immeasurable. __________

7. Every recycled bottle and can (to mean) a saving of resources. ____________

8. Not only an adult but also a child (to be) capable of helping the environment. ____________

9. Learning what to recycle, as well as being willing to do it, (to become) necessary. ____________

10. You and I each (to be) expected to do our part. ____________

C: Circle the subjects and underline the verbs. If the verb does not agree with the subject, cross it out and write the correct form on the line to the right. If the verb does agree, write *correct* on the line. (24g, j)

EXAMPLE Kyoto the historic capital of Japan, ~~are~~ really many cities in one. *is*

1. Has Ken and Sara ever visited Japan? ____________
2. There is several places they should see. ____________
3. It is cities like Kyoto that transmit Japanese culture. ____________
4. Japanese history seems alive here. ____________
5. There is more than two thousand temples in Kyoto. ____________
6. In the city are also castles and luxurious residences. ____________
7. There is peaceful Zen gardens. ____________
8. Japanese art and architecture reveals the history of the empire. ____________
9. Yet there is also a very modern city. ____________
10. From all over the world comes visitors to Kyoto.

D: Fill in the blanks on the right with the present-tense forms of the verbs in parentheses. (24h, i)

EXAMPLE Most of Chicago's visitors (to be) impressed by its architecture. *are*

1. The Chicago School (to be) a group of architects at the start of the twentieth century. ____________
2 Some (to be) known throughout the world. ____________
3. Not everyone in the group (to be) considered a genius. ____________
4. Yet all (to have) contributed to the appearance of the city. ____________
5. A number of buildings (to be) considered architectural landmarks. ____________
6. Many (to share) certain features like Chicago windows. ____________
7. One of the most famous styles (to be) Frank Lloyd Wright's Prairie House. ____________
8. A tour group visiting Chicago today (to be) sure to enjoy a drive down the Magnificent Mile. ____________

9. A family often (to prefer) a walking tour. ____________

10. Few (to be) exempt from the charms of a constantly building city. ____________

E: Circle the antecedent of each italicized *who*, *which*, or *that*. Then fill in the blanks on the right with the appropriate present-tense forms of the verbs in parentheses. (24l, k)

EXAMPLE The *Book of Kells* is one of many (manuscripts) *that* (to belong) to Trinity College, Dublin. *belong*

1. Its source is a mystery *that* (to continue) to baffle scholars. ____________
2. Anyone *who* (to see) it marvels at its brilliant illumination. ____________
3. The book, *which* (to be) considered a masterpiece, contains full-page illustrations of the Gospels. ____________
4. No one *who* (to study) the book can fail to be impressed by it. ____________
5. The paintings, *which* (to be) done in minute detail, retain their vivid colours. ____________
6. There is also decoration *that* (to appear) to have no relationship to the text. ____________
7. Some of the pictures, *which* (to stem) from unknown origins, seem strange for a religious book. ____________
8. One does not expect birds *that* (to wear) ecclesiastical garb. ____________
9. Nor does one expect the humour *that* (to pervade) some of the illustrations. ____________
10. The text, *which* (to be) written in beautiful script, combines two translations. ____________

F: Fill in the blanks on the right with the appropriate present-tense forms of the verbs in parentheses. (24l, m)

EXAMPLE Most people (to be) interested in learning more about themselves. *are*

1. Astrology (to seem) to satisfy some people's curiosity about why they are the way they are. ____________
2. Just twelve astrological signs (to show) all the complexities of people's personalities. ____________
3. A friend of mine, a proponent of astrology, (to argue) that there is a lot more to it than just the twelve signs. ____________

4 People who are more scientifically inclined (to look) to the Myers-Briggs Type Indicator (MBTI) to learn more about their personalities. ____________

5. The founders of the MBTI (to belong) to no particular school of psychology, but their findings are similar to those of Carl Jung. ____________

6. The MBTI (to make) sense to most people who take the test to learn about their personality types. ____________

7. Numerous companies (to publish) books about personality types. ____________

8. A psychologist (to deal) with issues of personality in a number of ways. ____________

9. But the average person (to get) some useful personal insight by taking some psychological tests published in self-help books. ____________

10. If you're curious about your personality traits, there's one way to find out about them. (To ask) a friend. ____________

G: Fill in the blanks on the right with the appropriate present-tense forms of the verbs in parentheses. (24a–m)

EXAMPLE Everyone (to dream) during sleep. *dreams*

1. No one (to know) why we (to dream). ____________

2. Dreams (to occur) during a special kind of sleep, known as REM. ____________

3. REM (to stand) for Rapid Eye Movement. ____________

4. A total of about two hours a night (to get) spent in this dream state. ____________

5. There (to be) many theories about why people dream and what the rapid movement of our eyeballs (to mean). ____________

6. Some (to suggest) that REM sleep occurs when the brain ids itself of unnecessary images. ____________

7. According to this theory, dreams (to represent) random signals. ____________

8. Others (to believe) that dreaming helps the brain establish patterns for thinking. ____________

9. Human newborns, they say, (to spend) about half their sleep time dreaming. ____________

10. The babies, who (to receive) huge amounts of new information every day, may be developing plans for processing what they see and hear. ____________

11. In contrast, the elderly (to devote) only 15 percent of their sleep time to dreaming. ____________

12. Why we dream and what dreams mean (to form) a big mystery. ____________

13 Psychologists (to think) dreams help people deal with emotional issues. ____________

14. The population often (to lack) the time necessary to cope with complicated emotional situations. ____________

15. For example, people in the middle of divorce often (to have) long, detailed dreams. ____________

16. In contrast, people with peaceful lives generally (to claim) their dreams are dull. ____________

17. Sigmund Freud said that dreams (to protect) us from painful truths. ____________

18. There (to exist) a radical new theory which (to propose) that dreams do something entirely different. ____________

19. While awake, people (to learn) about the environment, but in dreams the flow of new information about the world is cut off. ____________

20. Each dream (to combine) new information with information already in the brain, and new ways of dealing with the world (to be) rehearsed. ____________

Pronoun–Antecedent Agreement

EXERCISE 24-2

(24o–t)

Select a personal pronoun that agrees with the subject of each of these sentences. Write your answers on the lines to the right. Some items have more than one correct answer.

EXAMPLE A hiker should never forget to take __________ water bottle on the trail. *his or her*

1. Outdoor sports enthusiasts need to rehydrate ______ bodies regularly. ______________
2. One should not wait to feel dryness in ______ throat before drinking water. ______________
3. Rather, anyone engaged in physical exertion should sip fluids regularly as ______ continues with ______ activity. ______________
4. If a family goes on a long hike, ______ should carry enough water for each of ______ members. ______________
5. In practical terms, that means that a family should all carry ______ own water bottles. ______________
6. Neither an adult nor a child can do without ______ water supply on the trail. ______________
7. The Web site of Mountain Equipment Co-op (MEC) informs ______ members all about these things. ______________
8. Everyone who visits the site can find useful tips for ______ outdoor adventures. ______________
9. To purify water for drinking on the trail, many campers like to boil ______ water and pour it right into the bottle. ______________
10. This has led many of them to carry ______ water supply in polycarbonate plastic water bottles. ______________
11. All of the other available plastics melt or lose ______ shape when filled with boiling liquids. ______________
12. None of the others both holds ______ shape and resists odours as effectively. ______________
13. In late 2007, however, MEC stores removed all polycarbonate bottles from ______ shelves. ______________
14. MEC noted on ______ Web site that one of the compounds used in polycarbonate plastics mimics the hormone estrogen. ______________

15. A liquid or food can have ______ chemistry altered if the compound leaches out of the plastic. ____________

16. Either one, then, might have unexpected effects on the people who consume ______ , over time. ____________

17. MEC's Web site referred to a study of these effects that the federal government was conducting under ______ Chemical Management Plan. ____________

18. Any purchaser wanting to inform ______ further on the topic can follow the health and environmental links on the MEC Web site. ____________

Pronoun–Antecedent Agreement

EXERCISE 24-3

(24o–t)

Revise each of these passages so that all pronouns agree with their antecedents in person, number, and gender. You may also have to change verbs or other words. Some sentences can be revised in more than one way. Take the time to try several, and select the version you like best.

EXAMPLE: In our society, a person's success is often defined by what they do and what they own.
In our society, a person's success is often defined by what he or she does and what he or she owns.

1. Many people assume that a person who makes a lot of money as their happiness guaranteed.

____

____

2. However, a person who owns a lot of things is not necessarily as happy as they would like to be.

____

____

3. An individual who isn't able to buy much beyond life's necessities may not be happy with their life either.

____

____

4. How do most people define happiness and how can he or she achieve it?

____

____

5. The answer is that everyone has their own idea of what makes them happy.

____

____

6. Therefore, each individual should take time to reflect on what makes them happy.

____

____

7. One of the oldest and wisest sayings is "Know yourself." That is the only way to know what makes him or her happy.

____

____

8. It's also important to understand that no matter how much somebody may care for you, they are not responsible for your happiness. You are responsible for your own happiness.

____

____

9. To be happy, it seems that most people need more than just life's necessities, but he or she does not need nearly as much as he or she may think.

____

____

Identifying Adjectives and Adverbs

EXERCISE 25-1

(25a, b, d)

On the lines to the right, identify each of the italicized words as an adjective or adverb. (Following common usage, the titles of books also appear in italics; however, these are nouns, never adjectives or adverbs.)

EXAMPLE Rohinton Mistry won the Governor General's award for his *first* novel. ___*adjective*___

1. Agatha Christie is famous for her *mystery* novels. ________
2. She *also* wrote romantic novels, under a pen name. ________
3. Joseph Conrad was a *highly* respected English writer. ________
4. His *native* language was Polish. ________
5. He *always* had trouble speaking but not writing English. ________
6. *Gone with the Wind* was Margaret Mitchell's *only* book. ________
7. Upton Sinclair wrote *The Jungle* hoping to improve conditions in the *Chicago* stockyards. ________
8. In *his* book he called for large social and economic reforms. ________
9. Sinclair's work led *directly* to regulations governing food purity. ________
10. Each year, Canadian publishers introduce about 10 000 *different* books in both French and English. ________
11. The *typical* Canadian book author earns less than $10 000 a year from writing. ________
12. The federal government is a *major* supporter of Canadian publishing. ________
13. In 1979, *4479* writers belonged to writers' unions in Canada. ________
14. Only *recently* have women authors been widely accepted. ________
15. Many nineteenth-century English female authors became *widely* popular writing under men's names. ________
16. George Eliot was *really* Mary Anne Evans, while Charlotte Brontë wrote as Currer Bell and her sister Emily Brontë wrote as Ellis Bell. ________ ________
17. *Other* famous writers have also used pen names. ________
18. George Orwell was *actually* the pen name of Englishman Eric Arthur Blair. ________
19. Popular *romance* novelist Barbara Cartland also publishes under the name Barbara Hamilton McCorquodale. ________
20. Even Agatha Christie *sometimes* chose a pseudonym: Mary Westmacott. ________

Distinguishing Adjectives from Adverbs

EXERCISE 25-2
(25a, b, d)

From the choices in parentheses, select the correct modifier for each sentence. Write your answers on the lines to the right.

EXAMPLE Aspirin can cause a (severe, severely) upset stomach in some people. ___*severely*___

1. Pain sufferers (annual, annually) spend millions of dollars on aspirin. ____________
2. Over 200 kinds of headache medicines containing aspirin are (available, availably). ____________
3. Many of us feel taking aspirin can make us (good, well). ____________
4. However, aspirin has many (serious, seriously) side effects. ____________
5. Aspirin (common, commonly) causes bleeding in the stomach. ____________
6. This can make us feel (bad, badly). ____________
7. Bleeding occurs when an undissolved aspirin tablet lies on the (delicate, delicately) stomach wall. ____________
8. For most of us, the amount of blood lost is not (dangerous, dangerously). ____________
9. However, some (slow, slowly) dissolving tablets can cause prolonged bleeding, leading to great discomfort. ____________
10. (High, Highly) quality aspirin dissolves more quickly and is less likely to cause a problem. ____________
11. Aspirin has a (lengthy, lengthily) history. ____________
12. Our (ancient, anciently) ancestors chewed the leaves and bark of the willow tree. ____________
13. They contain a substance (chemical, chemically) related to aspirin. ____________
14. Aspirin itself was introduced as a painkiller and fever reducer more (recent, recently). ____________
15. Coming on the market in 1899, it (quick, quickly) became the best-selling nonprescription drug in the world. ____________
16. The tablet form so (popular, popularly) today was introduced by Bayer in 1915. ____________
17. Taking an aspirin a day has (late, lately) been claimed to be good for the heart. ____________

18. Some research shows that men who take aspirin (regular, regularly) after a heart attack are less likely to have another attack. __________ __________

19. Some healthy people have been (quick, quickly) to start taking aspirin daily. __________

20. Doctors advise us to think (careful, carefully) and get medical advice before we do this. __________

Using Comparatives and Superlatives

EXERCISE 25-3
(25e)

A: Fill in the comparative and superlative forms of the adjectives and adverbs listed on the left.

		Comparative	***Superlative***
EXAMPLE	tall	*taller*	*tallest*
1.	*bad*	______	______
2.	*badly*	______	______
3.	*forgiving*	______	______
4.	*free*	______	______
5.	*good*	______	______
6.	*gracefully*	______	______
7.	*handsome*	______	______
8.	*hot*	______	______
9.	*little*	______	______
10.	*loudly*	______	______
11.	*many*	______	______
12.	*much*	______	______
13.	*powerfully*	______	______
14.	*pretty*	______	______
15.	*quickly*	______	______
16.	*some*	______	______
17.	*sweetly*	______	______
18.	*sympathetically*	______	______
19.	*talented*	______	______
20.	*well*	______	______

B: Use the adjectives and adverbs above in sets of sentences that show how the three forms are related to changes in meaning. Use your own paper.

EXAMPLE I am tall. (positive)
I am taller than my sister. (comparative)
I am the tallest person in my family. (superlative)

Writing with Adjectives

<u>EXERCISE 25-4</u>

(25)

Write a paragraph describing someone, something, or someplace wonderful. Some suggestions: your favourite restaurant, your favourite movie star, an exciting amusement park, your most treasured possession.

Be sure to have a topic sentence (3e). Develop your idea with four to six sentences, each containing strong and appropriate adjectives and adverbs. Try not to use so many modifiers in any one sentence that the main idea gets lost.

Revising Fragments

EXERCISE 26-1
(26a–d)

A. Explain what is wrong with each fragment and then rewrite it as a complete sentence.

EXAMPLE celebrating his retirement this May
There is no subject, and celebrating *is not a conjugated verb.*
Alex will be celebrating his retirement this May.

1. When Alyssa arrived at work

2. whichever job offer comes first

3. joins the bowling league

4. on my desk

5. Fortunately, the tutor helping my sister

6. considered the best tennis doubles partner in town

7. that I hope to write

8. my least favourite course this semester

9. visiting with my family in Ireland

10. and write short stories

B. Write two corrected versions of each fragment. Be sure to use the fragment differently in each, and identify how you have used it (as illustrated in the parentheses below).

EXAMPLE preparing lectures
Preparing lectures / takes much of the professor's time. (subject)
The professor / who was preparing lectures / stayed up most of the night.(adjective)

1. gets to class on time

____

____

2. entered in the literary contest

____

____

3. to buy a textbook

____

____

4. when I took the exam

____

____

5. working to pay for university

____

____

6. studying for exams during spring break

____

____

7. Administrators, faculty, staff, and students

____

____

8. The power going off suddenly

____

____

9. who attends night classes

____

____

10. in the writing centre

____

____

Revising Fragments within Passages

EXERCISE 26-2
(26a–d)

A. Explain what is wrong with each fragment, and then rewrite it as a complete sentence.

EXAMPLE The history of the Internet is a fascinating one. The network that connects computers around the world. The Internet still continues to surprise.
The history of the Internet, the network that connects computers around the world, is a fascinating one. The Internet still continues to surprise.

1. When futurist and author Arthur C. Clarke predicted in the 1960s. He foresaw the development of a vast electronic "global library." Surprisingly, he said that it would be in place by the year 2000.

____

____

2. In fact, the origins of the Internet can be traced back to 1958. ARPA, the Advanced Research Projects Agency, was set up by the U.S. Department of Defense. As an arm of the military.

____

____

3. However, before ARPA began supporting networking research seriously. Leonard Kleinrock, a graduate student at the Massachusetts Institute of Technology, had already invented the technology of the Internet. Kleinrock's contribution is known as "packet switching."

____

____

4. A method of sending data as short, independent units of information. Packet switching was far more efficient than the system that it replaced. This was the traditional circuit-switched method.

____

____

5. Packet switching avoided the long periods of "silence" that occur when data is circuit switched. And can occupy as much as 99 percent of each transmission. Such delays prevent effective transmission of large files.

____

____

6. Packet-switching technology was used in the creation of ARPAnet. Which is the network that laid the foundation for the Internet. ARPAnet was inaugurated in 1969.

____

____

7. The US military was especially interested in packet switching. Because it sends messages along a complex network by any route available. Air force planners wanted a way to stay in control if a nuclear war destroyed most communications in the United States.

____

____

8. Soon after, in 1972, Ray Tomlinson, a computer engineer involved in the ARPAnet project. He invented electronic mail.

____

____

9. E-mail was the Internet's first "killer application." A slang term for software that is so useful, it creates a market for new hardware. People bought computers and modems just to have access to the Internet.

____

____

10. As academics and researchers in other fields began to use the network. ARPAnet was taken over by the NSF. This abbreviation represents the US National Science Foundation.

____

____

11. The NSF had created a similar network of its own. NSFnet, one of the many networks that had begun to introduce improvements in the technology. Among these improvements was the adoption of the transmission protocol known as TCP/IP.

____

____

12. In 1989, British scientist Tim Berners-Lee proposed the World Wide Web project. Web browsers would be able to communicate across the Internet. By adopting his HTTP, or Hypertext Transfer Protocol.

____

____

13. The Web gives users access to a vast array of documents connected to each other by hyperlinks. Electronic connections that link related pieces of information.

____

____

14. The World Wide Web gained rapid acceptance with the creation in 1993 of a Web browser called Mosaic. This program allowed users to search the Web using "point-and-click" graphics much more easily. Than with the original system of keyboard-based commands.

____

____

15. One of the developers of Mosaic, Marc Andreessen, went on to create Netscape Navigator. Which became the first commercially successful Web browser. Its success led to the development of several competing browsers, including many that can be downloaded for free.

____

____

16. James Gosling, who studied computer science in Calgary. Gosling became known as one of the best programmers in the world. By the early 1990s he sensed the need for a programming language that could integrate every "smart" machine and gadget into the Internet.

____

____

17. Gosling's solution was Java. A simple programming language designed to let programmers write applications for nearly any computing device. A major innovation in the new language was the "applet."

____

____

18. Applets are mini-programs that are downloaded along with Web pages. Which allow the downloading devices to interact and perform new sets of tasks. The resulting interactivity of devices and their software has created the wired world we are just getting to know.

____

____

Revising Fragments within Paragraphs

EXERCISE 26-3
(26a–d)

Circle the number of any fragments. Then correct each fragment by connecting it to a main clause or by adding words to complete it. Use your own paper.

A. [1]Paul Bertoia, an immigrant from near Udine in Friuli, the northeast of Italy.[2]Arrived alone in Toronto after World War I. [3]In search of work and relatives, he went on to Edmonton.[4]There he stayed in a boardinghouse/inn. [5]Known to its residents as the Roma Hotel. [6]One floor was occupied completely by Friulan sojourners. [7]And the next floor by Trevisans from a neighbouring region of Italy.[8]Each floor had its own cooking, dialect, card games, and camaraderie.[9]Even though the inn was named for Italy's capital and the native Edmontonians considered everyone in the building an Italian migrant. [10]When Mr. Bertoia boarded with kinfolk in Drumheller.[11]He associated chiefly with people from his home town near Udine. [12]And later, when he came to Toronto, became involved in benevolent organizations like the Fratellanza.[13]Which took in members.[14]From all over the Italian peninsula. [15]His ethnic reference group changed according to his setting.

—ADAPTED FROM ROBERT F. HARNEY, "Boarding and Belonging"

B. [1]The striped barber pole is a symbol left over from the times. [2]When barbers doubled as surgeons. [3]As early as the fifth century. [4]Roman barbers pulled teeth, treated wounds. [5]And bled patients.[6]Records show that in 1461 the barbers of London were the only people practising surgery. [7]In the city. [8]However, under Henry VIII, less than a hundred years later. [9]Parliament passed a law limiting barbers to minor operations. [10]Such as blood letting and pulling teeth. [11]While surgeons were prohibited from barbery and shaving. [12]The London barbers and surgeons were considered one group until 1745.[13]In France and Germany, barbers acted as surgeons. [14]Until even more recent times.

[15]Barbers usually bled their patients. [16]To cure a variety of ailments. [17]Because few people could read in those days. [18]Pictures were commonly used as shop signs. [19]The sign of the barber was a pole painted with red and white spirals. [20]From which was suspended a brass basin. [21]The red represented the blood of the patient. [22]The white, the bandage. [23]And the basin, the bowl used to catch the blood. [24]In Canada, the bowl is often omitted. [25]But it is still common on British barber poles. [26]Some American barbers added a blue stripe. [27]Probably to make the colours match the American flag.

Revising Comma Splices and Fused Sentences

EXERCISE 27-1
(27a–d)

A: Correct each comma splice or fused sentence in any of the ways shown in this chapter.

EXAMPLE Many people think of the Middle Ages they think of knights in shining armour.
When many people think of the Middle Ages, they think of knights in shining armour.

1. The average person contains about 250 grams of salt without it a person would die

2. When people began to farm obtaining the salt their bodies required became difficult, They began to seek sources of salt.

3. Salt has been used just like money, it was a medium of exchange.

4. The world's oceans are very salty, there's enough salt in them to bury Canada about one and a half kilometres deep.

5. Only five percent of salt is used as a seasoning most of the rest is used in industry.

6. We get some salt from the oceans most of it comes from salt mines.

7. People used to crave salt now so much is used in food production that we need to be careful not to consume too much of it.

B: Correct each comma splice or fused sentence in the way indicated.

EXAMPLE Salt can be deadly too much of it can kill fish and keep plants from growing. (Make into two separate sentences.)
Salt can be deadly. Too much of it can kill fish and keep plants from growing.

1. Salt is a major ingredient in pesticides and herbicides, they kill insects and plants. (Turn one part into a dependent clause.)

____

____

2. The Romans destroyed the city of Carthage they ploughed the ground with salt as a symbol of its desolation.
(Make into two separate sentences.)

____

____

3. Constructive or destructive, salt has many uses it is used far more than any other mineral.
(Add a semicolon and a conjunctive adverb.)

____

____

4. The Romans knew the value of salt as a commodity they named a major highway Via Salaria, Salt Road.
(Add a semicolon.)

____

____

5. The word *salary* comes from the word *salarium* it meant money used to pay soldiers. So they could buy salt.
(Turn one part into a dependent clause.)

____

____

6. Salt has long been used to preserve food the expression "salted away" means to. keep for a future time.
(Add a comma and a coordinating conjunction.)

____

____

7. Salt may become even more important to us than it already is we may be able to use it to bury radioactive waste.
(Add a semicolon.)

____

____

C: Correct each comma splice or fused sentence in four ways: (1) make each into two separate sentences by inserting a period; (2) add a semicolon; (3) add a coordinating conjunction to create a compound sentence—you will also need to add a comma unless the clauses are very short; (4) add a subordinating conjunction or relative pronoun—you may need to drop a word—to create a complex sentence.

EXAMPLE The tallest creates in the world are giraffes, they can grow to be five metres tall.
1. …giraffes. They can grow . . .
2. …giraffes, they can grow. . .
3. …giraffe,. for they can grow. . .
4. …giraffes that can grow.

1. Giraffes spend much of their time eating their favourite food, the whistling-thorn acacia tree, it satisfies their hunger and thirst.

____

____

____

____

2. To most people giraffes appear awkward and ungainly, they can race along at speeds up to 50 kilometres per hour.

____

____

____

____

3. People have greatly reduced the number of remaining giraffes, they need more protection. from poachers.

____

____

____

____

4. To establish identity, people have fingerprints, giraffes have distinctive patches of brown on their bodies.

____

____

____

____

5. Introduced to Rome by Julius Caesar in 46 BCE, the giraffe was billed as a camel leopard, its scientific name became Giraffa camelopardalis.

____

____

____

____

Revising Comma Splices and Fused Sentences within Passages

EXERCISE 27-2

(27a–d)

Find the comma splice or fused sentence in each passage. Correct each in any way shown in this chapter. You may need to change punctuation or wording, but try to keep the meaning of the original passage.

EXAMPLE Some of the most beautiful temples in the world are those of Angkor. Angkor is a Cambodian region it served as the capital of the ancient Khmer empire between the 9th and 15th centuries. The empire once extended into what are today Vietnam, Laos, and Thailand.

Some of the most beautiful temples in the world are those of Angkor. Angkor is a Cambodian region that served as the capital of the ancient Khmer empire between the 9th and 15th centuries. The empire once extended into what are today Vietnam, Laos, and Thailand.

1. King Jayavarman II introduced into the empire an Indian royal cult. The cult held that the king was related spiritually to one of the Hindu gods, consequently, the king was thought to fill on earth the role the gods had in the universe.

___

___

2. Each king was expected to build a stone temple. The temple, or wat, was dedicated to a god, usually Shiva or Vishnu, when the king died, the temple became a monument to him as well.

___

___

3. Over the centuries the kings erected more than seventy temples within 200 km^2. They added towers and gates they created canals and reservoirs for an irrigation system.

___

___

4. The irrigation system made it possible for farmers to produce several rice crops a year. Such abundant harvests supported a highly evolved culture, the irrigation system and the rice production were what we would call labour-intensive.

___

___

5. The greatest of the temples is Angkor Wat, it was built by Suryavarman II in the 12th century. Like the other temples, it represents Mount Meru, the home of the Hindu gods. The towers represent Mount Meru's peaks while the walls represent the mountains beyond.

____

____

6. The gallery walls are covered with bas-reliefs they depict historical events. They show the king at his court, and they show him engaging in activities that brought glory to his empire.

____

____

7. The walls also portray divine images. There are sculptures of *apsarases*, they are attractive women thought to inhabit heaven. There are mythical scenes on the walls as well.

____

____

8. One scene shows the Hindu myth of the churning of the Sea of Milk. On one side of the god Vishnu are demons who tug on the end of a long serpent, on the other are heavenly beings who tug on the other end. All the tugging churns the water.

____

____

9. Vishnu is the god to whom Angkor Wat is dedicated. In Hindu myth he oversees the churning of the waters, that churning is ultimately a source of immortality.

____

____

10. Another temple is the Bayon, it was built by Jayavarman Vll around A.D. 1200 Jayavarman Vll was the last of the great kings of Angkor. He built the Bayon in the exact centre of the city.

____

____

11. The Bayon resembles a step pyramid. It has steep stairs that lead to terraces near the top around its base are many galleries. Its towers are carved with faces that look out in all directions.

____

____

12. Jayavarman Vll was a Buddhist, the representations on Bayon are different from those on earlier temples. Some scholars think they depict a Buddhist deity with whom the king felt closely aligned.

____

____

13. To build each temple required thousands of labourers they worked for years. After cutting the stone in far-off quarries, they had to transport it by canal or cart. Some stone may have been brought in on elephants.

____

____

14. Once cut, the stones had to be carved and fitted together into lasting edifices, thus, in addition to requiring labourers, each project needed artisans, architects, and engineers. Each temple was a massive project.

____

____

15. Angkor was conquered by the Thais in the 1400s, it was almost completely abandoned. The local inhabitants did continue to use the temples for worship, however, and a few late Khmer kings tried to restore the city.

____

____

16. The Western world did not learn about Angkor until the nineteenth century, a French explorer published an account of the site. French archaeologists and conservators later worked in the area and restored some of the temples. More recent archaeologists have come from India.

____

____

17. Today the Angkor Conservancy has removed many of the temple statues. Some of the statues need repair, all of them need protection from thieves. Unfortunately, traffic in Angkor art has become big business among people with no scruples. There is even a booming business in Angkor fakes.

____

____

18. Theft is just one of the problems Angkor faces today, political upheaval has taken its toll. Although Angkor mostly escaped Cambodia's civil war, some war damage has occurred.

____

____

19. More damage has been done by nature, however, trees choke some of the archways, vines strangle the statues, and monsoons undermine the basic structures.

____

____

20. Today many Cambodians do what they can to maintain the temples of Angkor. They clean stones or sweep courtyards or pull weeds. No one pays them, they do it for themselves and their heritage.

____

____

Eliminating Misplaced and Dangling Modifiers

EXERCISE 28-1
(28a–e)

Underline all misplaced and dangling modifiers in this paragraph. Then revise the paragraph to eliminate them. You can change or add words and otherwise revise to make the material sensible.

[1]The art of carving or engraving marine articles, sailors developed scrimshaw while sailing on long voyages. [2]Practised primarily by whalers, sperm whale teeth were the most popular articles. [3]Baleen was another popular choice which was also called whalebone. [4]A sailor needed something to occupy his time with whaling voyages taking several years. [5]Imagination or available material only limited scrimshaw. [6]All kinds of objects were produced by the scrimshander, canes, corset busks, cribbage boards. [7]From whaling scenes to mermaids the sailor used everything to decorate his work. [8]A sailor doing scrimshaw often drew his own ship. [9]The most frequently depicted ship, the *Charles W. Morgan*, is, at present, a museum ship at Mystic Seaport. [10]It is possible to easily see it on a visit to Connecticut.

Eliminating Misplaced and Dangling Modifiers

EXERCISE 28-2
(28a–e)

A: Underline each misplaced modifier. Then revise the sentence, placing the modifier where it belongs.

EXAMPLE Inexperienced people are afraid to paint their own homes often.
*Inexperienced people are **often** afraid to paint their own homes.*

1. To paint one's house frequently one must do it oneself.

 ____

2. All homeowners almost try to paint at one time or another.

 ____

3. They try to usually begin on a bedroom.

 ____

4. They think no one will see it if they botch the job by doing so.

 ____

5. Most people can learn to paint in no time.

 ____

6. The uncoordinated should only not try it.

 ____

7. People have a distinct advantage that have strong arm muscles.

 ____

8. Prospective painters can always exercise lacking strength.

 ____

9. Novices need to carefully purchase all supplies, such as brushes, rollers, and drop cloths.

 ____

10. They must bring home paint chips exactly to match the shade desired.

 ____

11. It takes as much time nearly to prepare to paint as it does to do the actual job.

 ____

12. Painters are in for a surprise who think they are done with the last paint stroke.

 ____

13 Painters need to immediately clean their own brushes and put away all equipment.

____

14 They can be proud of their accomplishment in the long run.

____

15 Then can they enjoy only the results of their labour.

____

16. Painting one's own home can, when all is said and done, be extremely satisfying.

____

B: Revise each sentence to eliminate dangling modifiers. You may have to add or change a few words. If a sentence is acceptable as written, write *correct* on the line.

EXAMPLE Advising a group of young women in his neighbourhood, many discussions focusing on love problems were led by Samuel Richardson.
Advising a group of young women in his neighbourhood, Samuel Richardson led many discussions focusing on love problems.

1. Playing the role of a caring and wise father, the girls were told by Richardson how to handle various situations.

____

____

2. To help the girls, letters to their suitors were sometimes written for them by Richardson.

____

____

3 After writing a number of successful letters, the idea of writing a book of model letters occurred to Richardson.

____

____

4. To prepare the book, it included letters written as if from adults to sons, daughters, nieces, and nephews.

____

____

5 When ready to send advice, a letter was copied out by a parent, and just the names changed.

____

____

6. Bought by many, Richardson was a successful author.

7. While working on one letter, enough ideas for a whole book occurred to Richardson.

8. By writing a series of letters between a girl and her faraway parents, young readers would be entertained and instructed.

9. Upon finishing *Pamela, or Virtue Rewarded* in 1740, a new form of literature had been invented by Richardson.

10. After years of development, we call this form the novel.

11. Being a nasty person, Horace Walpole's only novel wasn't very attractive either.

12. Imitated by others for over 200 years, his *The Castle of Otranto* was the first gothic novel.

13. Although badly written, Walpole invented the themes, atmosphere, mood, and plots that have filled gothic novels ever since.

14. Featuring gloomy castles filled with dark secrets, people are entertained by gothic movies too.

Revising to Eliminate Shifts

EXERCISE 29-1

(29a–e)

A: Revise this paragraph to eliminate shifts in person and number. The first sentence should become "The next time you watch a western movie, notice whether it contains any sign language." Use your own paper.

The next time I watch a western movie, notice whether it contains any sign language. Some people consider sign language the first universal language. Although few people use them today, it is a Native North American language with a lengthy history. You can find some tribal differences, but basic root signs are clear to everyone who studies it.

Sign language differs from the signage used by hearing-impaired people. For instance, he indicates the forehead to mean *think* while a Sioux pointed to the heart. You also use extensive facial expression in speaking to someone with a hearing loss while Native North Americans maintained a stoic countenance. She believed the signs could speak for itself. Ideally you made the signs in round, sweeping motions. They tried to make conversation beautiful.

B: Revise this paragraph to eliminate shifts in verb tense. The first sentence should read "No one knows why sailors wear bell-bottom pants." Use your own paper.

No one knows why sailors wore bell-bottom pants. However, three theories were popular. First, bell-bottoms will fit over boots and keep sea spray and rain from getting in. Second, bell-bottoms could be rolled up over the knees, so they stayed dry when a sailor must wade ashore and stayed clean when he scrubbed the ship's deck. Third, because bell-bottoms are loose, they will be easy to take off in the water if a sailor fell overboard. In their training course, sailors were taught another advantage to bell-bottoms. By taking them off and tying the legs at the ends, a sailor who has fallen into the ocean can change his bell-bottom pants into a life preserver.

C: Identify the shift in each passage by writing its code on the line to the right: *1* for a shift in person or number, *2* in subject or voice, *3* in tense, *4* in mood, or *5* in discourse (confusing direct and indirect quotation). Then revise each sentence to eliminate the shift.

EXAMPLE When people speak of a fisherman knit sweater, you mean one from the Aran Isles. ____*1*____

When people speak of a fisherman knit sweater, they mean one from the Aran Isles.

1. The Aran Isles are situated off the coast of Ireland. Galway is not far from the Isles. __________

____

2. An islander has a difficult life. They must make their living by fishing in a treacherous sea. __________

____

3. They use a simple boat called a *curragh* for fishing. It is also used to ferry their market animals to barges. __________

____

4. Island houses stood out against the empty landscape. Their walls provide scant protection from a hostile environment. __________

____

5. In 1898 John Millington Synge first visited the Aran Isles. They are used as the setting for *Riders to the Sea* and other of his works. __________

____

6. Whether people see the Synge play or Ralph Vaughan Williams's operatic version of *Riders to the Sea*, you will feel the harshness of Aran life. __________

____

7. The mother, Maurya, has lost her husband and several sons. They are all drowned at sea. __________

____

8. When the body of another son is washed onto the shore, his sister identifies it from the pattern knitted into his sweater. __________

____

9. Each Aran knitter develops her own combination of patterns. The patterns not only produce a beautiful sweater, but they will have a very practical purpose. __________

____

10. The oiled wool protected the fishermen from the sea spray while the intricate patterns offer symbolic protection as well as identification when necessary. ____________

____

11. When you knit your first Aran Isle sweater, you should learn what the stitches mean. Don't choose a pattern just because it is easy. ____________

____

12. A cable stitch represents a fisherman's rope; winding cliff paths are depicted by the zigzag stitch. ____________

____

13. Bobbles symbolize men in a *curragh* while the basket stitch represented a fisherman's creel and the hope that it will come home full. ____________

____

14. The tree of life signifies strong sons and family unity. It was also a fertility symbol. ____________

____

15. When someone asks you did you knit your Aran Isle sweater yourself, you can proudly say that you did and you also chose the patterns. ____________

____

Eliminating Mixed Constructions, Faulty Predication, and Incomplete Sentences

EXERCISE 29-2
(29f–j)

A: Revise these mixed sentences to eliminate faulty predication and mixed constructions. It may be necessary to change, add, or omit words.

EXAMPLE Easter is when Russians traditionally exchanged eggs.
On Easter Russians traditionally exchanged eggs.

1. When one thinks of Carl Fabergé created Easter eggs for the tsars.

   ____

2. Because Fabergé was a talented goldsmith was the reason he was able to make exquisite objects.

   ____

3. Working for the court of Imperial Russia was able to combine craftsmanship and ingenuity.

   ____

4. The object of Fabergé pleased his clients by creating unique works of art.

   ____

5. When he included gems in his creations but they did not overshadow his workmanship.

   ____

6. In adapting enamelling techniques achieved a level seldom matched by other artisans.

   ____

7. With buyers in Europe expanded his clientele beyond the Russian royal family.

   ____

8. Because he had no money worries meant few restrictions on imagination.

   ____

9. Although Fabergé created other examples of the jeweller's art, but it is the Imperial Easter eggs for which he is most remembered.

   ____

10. In the most famous eggs contained surprises inside—a hen, a ship, a coach.

    ____

11. When one egg opened to reveal a model of a palace.

____

12. Because the most ambitious creation represented an egg surrounded by parts of a cathedral.

____

13. An artist is when one practises an imaginative art.

____

14. One reason Fabergé is so admired is because he was a true artist.

____

B: Revise these incomplete sentences to supply any carelessly omitted words or to complete compound constructions and comparisons clearly. Write *correct* if the sentence has no errors.

EXAMPLE Cuneiform was system of writing with wedgelike marks.
Cuneiform was a system of writing with wedgelike marks.

1. The use of cuneiform began and spread throughout ancient Sumer.

____

2. This picture language of the Sumerians is thought to be older than the Egyptians.

____

3. Like hieroglyphics, early cuneiform used easily recognizable pictures represent objects.

____

4. When scribes began using a wedge-shaped stylus, greater changes occurred.

____

5. The new marks were different.

____

6. They had become so stylized.

____

7. Early Sumerian tablets recorded practical things such lists of grain in storage.

____

8. Some tablets were put clay envelopes that were themselves inscribed.

____

9. Gradually ordinary people used cuneiform as much as official scribes.

____

10. *The Epic of Gilgamesh*, written in Akkadian cuneiform, is older than any epic.

____

11. The Code of Hammurabi recorded in cuneiform a more comprehensive set of laws.

____

12. No one could decipher cuneiform script until someone discovered the Record of Darius.

____

13. Because it was written in three languages, it served the same purpose.

____

14. Today we understand cuneiform as much, if not more than, we understand hieroglyphics.

____

C: Revise this paragraph, changing, adding, or deleting words as you judge best, in order to eliminate mixed and incomplete sentences. Circle the number of the one sentence that contains no errors. Use your own paper.

[1]Although wild rice may be the caviar of grains is not really rice. [2]It is, however, truly wild. [3]One reason is because it needs marshy places in order to thrive. [4]By planting it in prepared paddies can produce abundant crops. [5]Nevertheless, most wild rice grows naturally along rivers and lake shores northern US states and Canada. [6]In certain areas only Aboriginal people are allowed harvest the rice. [7]Connoisseurs think wild rice tastes better than any grain. [8]It is surely the most expensive. [9]Some hostesses serve it with Cornish hens exclusively, but the creative cook, with many dishes. [10]Try it in quiche or pancakes; your guests will be so pleased.

PART FIVE: WRITING EFFECTIVELY

Eliminating Wordy Sentence Structures

EXERCISE 30-1
(30c)

Revise these sentences to eliminate wordy sentence structures. You may need to delete expletives, change passive sentences to the active voice, reduce clauses to phrases or phrases to words, and/or replace weak, heavily modified verbs with strong direct verbs.

EXAMPLE It is Art Deco which became an international style in the 1920s and 1930s.
Art Deco became an international style in the 1920s and 1930s.

1. Art Deco took its name from an exposition that was held in Paris in 1925.

 ____

2. Art Deco may be defined as a style that used shapes that were bold and streamlined and that experimented with new materials.

 ____

3. In the 1920s Art Deco was influenced by public fascination with technology and the future.

 ____

4. In addition to architecture, which it dominated, the style could be found in designs for glassware, appliances, furniture, and even advertising art.

 ____

5. The Marine Building in Vancouver and the Chrysler Building in New York are exemplifications of the dynamic style of Art Deco.

 ____

6. After the crash of the stock market in 1929, Art Deco became less extravagant in its expression of modern ideas and themes.

 ____

7. There was a restraint and austerity in the Art Deco of the Great Depression.

 ____

8. Builders of architecture made use of rounded corners, glass blocks, and porthole windows.

 ____

9. They had a liking for roofs that were flat.

 ____

10. Buildings that had plain exteriors often were decorated with lavish care inside and had furniture to match.

 ____

Eliminating Unneeded Words

EXERCISE 30-2
(30b)

Revise these sentences to eliminate unneeded words and phrases.

EXAMPLE It seems that many cultures considered the first of May the official beginning of summer.
Many cultures considered the first of May the official beginning of summer.

1. As a matter of fact, the Romans gave sacrifices to the goddess Maia on the first day of the month named for her.

   ____

2. It seems that the Celts also celebrated May Day as the midpoint of their year.

   ____

3. One of the most important of the May Day celebrations that exist is the Maypole.

   ____

4. In a very real sense, the Maypole represented rebirth.

   ____

5. In Germany a Maypole tree was often stripped of all but the top branches for the purpose of representing new life.

   ____

6. In the case of Sweden, floral wreaths were suspended from a crossbar on the pole.

   ____

7. The English had a different type of tradition.

   ____

8. Holding streamers attached to the top of the Maypole, villagers danced around it in an enthusiastic manner.

   ____

9. In view of the fact that May Day had pagan beginnings, the Puritans disapproved of it.

   ____

10. Thus it was suppressed by Oliver Cromwell after the overthrow of Charles I.

    ____

Eliminating Redundancies

EXERCISE 30-3

(30d)

Revise these sentences to eliminate unnecessary repetition of words and redundant ideas. Retain helpful repetition.

EXAMPLE Stamps are small in size, and it takes many in number to make a good collection.
Stamps are small, and it takes many to make a good collection.

1. Many new collectors express astonished amazement at the number of stamps to be collected.

   ____

2. They get excited about each and every new stamp they acquire.

   ____

3. They hope to make their collections totally complete.

   ____

4. Soon it becomes perfectly clear that a complete collection is impossible.

   ____

5. Then they may take the pragmatic approach and be practical.

   ____

6. They limit their collections by confining them to one country, continent, or decade.

   ____

7. At that point in time, their collections will again provide great satisfaction.

   ____

8. It is a consensus of opinion that collecting stamps can be educational.

   ____

9. It can teach about past history or the geography of the earth.

   ____

10. Nevertheless, a new collector should not become discouraged by overstepping possibility and trying to collect too much.

    ____

Revising for Conciseness

EXERCISE 30-4

(30b–e)

Revise these paragraphs to eliminate wordiness, pointless repetitions, and redundancies. Combine sentences as necessary.

A: It was first in the 1980s that the computerized animation industry began to take off and attain growing success. Computerized animation is also widely known as digital animation. Among the earliest pioneers that first entered the animation field were two firms named Nelvana and CINAR. The former was founded in Toronto, and the latter one was founded in Montreal. These firms as well as others supplied animated programming to the television and film industries and enjoyed a large number of hits, while at the same time being awarded several awards. In fact, *ReBoot*, the first TV series to be made entirely with computer graphics, was made in the early 1990s in Vancouver. At the same time, Vancouver's Vertigo Technology, Montreal's Softimage, and Toronto's AliasWavefront developed the cutting-edge digital animation software that models and animates digital images. These are precisely the studios that brought the Terminator to life—again and again—and that put Forrest Gump into old, historic newsreels. Finally, Sheridan College in Ontario and Algonquin College, also in Ontario, have highly regarded programs in animation. Sheridan, as a matter of fact, was called by a writer in *Wired* magazine "the Harvard of animation schools."

B: Auguste Escoffier was the most famous chef at the turn of the century between 1880 and World War I. In a very real sense, he was the leader of the culinary world of his day. Until that point in time, the best chefs were found in private homes. With Escoffier came an era of fine dining at restaurants to which the nobility and wealthy flocked in order to eat well. After Escoffier joined César Ritz, the luxury hotel owner, they worked as a team together to attract such patrons as the Prince of Wales. Ritz had a tendency to make each and every guest feel personally welcome. It was Escoffier who added the crowning touch by preparing dishes made especially for guests. He created dishes for the prince and for celebrities such as those well known in the entertainment world. He concocted a soup which was called *consommé favori de Sarah Bernhardt* for the actress of the same name. There was an opera singer for whom he created *poularde Adelina Patti*. As a matter of act, another singer was fortunate to have more than one dish named for her. When Nellie Melba, an Australian singer, sang in *Lohengrin*, Escoffier served *pêches melba*, a combination of poached peaches and vanilla ice cream. To commemorate the swans of *Lohengrin*, he served the dessert in a swan that was made of ice. Melba toast was created by Escoffier during one of the periods when Melba was trying to diet. Today despite the fact that many people have not heard of Nellie Melba, they are familiar with melba toast. As a young army chef, Escoffier had to prepare horse meat and even rat meat for the purpose of feeding the troops. It is obvious that he left those days far behind him when he became the most renowned chef of his day.

Combining Sentences with Coordination

EXERCISE 31-1
(31a–d)

Combine these sentences using coordination. For the first five sentences, use the coordinating conjunction given; for the rest, use whatever coordinating conjunction you feel is most appropriate. It may be necessary to add or change a few words, but major rewriting is not needed.

EXAMPLE Television and multimedia have captured the world's attention. Newspapers are still influential and profitable. (But)
Television and multimedia have captured the world's attention, but newspapers are still influential and profitable.

1. Many Canadians made their fortunes as newspaper owners. Others bought newspapers after making their mark in other fields. (and)

____

____

2. Reformer George Brown wanted to promote his political ideals. He founded the *Globe* in 1844. (so)

____

____

3. K. C. Irving of New Brunswick founded a huge industrial empire based on oil refining, transportation, and pulp and paper. Later he added local newspapers to his holdings.(;)

____

____

4. Conrad Black liked to tell how he started his newspaper empire with a small loan. His wealthy family already had major business investments in other fields. (but)

____

____

5. We should not forget other Canadian newspaper tycoons such as the Thomsons and the Beaverbrooks. We should also not ignore lesser-known mavericks like Margaret "Ma" Murray, owner of the *Bridge River-Lillooet News*. (nor)

____

____

6. The Trudeau government was concerned that newspaper ownership was becoming concentrated in too few hands. In 1980 it set up a royal commission to study the problem.

___

___

7. Tom Kent was named head of the commission. He had been a newspaper editor and adviser to prime ministers.

___

___

8. Kent recommended that the government limit the size of newspaper empires. Soon Canadians would all be reading the same opinions written by employees of a small number of wealthy men.

___

___

9. Little was done about the Kent Commission recommendations. The newspaper empires continued to grow.

___

___

10. Kent did not know that his report would be ignored by the Trudeau government. Also, he could not have guessed that by the 1990s, Conrad Black would own the majority of Canada's daily newspapers.

___

___

11. Defenders of big newspaper chains say that size is a good thing. Only wealthy owners can afford the staff and resources to produce the best newspapers.

___

___

12. Some people also look back with nostalgia to the legendary days of the strong-willed newspaper boss. They argue that we can find their counterparts today only among opinionated media tycoons.

___

___

Combining Sentences with Subordination

EXERCISE 31-2
(31e–h)

Combine these sentences using subordination. For the first five sentences, use the subordinating conjunction or relative pronoun given; for the rest, use whatever subordinating conjunction or relative pronoun you feel is most appropriate. Some items have more than one correct answer, but most make sense only one way, so decide carefully which sentence comes first and where to place the subordinating conjunction or relative pronoun. It may sometimes be necessary to add or change a few words, but major rewriting is not needed.

EXAMPLE Many countries around the world started using fragrances.
Researchers found that fragrances have a stimulating effect on people. (after)
Many countries around the world started using fragrances after researchers found that fragrances have a stimulating effect on people.

1. A company in Toronto was one of the first ones to install a fragrancing unit in its office ventilation system. It was installed to control employee behaviour. (in order to)

   ____

   ____

2. The company was careful about which fragrances it introduced into the workplace. Some fragrances rev people up, and some calm them down. (because)

   ____

   ____

3. The scents were designed by Toronto-based Aromasphere, Inc. The company created a time-release mechanism to send the scents directly into the work area. (which)

   ____

   ____

4. Bodywise Ltd. in Great Britain received a patent for a fragrance. It began to market its scent, which contains androstenone, an ingredient of male sweat. (once)

   ____

   ____

5. The scent was adopted by a US debt-collection agency. Another agency in Australia reported that chronic debtors who receive scented letters were 31 percent more likely to pay than were those who received unscented letters. (after)

   ____

   ____

6. Researchers have recently discovered how much odour can influence behaviour. Smell is still the least understood of the five senses.

   ____

   ____

7. Aromasphere's employees have been asked to keep logs of their moods. They are in the workplace.

____

____

8. Researchers have raised many concerns about trying to change human behaviour. They feel that this kind of tampering may lead to too much control over employees.

____

____

9. Smells can have an effect on people. They may be completely unaware of what is happening.

____

____

10. Employees are forewarned, however, that they will be exposed to mood-altering fragrances. Such employees may protest against the introduction of such scents in the workplace.

____

____

11. Even psychiatric wards emit a scent. It makes the patients calm.

____

____

12. International Flavors and Fragrances of New York is the world's largest manufacturer of artificial flavours and aromas. It has developed many of the scents commonly used today.

____

____

13. It has even created a bagel scent. Bagels lose their aroma when they are contained in plexiglass.

____

____

14. There wasn't a true commercial interest in these products. Researchers began to understand somewhat the anatomy of smell.

____

____

15. It turns out that olfactory signals travel to the limbic region of the brain. Hormones of the automatic nervous system are regulated.

____

____

Expanding Sentences with Coordination and Subordination

EXERCISE 31-3
(31a–i)

Add to each sentence below in two ways. First add an independent clause, using a coordinating conjunction. Then add a dependent clause beginning with either a subordinating conjunction or a relative pronoun.

EXAMPLE Watching a movie is relaxing.
Watching a movie is relaxing, but sometimes I feel like doing something more exciting.
Watching a movie is relaxing after a long, stressful day at the office.

1. Surfing the Internet can be very frustrating.

____

2. Vacationing on the beach can be very dangerous.

____

3. Shovelling snow is wonderful exercise.

____

4. Installing a light fixture can be very easy.

____

5. Near closing time, the line at the bank can be incredibly long.

____

6. The cost of tuition keeps going up.

____

7. Training a dog can be a challenging task.

____

8. Putting together a photo album of a vacation is a great activity.

____

9. Cookbooks can be very intimidating to a beginner.

____

10. Photography is a competitive profession.

____

Using Coordination and Subordination in a Paragraph

EXERCISE 31-4
(31a–i)

These paragraphs are full of choppy sentences. Revise them using coordinating and subordinating conjunctions so that the sentences are smoother and more fully explain the relationships between ideas. Many correct versions are possible. Take the time to try several, and select the version you like best.

Senet is a game. It was played by ancient Egyptians. It was very popular. Egyptians began putting senet boards into tombs as early as 3100 BC. Tomb objects were intended for use in the afterlife. They give us a good idea of daily life.

Many senet boards and playing pieces have been found in tombs. The hot, dry air of the tombs preserved them well. Tomb paintings frequently show people playing the game. Hieroglyphic texts describe it. Numerous descriptions of the game survive. Egyptologists think it was a national pastime.

Senet was a game for two people. They played it on a board marked with thirty squares. Each player had several playing pieces. They probably each had seven. The number did not matter as long as it was the same for both. Opponents moved by throwing flat sticks. The sticks were an early form of dice. Sometimes they threw pairs of lamb knuckles instead. Players sat across from each other. They moved their pieces in a backward S line. The squares represented houses. They moved through the houses.

By the New Kingdom the game began to take on religious overtones. The thirty squares were given individual names. They were seen as stages on the journey of the soul through the netherworld. New Kingdom tomb paintings showed the deceased playing senet with an unseen opponent. The object was to win eternal life. The living still played the game. They played it in anticipation of the supernatural match to come.

Identifying Parallel Elements

EXERCISE 32-1
(32a–e)

Underline parallel words, phrases, and clauses.

EXAMPLE Many ancient writers <u>in Greece</u> and <u>in Rome</u> wrote about underwater ships.

1. They hoped these ships would be used for exploration and travel.
2. Leonardo Da Vinci felt that humanity would be destroyed by a great flood because of its proud and evil ways.
3. Therefore, just as earlier he had made plans for a helicopter, he made plans for an underwater ship.
4. However, the first working submarine was designed by a British mathematician and built by a Dutch inventor.
5. It was designed in 1578, built in 1620, and successfully tested from 1620 to 1624.
6. This submarine was equipped with oars, so it could be used either on the surface or below the surface.
7. King James I of England actually boarded the submarine and took a short ride.
8. James's praise soon made submarines the talk of the town and the focus of scientific investigation.
9. A much later model featured goatskin bags attached to holes in the bottom of the ship. When the vessel was to submerge, the bags would fill with water and pull the ship downward; when the vessel was to rise, a twisting rod would force water from the bags, and the lightened ship would surface.
10. David Bushnell, a student at Yale during the American Revolution, designed and built a war-submarine, the *Turtle*.
11. It was intended to sneak up on British warships and attach explosives to their hulls.
12. Despite successful launching and steering, the *Turtle* failed on its only mission when the pilot was unable to attach the explosives to the British target ship.
13. The first successful wartime submarines were developed by the South in the American Civil War: small, four-person ships called "Davids" and a full-sized submarine called the *Hunley*.
14. New submarines were designed throughout the nineteenth century, but providing dependable power and seeing to navigate remained problems for years.
15. The development of the gasoline engine and the invention of the periscope solved these problems before the beginning of World War I.

Writing Parallel Elements

EXERCISE 32-2

(32a–e)

Fill in the blanks with words, phrases, or clauses, as appropriate.

EXAMPLE Many people enjoy watching TV once in awhile, especially when they are *physically, and mentally, exhausted.*

1. Sometimes after a demanding day at work, it's relaxing to turn on the TV, _______________, and _______________.
2. TV shows can be _______________ and _______________.
3. Because there are more channels than ever before, channel surfing can be _______________ or _______________.
4. _______________ and _______________ are ways some people describe TV viewing.
5. Others describe TV viewing as _______________ and _______________.
6. Those people claim that finding a _______________ TV show is much more difficult than finding a _______________ one.
7. But the wonderful range of programs now available means that people of all _______________ and _______________ can find something they want to watch on TV.
8. Like anything else, watching too much TV may cause _______________, and _______________ problems.
9. Just be sure to balance TV viewing with physical activities such as _______________ and _______________.
10. Also be sure to balance TV viewing with mental activities such as _______________ or _______________ a puzzle.
11. It can be upsetting when your favourite TV show is scheduled while you are away from home either _______________ or _______________ errands.
12. However, many people are adept at recording the TV shows they want to _______________ or can't bear to _______________.
13. TV is especially important for people who live in rural areas where live _______________ and sports _______________ are rare.
14. These people can enjoy an evening at the Bell Centre or at Vancouver's Chan Centre for the Performing Arts in the _______________ and _______________ of their own homes.
15. In spite of what naysayers may think of TV, I would rather _______________ one than not _______________ one.

Varying Sentence Beginnings by Varying Subjects

EXERCISE 33-1

(33f)

Revise each sentence so that it begins with the word or words given.

EXAMPLE For many people, building a house is challenging and rewarding.
Building a house: Building a house is challenging and rewarding for many people.

1. Choosing a house plan is the first task.
   The first task: ____________________

2. It's difficult to choose just the right plan among all the architectural styles and floor plans.
   To choose: ____________________

3. Next people can get their finances in order by talking to loan officers at different banks.
   By talking: ____________________

4. The bank that gives the lowest interest rate is the bank most people want to borrow from.
   Most people: ____________________

5. A contractor who is trustworthy and competent is every homeowner's dream come true.
   Every homeowner's: ____________________

6. It's time to begin building the house once all the permits have been signed by city officials.
   Once all: ____________________

7. As the contract clears the lot and lays the foundation, the homeowners get a little break.
   The homeowners: ____________________

8. For the homeowners, choosing all the materials and colours to use in a new home is exciting and demanding.
   Choosing: ____________________

9. People who are building a new home should do lots of shopping before the contractor calls and asks if they have their flooring, counters, cabinets, and paint colours picked out.
   Before the contractor: ____________________

10. What went right, what changes they made, and what they would do differently if they could go back in time and build their house again are stories people enjoy telling to friends.
    Stories people enjoy telling: ____________________

Expanding Sentences with Modifiers

EXERCISE 33-2
(33d)

A: Expand these simple sentences in the ways stated in parentheses.

EXAMPLE The city seems busy.
(prepositional phrase) *The city seems busy in the mornings.*

1. The children walk to school.

   (adjective) ____________________

   (adverb clause) ____________________

   (participial phrase) ____________________

2. Shopkeepers open their stores.

   (adjective) ____________________

   (adverb clause) ____________________

   (participial phrase) ____________________

3. People go shopping.

   (adjective) ____________________

   (adverb clause) ____________________

   (participial phrase) ____________________

4. Delivery trucks are seen.

   (adjective) ____________________

   (adverb clause) ____________________

   (participial phrase) ____________________

5. The coffee shops are crowded.

   (adjective) ____________________

   (adverb clause) ____________________

   (participial phrase) ____________________

B: Add the several elements given to each of the following sentences.

EXAMPLE The astronaut was welcomed home.
(adjective modifying *astronaut*; adverb modifying *was welcomed*; prepositional phrase modifying *home*)
The *brave* astronaut was *warmly* welcomed home *from space.*

1. The celebration included a parade.
(adjectives modifying *celebration* and *parade*; prepositional phrase modifying *parade*)

____

2. The crowd was dressed in shorts and shirts.
(absolute phrase; adjective modifying *shirts*)

____

3. The mayor stopped traffic.
(adjective clause modifying *mayor*; adverb clause)

____

4. The astronaut rode in a car.
(adjectives modifying *astronaut* and *car*; adverb modifying *rode*)

____

5. Youngsters tried to get autographs.
(adverb clause; adjective clause modifying *youngsters*)

____

6. The mayor gave a speech.
(absolute phrase; two adjectives modifying *speech*)

____

7. Everyone cheered.
(two adverb clauses)

____

8. The celebration ended.
(prepositional phrase modifying *ended*)

____

9. Everyone headed home.
(participial phrase modifying *everyone*)

____

10. The street cleaners came out.
(prepositional phrase modifying *came out*; adverb clause)

____

Revising to Emphasize the Main Idea

EXERCISE 33-3
(33a–f)

Using sentence combining, revise each passage into one or two sentences that emphasize the main idea. To do this, select the most effective subject for the sentence; stay in the active voice whenever possible; use a variety of sentence types (simple, compound, complex, compound-complex) and modifiers; and change clauses into phrases where practical.

EXAMPLE Retail chain stores are closing outlets. Firms are laying off many employees. There is a shift from intimidation to collaboration among workers and their bosses.
Because retail chain stores are closing outlets and firms are laying off many employees, there is a changed relationship between some workers and their bosses.

1. There is a new emphasis on teamwork. There is a new emphasis on trust in the workplace. Managers hope that the new shift in attitude will benefit their businesses.

____

____

2. Companies are trying to make a difference. They are experimenting with group talks among employees. These groups discuss issues dealing with workers as individuals and as team members.

____

____

3. The talks are very helpful for managers. The workers involved are those who are still with the company. They have survived the massive cutbacks and need a boost in morale.

____

____

4. These experimental groups also break down barriers in the workplace. These barriers tend to separate one department from another. This separation takes away any feelings of teamwork and cooperation.

____

____

5. Teamwork is critical for companies that want to regain competitiveness. These groups strive to remove obstacles that prevent communication and respect among workers. Teamwork is a necessary step in the right direction.

____

____

Practising English Usage

EXERCISE 34-1

(34)

Choose any ten entries from the Usage Glossary of the *Simon & Schuster Handbook for Writers*, Fifth Canadian Edition. Compose a paragraph, on a topic of your choice, that contains all the words that are explained or defined in each of your ten entries. If you decide to choose an entry containing words that the glossary calls "nonstandard," work those words into your paragraph in a way that points out that they are nonstandard. (You may consider writing a piece of dialogue to accomplish that.) Note that humour, wordplay, and punning are acceptable in this exercise—and may even be hard to avoid in some cases.

Recognizing Levels of Formality

EXERCISE 35-1
(35b)

Different levels of formality are appropriate in different situations. Decide which level (informal, medium, between medium and formal, and formal) best fits each of these situations.

	Level of Formality
EXAMPLE a letter requesting the list of winners in a sweepstakes	*Medium*
1. a note to a friend asking him or her to take a package to the post office for you	______________
2. a chemistry lab report	______________
3. a petition to have a candidate's name added to the election ballot	______________
4. an invitation to a community activist to speak to your daughter's grade six class.	______________
5. the valedictorian's speech at a college graduation ceremony	______________

Now select three of these documents, each calling for a different level of formality, and write them. Use your own paper.

Understanding Differences in Denotation and Connotation

EXERCISE 35-2
(35e)

A: Underline the most appropriate word from the pair given in parentheses. If you are unsure, consult your Dictionary's synonymy. (A synonymy is a paragraph comparing and contrasting words.)

EXAMPLE The sky was (<u>clear</u>, transparent), with not a cloud in sight.

1. The sergeant (instructed, commanded) his men to clean the barracks.
2. The plane remained (complete, intact) after passing through the severe storm.
3. The dictator was (conquered, overthrown) by his own brother.
4. Astronomy calls for great (accuracy, correctness).
5. After he fell into the cesspool, his suit was so (soiled, foul) it could not be cleaned.
6. The inheritance was (divided, doled out) among her sisters.
7. The crowd (dissipated, dispersed) once the ambulance took away the accident victim.
8. The tenants (withheld, kept) their rent in protest over the long-broken boiler.

9. Most fashion models are (lofty, tall).

10. The patient was (restored, renovated) to health by physical therapy.

11. Because of his (immoderate, exorbitant) behaviour, the young man was thrown out of the restaurant.

12. The committee voted to (eliminate, suspend) voting on the budget until the missing members could be located.

13. The coach talked to the team in the (capacity, function) of a friend.

14. The family (donated, bestowed) its time to help restore the fire-damaged day-care centre.

15. The practical joker (tittered, guffawed) as his victim slipped on a banana peel.

16. The professor (praised, eulogized) the class for its good work on the midterm examination.

17. Sometimes people offer (premiums, rewards) to help capture dangerous criminals.

18. The guest wondered if it would be (impolite, boorish) to ask for a third piece of pie.

19. The man (clandestinely, secretly) took his wife's birthday present into the attic.

20. The lifeguard's (skin, hide) was dry from overexposure to the sun.

B: The following words are synonymous, but not all are equally appropriate in every situation. Check the precise meaning of each word, and then use each in a sentence. Your dictionary may have a synonymy (a paragraph comparing and contrasting all the words) listed under one of the words, so check all the definitions before writing your sentences.

EXAMPLE laughable *The travel book was laughable, because the author had never left the tour bus.*

amusing *We spent an amusing afternoon riding in an old, horse-drawn carriage.*

droll *The political commentator had a droll sense of humour.*

comical *The clowns in the circus were truly comical.*

1. danger ______________________________

peril ______________________________

hazard ______________________________

risk ______________________________

2. rich ______________________________

wealthy ______________________________

affluent ______________________________

opulent ______________________________

3. speak ____________________

talk ____________________

converse ____________________

discourse ____________________

4. think ____________________

reason ____________________

reflect ____________________

speculate ____________________

deliberate ____________________

5. irritable ____________________

choleric ____________________

touchy ____________________

cranky ____________________

cross ____________________

Using Concrete, Specific Language

EXERCISE 35-3

(35f)

A: Reorder the words in each list so they move from most general to most specific.

Example	cola	*beverage*
	pop	*pop*
	Coca-Cola	*cola*
	beverage	*Coca-Cola*

1. sandwich ____________

   food ____________

   cheese sandwich ____________

   Swiss cheese on rye ____________

2. The Bay ____________

   store ____________

   business ____________

   department store ____________

3. bill ____________

   record club charges ____________

   letter ____________

   mail ____________

4. clothing ____________

   jeans ____________

   pants ____________

   stone-washed jeans ____________

5. land ______
tropical paradise ______
islands ______
Hawaii ______

6. cookbook ______
The Joy of Cooking ______
how-to book ______
book ______

7. lion ______
carnivore ______
cat ______
animal ______

8. television show ______
entertainment ______
satire ______
The Royal Canadian Air Farce ______

9. *The Blue Boy* ______
painting ______
art ______
portrait ______

10. sports ______
100-metre dash ______
running ______
track ______

B: The italicized word or phrase in each sentence below is too abstract or general. Replace it with a word (or words) that is more specific or concrete. Use the lines to the right.

EXAMPLE The *beast* escaped from the zoo. *ferocious leopard*

1. He's very proud of his new *car*. ______
2. They planted *bushes* along the edge of the walk. ______
3. The milk tasted *funny*. ______
4. Proudly, she *walked* onto the stage. ______
5. My aunt lives in the *West*. ______
6. *Somebody* asked me to deliver these roses to you. ______
7. She wrote a book about *history*. ______
8. A *bird* flew into the classroom. ______
9. To be successful, an accountant must be *good*. ______
10. The Mounties caught *their man*. ______
11. The dancer *hurt* her ankle. ______
12. He received *jewellery* as a birthday present. ______
13. The engine made a *strange* sound. ______
14. He thought Economics class was a *pain*. ______
15. The nurse was very *nice* to the patients. ______
16. After practice, we went to *a movie*. ______
17. His new dining room set was delivered *damaged*. ______
18. The building is *a mess*. ______
19. I want to get a *good* job after graduation. ______
20. The doctor gave *everyone* a booklet about how to quit smoking. ______

Avoiding Slang, Colloquial, and Overly Formal Language

EXERCISE 35-4
(35b, h)

Underline the word in each sentence that best suits an academic style. You may need to check your dictionary for usage labels.

EXAMPLE That academic advisor fails to motivate students because she is (stuck-up, aloof).

1. My anthropology professor is a brilliant (guy, man).
2. The food in the main dining hall is barely (edible, comestible).
3. (Hey, Please) shut off the lights when leaving classrooms.
4. The Dean of Faculty will (address, parley with) the audience at graduation.
5. (Regardless, Irregardless) of the weather, the honours and awards ceremony will be held on Thursday evening.
6. All students must wear skirts or (britches, slacks) under their graduation robes.
7. The elevator is reserved for faculty and (educands, students) with passes.
8. Remind your guests to park their (cars, wheels) in the visitors' lot.
9. Anyone parking a (motorcycle, chopper) on campus should chain it to the rack in the parking field.
10. Relatives may stay overnight in the (dormitories, dorms) provided they have written in advance and (checked in, touched base) with the house parents.

Revising Sentences for Appropriate Language

EXERCISE 35-5
(35h)

Revise these sentences using language appropriate for academic writing

EXAMPLE It stinks that I can't go skydiving more often.
It's a shame that I can't go skydiving more often.

1. Before I tried skydiving, I thought skydivers were nuts.

   ____

2. It seemed so out there.

   ____

3. But now I've done it, I think it's a blast.

   ____

4. The day of the jump, I was totally stoked.

   ____

5. My friends were pretty weirded out on my account, though.

____

6. But then, they're such wusses.

____

7. I thought I was going to barf just before I jumped out the plane.

____

8. But it was great—it blew me away.

____

9. It has to be way cooler than bungee-jumping, which is, like, blink and you've missed it.

____

10. Yeah, skydiving definitely rocks.

____

Revising Slanted Language

EXERCISE 35-6
(35h)

Here is the opening paragraph of a very slanted letter to the editor. Revise it, using moderate language. Try to convince the reader that you are a reasonable person with a valid argument.

Dear Editor:

I just read your ridiculous article on the proposed opening of a hazardous waste storage depot just outside town. Are you crazy? Anyone who would propose such a deadly project has no soul. Those city council members who are sponsoring this monstrous facility obviously have the brains of fruit flies. If they had bothered to do a little research, they would have discovered that dreadful things can happen to any poor community that lets such a depot be forced upon it.

Revising for Appropriate Figurative Language

EXERCISE 35-7
(35d, h, j)

Revise these sentences by replacing clichéd or inappropriate language or mixed metaphors with fresh, appropriate figures of speech. You may want to reduce the number of figures of speech in a sentence, or you may sometimes feel a message is best presented without any figurative language.

EXAMPLE In high school, I decided that an actor's life is as good as it gets.

In high school, I decided that I wanted to be an actor. [*As good as it gets* is a cliché.]

1. Once I began acting, I was bowled over while walking on air.

___

2. I took to the stage like a duck to water.

___

3. My lines stuck to my brain like glue.

___

4. Sometimes the famous lines I spoke filled me with an awe and left me speechless.

___

5. When I danced on stage, I met with success at every turn.

___

6. My singing was out of sight.

___

7. At every audition I came out smelling like a rose.

___

8. In all its days, my high school had never seen an actor like me.

___

9. Being in a television commercial was the first step in my meteoric rise to fame.

___

10. The commercial was about a new and improved, never before seen product.

___

11. After that, my agent's cell phone rang off the hook.

___

12. My schedule became a constant flow of stops for public appearances.

___

13. During these public appearances, I had to sign autographs until the cows came home.

___

14. I soon learned that being rich and famous isn't all it's cracked up to be.

___

15. But my passion for acting is like a tide that never stops rising.

___

Using Figurative Language

EXERCISE 35-8

(35d, h, j)

Using new, appropriate figures of speech, write a sentence describing each of the following.

Example a fast train
Disappearing like the vapour trail of a jet, the train sped into the distance.

1. a graceful horse

____

2. a run-down shack

____

3. a terrible dance band

____

4. greasy french fries

____

5. being awakened by your alarm clock

____

6. a professor who requires too much work

____

7. a salesperson with a phony smile

____

8. a hot day in the city

____

9. something that is very late

____

10. an unpleasant singing voice

____

Eliminating Artificial Language

EXERCISE 35-9
(35h, k, l)

A: "Translate" these sentences into standard academic English by eliminating inappropriate jargon and euphemisms. You may need to refer to your dictionary.

EXAMPLE We were blessed with four centimetres of precipitation last night.
We got four centimetres of rain (or snow) last night.

1. After falling, the child sustained a severe hematoma of the patella.

   ____

2. Operators of automotive vehicles should be sure to utilize their seat belts before engaging engines.

   ____

   ____

3. Although she was in a family way, she continued in the fulfillment of her familial and employment responsibilities.

   ____

   ____

4. The municipal public-thoroughfare contamination controllers are on unauthorized, open-ended leave.

   ____

   ____

5. The dean has asked department heads to interface with him.

   ____

B: Find a piece of published writing that you feel uses pretentious language, unnecessary jargon, unnecessary euphemisms, and/or bureaucratic language. Likely sources are newsletters, business memos and reports, political mailings, solicitations for charity, and sales brochures. Be prepared to say in what ways the language is artificial and what problems that language can create for readers. Then rewrite the piece using appropriate language. Submit the original and your revision to your instructor.

Correcting Common Spelling Errors

EXERCISE 36-1
(36b–f)

Underline the misspelled word in each sentence, and spell it correctly on the line to the right. If a sentence has no misspellings, write *correct* on the line.

EXAMPLE Some exceptions to spelling rules are wierdly irregular. ___*weirdly*___

1. The letter carrier retired after being biten by the same dog for the seventh time. ____________
2. The counterfeiter pleaded innocent, saying he had been frammed. ____________
3. In the committee's judgment, the fair succeeded because of extremely efficient managment. ____________
4. The scientists received news from a reliable source about an important foriegn discovery. ____________
5. We had hoped to buy a new dinning room set with our winnings from the quiz show we competed on last month. ____________
6. It seems incredable that, after trailing in the polls for weeks, our candidate managed finally to win the election. ____________
7. Running, swimming, and jumpping rope are all ways to increase the heart's endurance. ____________
8. Many foreign-born workers have little liesure time because they often hold two or even three jobs, all paying low salaries. ____________
9. Because we did not think the payments were affordable, we reluctently postponed repairing the leaky ceiling. ____________
10. The disatisfied customers tried to return the chipped benches to the manufacturer, but the factory was permanently closed. ____________
11. The young man received a commendation from the community for his incredibly couragous performance in rescuing disabled children from an overturned bus. ____________
12. When he was layed off from work, he filed a grievance with his union representative and then proceeded to the unemployment office. ____________
13. After carefully painting the attic stairs, my brother-in-law realized he had closed off his route of escape, and he was traped upstairs until the paint dried. ____________

14. When I was younger, I use to want to take drum lessons until I realized how tiring practising the drums could be. ____________

15. The professor stated that she would return illegable papers without commenting on them, and she encouraged students to type all work carefully. ____________

16. Although the street was usually gloomy, every New Year's Eve it magicly transformed itself into a joyful scene for a few hours. ____________

17. According to some philosophies, the world is constantly changing and it is pointless to expect anything to be permanant. ____________

18. The neighbourhood children voted to coordinate a carwash and use the procedes to buy durable playground equipment. ____________

19. The chef advertised in the classified section of the newspaper for a relieable dessert-maker. ____________

20. The school aide was payed a bonus for her invaluable assistance during the ice storm. ____________

21. In some cultures, it is beleived that the ghosts of ancestors take up residence in the family home. ____________

22. One of the most appealing aspects of watching team sports is seeing the interraction among the players on the field. ____________

23. The most boring part of working in a department store is taking part in periodic inventorys of the available merchandise. ____________

24. Each autumn, people tragically injure themselves in avoidable falls on rain-soaked leafs. ____________

25. *Star Wars* was a very well-received and profitible movie, and it set the pattern for many imitations. ____________

Writing Plural Nouns

EXERCISE 36-2
(36c)

Write the plural forms of these nouns.

EXAMPLE lamp *lamps*
attorney at law *attorneys at law*

1. orange ______
2. kiss ______
3. stray ______
4. Iife ______
5. radio ______
6. pair ______
7. speech ______
8. fly ______
9. monkey ______
10. piano ______
11. mother-in-law ______
12. datum ______
13. ice skate ______
14. herself ______
15. echo ______
16. half ______
17. child ______
18. woman ______
19. phenomenon ______
20. mouse ______

Adding Suffixes

EXERCISE 36-3
(36d)

A: Combine these suffixes and roots. If in doubt about the spelling, look up the word in your dictionary.

EXAMPLE awake + ing *awaking*

1. motivate + ion ______
2. guide + ance ______
3. notice + able ______
4. grace + ful ______
5. true + Iy ______
6. accurate + Iy ______
7. mile + age ______
8. argue + ment ______
9. drive + ing ______
10. outrage + ous ______

What basic rules govern the combining of roots ending in *e* and suffixes?

______

______

B: Combine these suffixes and roots. If in doubt about the spelling, look up the word in your dictionary.

EXAMPLE carry + ing *carrying*

1. duty + ful ______
2. play + ing ______

3. dry + er ____________

4. supply + ed ____________

5. noisy + est ____________

6. stray + ed ____________

7. sloppy + er ____________

8. gravy + s ____________

9. happy + ness ____________

10. buy + ing ____________

What basic rules govern the combining of roots ending in *y* and suffixes?

____

____

C: Combine these suffixes and roots. If in doubt about the spelling, look up the word in your dictionary.

EXAMPLE trap + ed *trapped*

1. grip + ing ____________
2. mend + able ____________
3. steam + ed ____________
4. begin + er ____________
5. plant + ing ____________
6. stop + er ____________
7. pour + ed ____________
8. split + ing ____________
9. occur + ence ____________
10. refer + ence ____________

What basic rules govern the doubling of final consonants when a suffix is added?

____

____

Distinguishing Between ei and ie

EXERCISE 36-4

(36e)

Fill in the blanks with *ei* or *ie*. Because there are frequent exceptions to the rule, check your dictionary whenever you are in doubt.

EXAMPLE anc *ie* nt

1. bel_____ve
2. rec_____ve
3. n_____ther
4. c_____ling
5. for_____gn
6. f_____ld
7. counterf_____t
8. w_____rd
9. fr_____ght
10. n_____ce

Writing Sentences with Homonyms and Commonly Confused Words

EXERCISE 36-5
(36f)

Use each word below in a sentence that clearly demonstrates its meaning.

EXAMPLE its *Every plan has its disadvantages.*
it's *It's too late to go out for pizza.*

1. already ____
   all ready ____
2. its ____
   it's ____
3. than ____
   then ____
4. they're ____
   their ____
   there ____
5. to ____
   two ____
   too ____
6. your ____
   you're ____
7. passed ____
   past ____
8. quiet ____
   quite ____
9. through ____
   threw ____
   thorough ____
10. whose ____
    who's ____

Recognizing Homonyms and Commonly Confused Words

EXERCISE 36-6

(36f)

Underline the word within parentheses that best fits each sentence.

EXAMPLE (<u>Accepting</u>, Excepting) and following some (advise, <u>advice</u>) can make travelling a (hole, <u>whole</u>) lot of fun.

1. When (your, you're) travelling, the key (to, two, too) enjoying yourself is to relax.
2. (Weather, Whether) of any kind, (reign, rain, rein), cold, or heat, shouldn't (affect, effect) you.
3. Pack (cloths, clothes) that are suitable to (wear, where) (where, wear) you'll be staying.
4. (Buy, By) clothes that don't (weigh, way) (to, two, too) much and (which, witch) remain wrinkle-free.
5. Whether you're travelling for business or pleasure, you don't want to (waist, waste) time ironing.
6. When you travel on vacation, pack some (stationary, stationery) so you (rite, write, right) to your loved ones, and take a (dairy, diary) to record your adventures.
7. If you're leaving the (county, country), you can't be (already, all ready) until you have your passport.
8. Of (course, coarse), you should arrive at the airport in plenty of time to (bored, board) the (plain, plane).
9. Most airline (personal, personnel) are glad to be of (assistants, assistance) to customers, so don't be afraid to ask them questions.
10. If flying makes you nervous, choose an (aisle, isle) seat and remember to (breath, breathe) deeply and swallow often during the (assent, ascent) and (descent, dissent).
11. The (affect, effect) of breathing and swallowing is that (you're, your, yore) ears won't hurt as much.
12. Again, the (hole, whole) idea of travelling is to relax and enjoy it.
13. Whether you visit a famous (capitol, capital) or a (desert, dessert) resort, allow positive thoughts to (dominate, dominant) your mind.
14. (Its, It's) often fun to (meat, meet) some of the other guests (where, were) you are staying.
15. After all, it's only (human, (humane) to want to (hear, here) from those who have been (through, threw) exciting adventures and who have (scene, seen) wonderful (cites, sites, sights).
16. The (presence, presents) of a few friendly faces (there, they're, their) can make it seem as though you've (already, all ready) been to a place before.
17. Here is some more (council, counsel) regarding travelling that (may be, maybe) helpful: Be prepared to spend money.
18. It's possible to travel on a tight budget, but to (ensure, insure) a good time, have extra spending money.
19. You'll (altar, alter) your spending habits when travelling because you'll spend more on (fares, fairs) for transportation.
20. You won't need to (break, brake) the bank, but you'll probably want to (by, buy) a few (presents, presence) for your family and friends.
21. A final (peace, piece) of (advice, advise) regards delays while travelling.
22. Being (stationary, stationery) while travelling can leave you (quiet, quite) (board, bored) and irritable.
23. Keep your positive attitude and sense of humour no matter how your (patients, patience) may be tried.
24. Your (since, sense) of humour may keep other upset passengers from making a (seen, scene).
25. Once the delay and inconvenience have (passed, past), you'll be more (conscience, conscious) of the (principle, principal) that you cannot control what happens, but you can control your reactions to what happens.

Writing Compound Nouns and Adjectives

EXERCISE 36-7
(36g)

Using your dictionary, rewrite each of these compound words as a single word, as a hyphenated word, or as two separate words. If more than one form is correct, be prepared to explain.

EXAMPLE foot ball <u>*football*</u>

1. open heart surgery ____________
2. free for all ____________
3. high school ____________
4. pear shaped ____________
5. bird house ____________
6. accident prone ____________
7. pot hole ____________
8. bathing suit ____________
9. bread winner ____________
10. hand made ____________
11. head ache ____________
12. head cold ____________
13. head phone ____________
14. head to head ____________
15. head stone ____________
16. free agent ____________
17. free hand ____________
18. free form ____________
19. free spoken ____________
20. free style ____________

PART SIX: USING PUNCTUATION AND MECHANICS

Supplying Appropriate End Punctuation

EXERCISE 37-1
(37a–e)

A: Circle all inappropriate end punctuation: periods, exclamation marks, and question marks. Then on the line to the right, copy the final word of the sentence and add the appropriate end punctuation. If the end punctuation is correct as is, write *correct* on the line.

EXAMPLE Many people wonder why nurses wear white?	*white*
1. Have you ever wondered why doctors wear blue or green while operating.	________
2. White is the traditional symbol of purity!	________
3. It is also easier to keep clean because it shows dirt.	________
4. Surgeons wore white during operations until 1914?	________
5. Then one surgeon decided that the sight of red blood against the white cloth was disgusting!	________
6. He preferred—would you believe?—a spinach green that he felt reduced the brightness of the blood?	________
7. After World War II, surgeons began using a different shade of green!	________
8. Called minty green, it looked better under the new lighting used in operating rooms.	________
9. The latest colour is a blue-grey!	________
10. Why did the doctors change again.	________
11 Do you believe they did it because this blue shows up better on television than green does.	________
12. Believe it or not.	________
13. The surgeons appear on in-hospital television demonstrating new techniques to medical students!	________

B: Add end punctuation to this paragraph as needed.

Do you know who Theodor Seuss Geisel was Sure you do He was Dr. Seuss, the famous author of children's books After ten years as a successful advertising illustrator and cartoonist, Seuss managed to get his first children's book published *And to Think That I Saw It on Mulberry Street* was published in 1937 by Vanguard Press It had been rejected by 27 other publishers I wonder why They certainly were foolish What's your favourite Dr. Seuss book Mine is *The Cat in the Hat,* published in 1957 Everyone has a favourite And I do mean *everyone* His books have been translated into 17 languages, and by 1984 more than a hundred million copies had been sold worldwide In fact, in 1984 Seuss received a Pulitzer Prize for his years of educating and entertaining children How fitting Sadly, Dr. Seuss died in 1991 We will all miss him

Writing Sentences with Appropriate End Punctuation

EXERCISE 37-2

(37a–e)

Write a sentence to illustrate each of these uses of end punctuation.

EXAMPLE an emphatic command

Wipe that grin off your face!

1. an indirect question

____

2. a mild command

____

3. a direct question

____

4. an abbreviation

____

5. a declarative sentence containing a direct quotation

____

6. an exclamation

____

7. a declarative statement

____

8. an emphatic command

____

9. a declarative sentence containing a quoted direct question

____

10. a declarative sentence containing an indirect quotation

____

11. a declarative sentence containing a quoted exclamation

____

Using Commas in Compound Sentences

EXERCISE 38-1
(38b)

A: Rewrite the following sentences, inserting commas wherever coordinating conjunctions are used to join sentences. If a sentence does not need any additional commas, write *correct* on the line.

EXAMPLE Some people consider slime moulds protozoans but most scientists class them with the fungi.
Some people consider slime moulds protozoans, but most scientists class them with the fungi.

1. Slime moulds move by creeping along and sometimes they seem to flow.

   ____

2. They have a stationary stage, however and then they are more plantlike.

   ____

3. An observer seldom sees much of the mould's body or plasmodium for it stays beneath decaying matter.

   ____

4. The main part contains several nuclei but has no cell walls.

   ____

5. Like an amoeba, its protoplasm moves in one direction and then it goes in another.

   ____

6. Not only do slime moulds come in many colours but they also come in many types.

   ____

7. Some grow on long stalks while others are stalkless.

   ____

8. Some kinds are very small and can only be seen through a microscope.

   ____

9. Most slime moulds grow on decaying wood yet some grow directly on the ground.

   ____

10. A mould depends on water so it will dry up if it lacks moisture.

   ____

11. Most mature moulds change into sporangia and the sporangia each contain many spores.

____

12. Scientists know that the wind carries the spores and that they eventually germinate and form new moulds.

____

13. The slime-mould species *Fuligo* has the largest sporangia and they dwarf others by comparison.

____

14. Either they appear to be large sponges on the ground or they look like dark holes in the grass.

____

B: Combine the following sentences by using the coordinating conjunctions given in parentheses. Remember to use a comma before each coordinating conjunction used to join two sentences.

EXAMPLE Most slime moulds live in the woods.
They like soil with high humus content. (and)
Most slime moulds live in the woods, and they like soil with high humus content.

1. Some, however, leave the forest.
They live on cultivated plants. (and)

____

2. They can cause clubroot of cabbage.
They can create powdery scab of potato. (or)

____

3. Slime moulds sound disagreeable.
Some are quite attractive. (yet)

____

4. One form produces unappealing stalks.
The stalks are topped with tiny balls. (but)

____

5. The balls appear to be woven.
They look rather like baskets. (so)

____

6. The woven balls are really sporangia.
They contain spores for distribution. (and)

____

7. Another form looks like tiny ghosts.
Its white moulds could be small sheeted figures. (for)

____

8. Serpent slime mould is yellow.
It can look like a miniature snake on top of a decaying log. (and)

____

9. One would have to work hard to find it on the Prairies.
It is most common in the tropics. (for)

____

10. After one learns about slime moulds, they no longer seem disgusting.
They do not even seem disagreeable. (nor)

____

Using Commas after Introductory Elements

EXERCISE 38-2

(38c)

A: Applying the rules regarding commas and introductory elements, rewrite these sentences, inserting commas as needed. If any sentence does not need an additional comma, write *correct* on the line.

EXAMPLE Known as the Empty Quarter the Rub al-Khali is the largest of the deserts in Saudi Arabia.
Known as the Empty Quarter, the Rub al-Khali is the largest of the deserts in Saudi Arabia.

1. In fact it is the largest continuous body of sand in the world.

    ____

2. Extending over 650 000 square kilometres the Rub al-Khali composes more than one-third of Saudi Arabia.

    ____

3. As a point of comparison Saskatchewan is just slightly larger.

    ____

4. Because it is almost completely devoid of rain the Rub al-Khali is one of the driest places on the planet.

    ____

5. Despite the existence of a few scattered shrubs the desert is largely a sand sea.

    ____

6. However its eastern side develops massive dunes with salt basins.

    ____

7. Except for the hardy Bedouins the Rub al-Khali is uninhabited.

    ____

8. Indeed it is considered one of the most forbidding places on earth.

    ____

9. Until Bertram Thomas crossed it in 1931 it was unexplored by outsiders.

    ____

10. Even after oil was discovered in Arabia exploration in the Empty Quarter was limited.

    ____

11. Losing heavy equipment in the deep sand made such exploration expensive.

____

12. To facilitate exploration huge sand tires were developed in the 1950s.

____

13. Shortly thereafter drilling rigs began operating in the Rub al-Khali.

____

14. We now know that the Empty Quarter sits on huge reserves of oil.

____

15. As it turns out the Empty Quarter is not so empty after all.

____

B: Applying the rules governing commas and introductory elements, insert commas as needed in this paragraph.

[1]As might be expected the Rub al-Khali is hot all year round. [2]In contrast the Gobi Desert is hot in the summer but extremely cold in the winter. [3]Located in China and Mongolia the Gobi is twice the size of Saskatchewan. [4]Unlike the Rub al-Khali the Gobi has some permanent settlers. [5]Nevertheless most of its inhabitants are nomadic. [6]To avoid the subzero winters the nomads move their herds at the end of summer. [7]When the harsh winters subside they return to the sparse desert vegetation.

Using Commas in Series and with Coordinate Adjectives

EXERCISE 38-3

(38d–e)

A: In each sentence, first underline all items in series and all coordinate adjectives. Then rewrite each sentence, adding any necessary commas. If no commas are needed, explain why.

EXAMPLE Vicunas guanacos llamas and alpacas are all South American members of the camel family.
Vicunas, guanacos, llamas, and alpacas are all South American members of the camel family.

1. The vicuna, the smallest member of the camel family, lives in the mountains of Ecuador Bolivia and Peru.

   ____

2. The guanaco is the wild humpless ancestor of the llama and the alpaca.

   ____

3. The llama stands 1.25 metres tall is about 1.25 metres long and is the largest of the South American camels.

   ____

4. A llama's coat may be white brown black or shades in between.

   ____

5. Indians of the Andes use llamas to carry loads to bear wool and to produce meat.

   ____

6. Llamas are foraging animals that live on lichens shrubs and other available plants.

   ____

7. Because they can go without water for weeks, llamas are economical practical pack animals.

   ____

8. The alpaca has a longer lower body than the llama.

   ____

9. It has wool of greater length of higher quality and of superior softness.

   ____

10. Alpaca wool is straighter finer and warmer than sheep's wool.

    ____

B: Write complete sentences as described below. Take special care to follow the rules governing the use of commas in lists and between coordinate adjectives.

EXAMPLE Mention three favourite holidays.
My favourite holidays are Christmas, New Year's Day, and Easter.

1. Give at least three reasons to spend those holidays with relatives.

____

____

2. List your three favourite fast foods.

____

____

3. Mention your four preferred vacation activities.

____

____

4. Using two or three coordinate adjectives, describe a pet.

____

____

5. Use a series of adjectives to describe a favourite movie.

____

____

6. Use a series of prepositional phrases to tell where the groom found rice after the wedding.

____

____

7. Using a series of verbs or verb phrases, tell what John does at his fitness centre.

____

____

8. Use coordinate adjectives to describe John's improved appearance as a result of working out.

____

____

Using Commas with Nonrestrictive, Parenthetical, and Transitional Elements

EXERCISE 38-4
(38f–g)

Rewrite these sentences to punctuate nonrestrictive clauses, phrases, appositives, and transitional expressions. If a sentence needs no commas, write *correct* on the line.

EXAMPLE Ballet a sophisticated form of dance is a theatrical art.
Ballet, a sophisticated form of dance, is a theatrical art.

1. A ballet contains a sequence of dances that are performed to music.

____

____

2. The dances both solos and ensembles express emotion or tell a story.

____

____

3. The person who composes the actual dance steps is the choreographer.

____

____

4. A ballet's steps called its choreography become standardized over many years of performance.

____

____

5. The choreographer Marius Petipa created the blend of steps still used in most productions of *Swan Lake*.

____

____

6. The steps all with French names combine solos and groups.

____

____

7. The *corps de ballet* the ballet company excluding its star soloists may dance together or in small ensembles.

____

____

8. One soloist may join another for a *pas de deux* a dance for two.

9. Ensemble members not just soloists must be proficient at *pliés* and *arabesques*.

10. Children wanting to become professionals must practise for years.

11. It is important therefore to start lessons early.

12. In Russia which has some of the most stringent ballet training students begin at age three.

Expanding Sentences with Restrictive and Nonrestrictive Elements

EXERCISE 38-5
(38f)

Expand each sentence twice: first with a restrictive word, phrase, or clause, and then with a nonrestrictive word, phrase, or clause. Place commas as needed.

EXAMPLE I just moved into the neighbourhood.

1. (restrictive) *I just moved into the neighbourhood that I'd been considering.*
2. (nonrestrictive) *I just moved into the neighbourhood, which I'd been hoping to do for some time.*

1. My neighbours are kind.

____

____

2. They help one another.

____

____

3. They are friendly to strangers.

____

____

4. The houses and yards are well kept.

____

____

5. Trees line the streets.

____

____

6. Many of the neighbourhood families have pets.

____

____

7. The pets are friendly.

____

____

8. The park is one street away.

____

____

9. The park has a playground.

____

____

10. The neighbourhood children play in the park.

____

____

Using Commas with Quotations

EXERCISE 38-6
(38h)

Using the rules governing commas to attach quotations to their speaker tags, place commas in these sentences.

EXAMPLE According to Aristotle "The actuality of thought is life."
According to Aristotle, "The actuality of thought is life."

1. George Sand was most accurate when she said "Life in common among those people who love each other is the ideal of happiness."
2. "I find that I have painted my life—things happening in my life—without knowing" said the wise Georgia O'Keeffe.
3. "I slept and dreamed that life was beauty" said Ellen Sturgis Hooper. "I woke—and found that life was duty."
4. In passing, a professor said to a student "Life, dear friend, is short but sweet."
5. "Life's a tough proposition" declared Wilson Mizner "and the first hundred years are the hardest."
6. "Life" said Forrest Gump "is like a box of chocolates: You never know what you're going to get."
7. "That it will never come again is what makes life so sweet" observed Emily Dickinson.
8. "May you live all the days of your life" advised Jonathan Swift.
9. William Cooper was right when he said "Variety's the spice of life."
10. "Live all you can; it's a mistake not to" said Henry James.

Using Commas in Dates, Names, Addresses, and Numbers

EXERCISE 38-7
(38i)

Rewrite the following sentences, inserting commas (or spaces, if required) to punctuate dates, names, addresses, and numbers. If a sentence is correct as written, write *correct* on the line.

EXAMPLE January 1 1975 was the beginning of a momentous year.
January 1, 1975, was the beginning of a momentous year.

1. In the northwest part of China, more than 6000 pottery figures were found.

____

2. Construction workers uncovered a terra cotta army in July 1975.

____

3. The life-sized warriors and horses had been buried for 2200 years.

____

4. The figures were in a huge tomb near the city of Xian China.

____

5. Archaeologists also unearthed almost 10000 artifacts from the excavation site.

____

6. It did not take John Doe Ph.D. to realize that this was an extraordinary find.

____

7. Some of the figures were displayed in Quebec City, Quebec nearly thirty years later.

____

8. Running from 5 December 2001 to 2 September 2002, the exhibit featured 130 objects from the imperial tombs of China.

____

9. The exhibit was open from 9 a.m. to 10 p.m. daily.

____

10. To get tickets, one could write to Musée de la Civilisation 85 Dalhousie Street Quebec City Quebec G1K 7A6.

____

Adding Commas

EXERCISE 38-8
(38b–j)

A: Rewrite the following sentences, inserting commas as needed. If a sentence is correct as written, write *correct* on the line.

EXAMPLE Ancient writers both Greek and Roman wrote about the seven wonders of the world.
Ancient writers, both Greek and Roman, wrote about the seven wonders of the world.

1. One was the statue of Olympian Zeus which was covered with precious stones.

____

2. Unfortunately it was taken to Constantinople in A.D. 576 and there destroyed by fire.

____

3. The Hanging Gardens of Babylon built for Nebuchadnezzar were considered a wonder.

____

4. They were probably irrigated terraces connected by marble stairways.

____

5. To lift water from the Euphrates slaves had to work in shifts.

____

6. The Colossus of Rhodes was a huge impressive statue built to honour the sun god Helios.

____

7. Constructed near the harbour it was intended to astonish all who saw it.

____

8. Another wonder was the lighthouse at Alexandria Egypt.

____

9. Because it stood on the island of Pharos the word *pharos* has come to mean lighthouse.

____

10. After the death of Mausolus king of Caria his widow erected a richly adorned monument to honour him.

____

11. With sculptures by famous artists the Mausoleum at Halicarnassus amazed the ancient world.

____

12. The Temple of Artemis at Ephesus an important lonian city was also considered a wonder.

____

13. It was burned rebuilt and burned again.

____

14. Some wonders such as the Colossus and the Mausoleum were destroyed by earthquakes.

____

15. Of the seven works that astounded the ancients only the pyramids of Egypt survive.

____

B: Add commas as needed. You will not need to add any words or other marks of punctuation.

[1]St. Andrews Scotland is an old city.[2]Named for a Christian saint the city was once an object of devout pilgrimage. [3]Its cathedral the largest in Scotland is now a ruin. [4]It was destroyed in 1559 by followers of the reformer John Knox. [5]AII the revered carefully preserved relics of St. Andrew disappeared. [6]Although the castle of St. Andrews also lies in ruins it preserves two fascinating remnants of medieval history. [7]One is a bottle-shaped dungeon and the other is a countermine. [8]When attackers tried to mine under castle walls defenders tried to intercept the tunnel with a countermine. [9]Interestingly one can actually enter both mine and countermine. [10]The University of St. Andrews which is the oldest university in Scotland was established in 1412.[11]From all parts of the globe students come to study there. [12]Nevertheless most people who think of St. Andrews associate it with golf. [13]Even golf at St. Andrews is old the first reference dating to January 25 1552. [14]The famous Old Course is only one of four courses from which the avid golfer may choose.[15]St. Andrews is still an object of pilgrimage but today's pilgrims come with drivers wedges and putters.

EXERCISE 38-9
(38k)

Revise this paragraph, eliminating any unnecessary commas. You will not need to add any words or marks of punctuation.

[1]Originally, a slightly offbeat country singer, k.d. lang, has continued to push the boundaries. [2]Kathryn Dawn Lang, born in 1961 in Consort, Alberta, made her mark by bringing a punk sensibility to the interpretation of the songs of the US country star, Patsy Cline. [3]After joining with fiddler, guitarist, and composer, Ben Mink, in 1985, lang began to show her full range of tonality, and emotion. [4]Since then, the two of them, and especially lang, have won several, major, recording awards. [5]A brave public figure, lang was not afraid, to reveal her sexual orientation when most gay performers were still keeping their sexuality a secret.[6]Further, she did not hesitate to proclaim, her vegetarianism in Alberta's ranching country.[7]Following her surprising collaboration with aging, jazz singer Tony Bennett, lang took yet another direction.[8] In summer, 2004, she released an album of Canadian folk, and, popular music standards, *Hymns of the 49th Parallel.* [9]This intensely, personal project allowed lang to reveal new depths in her vocal style and even in the meaning, of the songs, which include, well-known pieces by Leonard Cohen, Joni Mitchell, Neil Young, Jane Siberry, and others.

Adding and Deleting Commas

EXERCISE 38-10

(38b–k)

Rewrite this paragraph, adding or deleting commas as needed. You will not have to change any words or other marks of punctuation. Number each change you make, and on the lines below, indicate the reason for each addition or omission.

Money, in terms of its value is really a matter, of trust and confidence in the government. By definition money is anything that society, accepts as having value. With such a broad definition it is not surprising, that money has, throughout history taken on some forms that were both creative and unique. Precious stones, fish hooks, nails livestock, throwing knives, and axe-heads, are just a few examples of money that is equivalent to ours today. In a successful, society, money must serve three, basic functions: It must serve as a store of wealth a medium of exchange and a unit against which items are valued. Forms of money, must be portable, easy to store durable, and relatively hard to acquire. Successful forms of money, like gold and silver have all these qualities. However, trust is also, necessary in a society such as ours that uses paper money. Although the paper itself is of little value we trust that a bill is, worth the number printed on the front of it.

Commas Added	Commas Deleted

Using the Semicolon

EXERCISE 39-1

(39a–f)

A: Insert semicolons where needed. They may be placed where there is now no punctuation, or they may replace commas. Some sentences may require more than one semicolon. If an item is correct, write *correct* in the left margin.

EXAMPLE Vision is our most important sense; we get most of our information about the world by seeing.

1. The sclera is the outer cover of the eye, it helps the eye keep its shape because the sclera is fairly hard.
2. The choroid is just inside the sclera it keeps out unneeded light.
3. The pupil is the opening in the eye this is where the light enters.
4. The cornea is the clear cover of the pupil, therefore, light can enter the eye.
5. The pupil is opened or closed by muscles in the iris, in fact, in bright light the iris closes to decrease the amount of light entering, in low light, it opens to increase the light.
6. After passing through the pupil, light shines on the retina, which sends messages to the brain.
7. The retina contains cells, cones and rods, which are outgrowths of the brain when light strikes them, nerve impulses travel to the brain.
8. The optic nerve connects the eye to the brain, thus any damage to the nerve can cause blindness.
9. Cone cells give us colour vision, they are most effective in the day.
10. Rods are sensitive to low light they are involved in night vision.

B: This paragraph is missing seven semicolons. Insert them where needed.

Hearing is based on sound waves these are pressure changes spreading out from a vibrating source. If we could see sound waves, they might remind us of ripples on water like ripples, sound waves vary in number, size, and speed. When these waves reach us, our ears and brain translate them into pitch, loudness, and timbre. Pitch is the number of wave vibrations per second it determines whether a tone is high or low, whether a singer is a soprano or an alto. Loudness is a measure of the intensity of the waves this is called their amplitude. When we turn up the volume on the stereo, we are raising the amplitude. Sound intensity is measured in decibels. Any sound registering over 130 decibels is painful however, people still listen to loud music or live near railroad tracks. Timbre is hard to describe in everyday language in physics terms, however, timbre is the main wavelength plus any other wavelengths that may come from a particular source. Timbre explains why a note played on a violin sounds different from the same note played on an electric guitar or why two people singing the same note sound different. Physics defines noise as too many unrelated frequencies vibrating together nevertheless, people still disagree over whether some sounds are noise or exciting music.

Using the Semicolon and the Comma

EXERCISE 39-2

(38, 39)

Add commas or semicolons as needed to fill in the blanks appropriately.

EXAMPLE One out of every twenty-five people is colourblind ______,______unable to tell certain colours apart.

1. Colourblindness is inherited _____ it appears more often in men than in women.
2. The most common colourblindness is the inability to tell red from green _____ but more than green and red are involved.
3. Different colours, the result of differences in light wavelengths, create a spectrum _____ the spectrum of colours is red, orange, yellow, green, blue, indigo, and violet.
4. People who are severely red-green colourblind cannot "see" any colours at that end of the spectrum _____ that is _____ they cannot tell the difference between blue-greens, reds, or yellow-greens.
5. Colourblindness varies from person to person _____ people who can distinguish red from green a little are called colour-weak.
6. Some people have no cone cells (the cells that send signals about colour to the brain) _____ so they are completely colourblind.
7. They have achromatism _____ a rare condition.
8. Such people can see only black, white, and greys _____ what a boring view of the world.
9. However, their problem is much more serious than this _____ they also have trouble focusing on objects.
10. The part of the eye that usually receives images is the fovea, which contains the cone cells _____ achromatics' foveas are blank and cannot receive images.
11. To compensate, they look at objects off centre _____ to pick up images with their rod (black and white) cells.
12. It is possible to be colourblind and not know it _____ how can people miss what they have never known?
13. There are several tests for colourblindness _____ most involve seeing (or not seeing) a number or word written on a background of a complementary colour for example, a red *48* on a green background.

Using the Colon

EXERCISE 40–1
(40a–e)

Rewrite the following sentences, adding colons as needed. If no colon is needed, write *correct* in the left margin.

EXAMPLE A survey once identified Canadian parents' favourite names for their babies Michael and Jessica.
A survey once identified Canadian parents' favourite names for their babies: Michael and Jessica.

1. People believe that Napoleon was short, but he was average height 5'6".
2. According to an ABC News-Harris Survey, US males' three favourite free-time activities are as follows eating, watching TV, and fixing things around the house.
3. According to the same survey, females' favourite activities include eating, reading books, and listening to music.
4. If you want my opinion, these are the most common street names in Canada, Queen, King, Elm, and Maple.
5. I plan to call my autobiography *Burrowing The Adventures of a Bookworm*.
6. The train, 20 minutes late, was due at 640.
7. She said just what we were fearing "I forgot to tell you—classroom participation also counts."
8. When walking alone at night, remember one thing Be alert!
9. The nineteenth century was a bad time for Turkey It lost three wars to Russia and three to Egypt, and it lost control over Greece.
10. Few animals eat humans, but those that do include the following polar bears, crocodiles, giant squid, leopards, lions, piranhas, sharks, and tigers.

Writing Sentences with the Colon

EXERCISE 40-2
(40a–e)

Write complete sentences in answer to these questions. Use a colon in each sentence.

EXAMPLE What time do you wake up?
I wake up at 5:45.

1. What is the full title and subtitle of one of your textbooks?

____

2. What are your favourite classes? (Use the expression *as follows*.)

____

3. What is your advice to someone going to a job interview?

____

4. Who are the star players on your favourite team?

____

5. What streets or geographical features mark the borders of your campus?

____

____

Using the Apostrophe in Possessive Nouns

EXERCISE 41–1
(41b–c)

Write the possessive forms, singular and plural, for each of the following words. If you are unsure how to form the plural of any word, see your dictionary or section 22c.

		Singular Possessive	Plural Possessive
Example	cow	*cow's*	*Cows'*
1	sheep	______	______
2.	pony	______	______
3.	turkey	______	______
4.	lion	______	______
5	mouse	______	______
6.	she	______	______
7.	gorilla	______	______
8.	goose	______	______
9.	gnu	______	______
10.	ox	______	______
11.	you	______	______
12.	buffalo	______	______
13.	zebra	______	______
14.	ibex	______	______
15.	fly	______	______
16.	I	______	______
17.	giraffe	______	______
18.	dodo	______	______
19.	zoo	______	______
20.	zoo keeper	______	______
21.	he	______	______
22.	farm	______	______
23.	farmer	______	______
24.	ranch	______	______
25.	it	______	______

Using the Apostrophe in Possessive Expressions

EXERCISE 41–2
(41b–c)

Rewrite each of these noun phrases as a possessive noun followed by another noun.

EXAMPLE The eye of the mind
The mind's eye

1. the work of a day

2. the worth of a dollar

3. the hooves of a horse

4. the hooves of several horses

5. the business of nobody

6. the share of the lion

7. the meow of the cat

8. the weights of the bodybuilder

9. the mail of the neighbour

10. the mail of the neighbours

11 the laptop of the boss

12 the anniversary of my sister-in-law

Using the Apostrophe in Contractions

EXERCISE 41-3
(41d)

Write contractions of the following expressions.

EXAMPLE he + is = *he's* __________

1. are + not = __________
2. will + not = __________
3. let + us = __________
4. he + had = __________
5. was + not = __________
6. you + would = __________
7. did + not = __________
8. I + will = __________
9. what + is = __________
10. I + am = __________
11. is + not = __________
12. would + not = __________
13. can + not = __________
14. does + not = __________
15. I + have = __________
16. you + are = __________
17. there + is = __________
18. we + would = __________
19. were + not = __________
20. they + are = __________
21. it + is = __________
22. we + have = __________
23. she + will = __________
24. we + are = __________
25. do + not = __________

Using Apostrophes

EXERCISE 41-4
(41b–g)

Insert apostrophes as needed. If no apostrophes are called for in a sentence, write *correct* in the left margin.

EXAMPLE The detective storys roots go back to at least 1841.
<u>*The detective story's roots go back to at least 1841.*</u>

1. The modern detective story began with Edgar Allan Poes "The Murders in the Rue Morgue."
2. Its detective reappeared in "The Mystery of Marie Rogêt" in 1842–43.
3. The authors last pure detective story was "The Purloined Letter."
4. The three stories featured amateur detective C. August Dupins ability to solve crimes by using logic.
5. Poe didnt use the word *detective* in the stories.
6. The publics response was not enthusiastic, perhaps because the heros personality was unpleasant.
7. This may explain why there werent any more detective stories by Poe.
8. Twenty years later, in 66, a Frenchman revived the detective story, and this time it was a great success.
9. Soon after, Englishman Wilkie Collins published *The Moonstone*.
10. Collins book was the first full-length detective novel in English.
11. The books hero was a professional detective who grew roses when he wasnt working.
12. *The Moonstones* hero had a better personality than Dupin, so the publics acceptance of him is understandable.
13. Charles Dickens, Collins friend, was writing a mystery novel when he died.
14. The fragment of *The Mystery of Edwin Drood* has been studied for years, but no ones been able to figure out how Dickens planned to explain the mystery.
15. Its been one of my favourite literary puzzles for years.
16. Arthur Conan Doyles Sherlock Holmes made his debut in "A Study in Scarlet" in 1887.
17. Holmes popularity really dates from July 1891, when "A Scandal in Bohemia" was published.
18. Peoples attention was finally captured, and they demanded more and more stories featuring Holmes.

19. Conan Doyle became so tired of the character that he wrote about Holmes death, killing him in a fall over a waterfall.

20. The readers outcry was so great that Holmes was brought back for more stories in 1902.

21. Then in 1905, Holmes earlier absence was explained.

22. The explanation was weak, but the fans couldnt have been happier.

Using Quotation Marks

EXERCISE 42-1
(42b–i)

Insert additional quotation marks as needed. Use double quotation marks unless single quotation marks are specifically needed. Remember to place quotation marks carefully in relation to other marks of punctuation. If a sentence needs no additional quotation marks, write *correct* in the left margin.

EXAMPLE Speaking of an old friend, Winston Churchill said, In those days he was wiser than he is now; he used frequently to take my advice.
Speaking of an old friend, Winston Churchill said, "In those days he was wiser than he is now; he used frequently to take my advice."

1. According to Chesterfield, Advice is seldom welcome.
2. "If you are looking for trouble, offer some good advice, says Herbert V. Prochnow.
3. Marie Dressler was right: No vice is so bad as advice.
4. Someone once remarked, How we do admire the wisdom of those who come to us for advice!
5. "Free advice, it has been noted, is the kind that costs you nothing unless you act upon it."
6. "The only thing to do with good advice is to pass it on; it is never of any use to oneself," believed Oscar Wilde.
7. I sometimes give myself admirable advice, said Lady Mary Wortley Montagu, but I am incapable of taking it.
8. Says Tom Masson, " 'Be yourself! is the worst advice you can give to some people.
9. The Beatles' song With a Little Help from My Friends contains some good advice.
10. Do you seriously advise me to marry that man?
11. My uncle advised me, The next time you are depressed, read Lewis Carroll's poem *Jabberwocky*.
12. Do you recall the Beach Boys' words: Be true to your school?
13. Many marriage counsellors advise us never to go to sleep angry with our mate.
14. However, comedian Phyllis Diller suggests, Never go to bed mad. Stay up and fight.
15. Rachel Carson advised, The discipline of the writer is to learn to be still and listen to what his subject has to tell him.
16. If I had to give students advice in choosing a career, I would tell them to select a field that interests them passionately.

Writing Direct Quotations

EXERCISE 42-2
(42b, h)

Rewrite these indirect quotations as direct quotations. You will need to add commas, colons, capitals, and quotation marks. If necessary, change pronouns and verbs to suitable forms.

EXAMPLE The chair said that she had an important announcement.
The chair said, "I have an important announcement."

1. She said that the committee had received an anonymous donation.

____

2. She told them the donation was $5000.

____

3. She ended by saying that the big problem was deciding how to spend the money to help the community. [Make this a split quotation.]

____

4. The treasurer suggested that the money should be used to repair town hall.

____

5. Someone shouted out that that was stupid.

____

6. After much discussion, the committee agreed, and the minutes read that the money would be used to make the library handicapped-accessible.

____

Writing Properly Punctuated Dialogue

EXERCISE 42-3
(42b–h)

Write an original dialogue using proper punctuation and appropriate pronouns and verb tenses. Select one of the following situations, letting each person speak at least three times. Remember to start a new paragraph each time the speaker changes. Use your own paper.

1. You are asking your boss for a raise.
2. You are asking one of your parents for advice.
3. You are trying to talk a traffic officer out of giving you a ticket.
4. You and your boyfriend/girlfriend are trying to decide what movie to see.
5. You are trying to convince your younger brother/sister not to drop out of high school.

Using Dashes, Parentheses, Brackets, Ellipses, and Slashes

EXERCISE 43-1
(43a–e)

Add dashes, parentheses, brackets, ellipses, or slashes as needed. If more than one kind of punctuation is possible, choose the one you think best. Be prepared to explain your decision.

EXAMPLE I'll pay by Do you accept cheques?"

"I'll pay by—Do you accept cheques?"

1. Niagara Falls is not the tallest waterfall in Canada Della Falls, British Columbia, is.
2. The next tallest waterfalls are 2 Takakkaw Falls, British Columbia, 3 Hunlen Falls, British Columbia, and 4 Panther Falls, Alberta.
3. Niagara Falls is relatively low it stands about one-seventh the height of Della Falls.
4. Greenland the largest island in the world was given its name by Eric the Red in 985.
5. The name was a masterstroke of publicity convincing settlers to come to what was actually an ice-covered wasteland.
6. Let's go to Quebec for Carniv Oops! I have exams that week.
7. The most expensive part of a trip the airfare can be reduced by careful planning.
8. Contest rules say "The winner must appear to claim his her prize in person."
9. "Broadway my favourite street is a main artery of New York—the hardened artery," claimed Walter Winchell. [Note: *my favourite street* is not part of the quotation.]
10. Punctuate the shortened version of the following quotation: "Too often travel, instead of broadening the mind, merely lengthens the conversation," said Elizabeth Drew. "Too often travel merely lengthens the conversation," said Elizabeth Drew.
11. Northern Ontraio sic has some spectacular parks for camping.
12. Once a camper has been there, he she will always want to return.
13. I can say only one thing about camping I hate it.
14. We leave as soon as Have you seen the bug spray? we finish packing.
15. "Let's take Highway 69 across" "Are you crazy?"
16. Finding an inexpensive hotel motel isn't always easy.
17. Motels named from a combination of *motorist* and *hotel* are usually cheaper than regular hotels.
18. When travelling, always remember to a leave a schedule with friends, b carry as little cash as possible, and c use the hotel safe for valuables.

Using Assorted Punctuation

EXERCISE 43-2
(43–49)

A: Add missing punctuation or change mistaken punctuation as needed. There may be more than one choice possible. If so, use the punctuation mark you think best. Be prepared to explain your answers.

The cheetah, is the fastest animal on earth, it can accelerate from 1.6 kilometres an hour to 65 kilometres an hour in under two seconds. Briefly reaching speeds of up to 110 kilometres an hour. Its stride, may during these bursts of speed, be as much as (7 metres). To help it run at these speeds: the cheetah is built unlike any of the other large cats—powerful heart, oversized liver, long, thin leg bones, relatively small teeth, and a muscular tail (used for balance. Unlike other cats; it cannot pull in its claws. They are blunted by constant contact (with the earth), and so are of little use, in the hunt. The cheetah—instead, makes use of a strong dewclaw on the inside of its front, legs to grab and hold down prey.

B: Add whatever punctuation is needed to this completely unpunctuated paragraph. Be sure to add capital letters as needed too. If more than one kind of punctuation is suitable, select the best one. Be prepared to explain your choices.

Have you ever built an inukshuk if you have you may be among the countless people to have borrowed this ancient Inuit symbol using it for some purpose of your own corporations government agencies and Vancouvers Olympic Committee have used it a communications network that when it was founded actually excluded the home of the inukshuk Nunavut and the Northwest Territories from its reach calls itself Inukshuk drivers on country highways encounter hundreds of these simple constructions stones flat ones are normally used that are piled up to resemble a human form with arms extended sometimes these appear to be an eco friendly alternative to roadside graffiti in southern Canada for the people of the far north however the inukshuks purpose is a practical one to serve as a landmark for travellers and hunters on the featureless tundra traditionally it can also do the following things mark hunting and fishing spots indicate navigable channels and waterways and simply proclaim ones presence on the land the CBCs Historica Minutes named after the educational foundation that provides the funding for these 60-second TV and radio spots include a vignette about an injured mountie in the 1930s the scene is the far north the mountie is being cared for by a group of Inuit he puzzles over the thing they build out of boulders as they prepare to move on to a new encampment a boy explains Now the people will know we were here

Dividing Words at the Ends of Lines

EXERCISE 43-3
(43g)

Using your dictionary, rewrite each word on the line to its right. Use a slash to indicate the best place to divide the word at the end of a line. Some words may be broken in more than one place. Pick the best place, and use dots to indicate all other syllable breaks. If the word cannot be divided, write it out as one unit.

EXAMPLES	signalled	*sig/nalled*
	brake	*brake*
	sledgehammer	*sledge/ham•mer*

1. sleepless ____________
2. slenderize ____________
3. referee ____________
4. phlegm ____________
5. palate ____________
6. muscle-bound ____________
7. indecent ____________
8. Hollywood ____________
9. expiration ____________
10. echo ____________
11. cuckoo ____________
12. cough ____________
13. butte ____________
14. avocado ____________
15. avoirdupois ____________
16. loose ____________
17. cattail ____________
18. enrol ____________
19. grouch ____________
20. progressing ____________
21. sleeve ____________
22. sapsucker ____________
23. Polynesia ____________
24. palace ____________
25. nonresident ____________
26. increase ____________
27. however ____________
28. gesticulate ____________
29. emerge ____________
30. cubic ____________
31. colourless ____________
32. caretaker ____________
33. buttermilk ____________
34. await ____________
35. antacid ____________
36. mother-in-law ____________
37. trousseau ____________
38. midget ____________
39. controlling ____________
40. farther ____________

Using Capital Letters

EXERCISE 44-1

(44a–e)

A: Select the passage in each pair that needs capital letters. Then rewrite the passage correctly on the line provided.

EXAMPLE (a) going to the city next summer
(b) going to winnipeg in june
(b) going to Winnipeg in June

1. (a) prime minister laurier
   (b) the seventh prime minister

   ____

2. (a) the ancient gods
   (b) god's love

   ____

3. (a) the board of broadcast governors
   (b) a government board

   ____

4. (a) a meeting in the afternoon
   (b) a meeting on friday

   ____

5. (a) my favourite aunt
   (b) my aunt clara

   ____

6. (a) when i graduate
   (b) when we graduate

   ____

7. (a) the musical ride
   (b) ceremonial ride to music

   ____

8. (a) mother teresa
   (b) my mother

   ____

9. (a) dinner at a fine restaurant
   (b) dinner at the steak palace

   ____

10. (a) english 202
    (b) a literature course

11. (a) across the main street
    (b) across main street

    ____

12. (a) the edmonton oilers
    (b) a hockey team

    ____

13. (a) a group of seven artists
    (b) the group of seven

    ____

14. (a) west of town
    (b) a town in the west

    ____

15. (a) a college in british columbia
    (b) a college on the coast

    ____

16. (a) "the gift of the magi"
    (b) a story about sacrifice

    ____

17. (a) learning a second language
(b) learning french

____

18. (a) victoria township medical centre
(b) the local hospital

____

19. (a) stars shining in the sky
(b) the moon and venus shining in the sky

____

20. (a) the st. lawrence river
(b) the polluted river

____

B: Rewrite these sentences on the lines provided, adding or deleting capital letters as needed. If no capitals are needed, write *correct* on the line.

EXAMPLE My uncle Peter and my Aunt are visiting.
My Uncle Peter and my aunt are visiting.

1. The Spring semester starts in february.

2. They live ten kilometres North of Elm street.

3. The Hotel has 450 rooms.

4. Green, the Ambassador, had a meeting with Foreign Minister Ramirez.

5. I want to visit lake Louise to go Skiing.

6. The bible is full of great adventures.

7. They plan to open an italian restaurant Downtown.

8. The new democratic party believes in the democratic system.

9. The teachers' union campaigned for better textbooks.

10. Springfield high school has a large pta.

11. Texans will always Remember the Alamo.

12. Travelling around the cape of Good Hope is dangerous.

13. Rembrandt's "Aristotle contemplating the bust of Homer" is one of his best known paintings.

____

14. The Manitoba Theatre centre is in Winnipeg.

____

15. Tickets to the grey cup were not available at the Stadium.

____

Using Italics

EXERCISE 44-2
(44f–h)

A: Select the passage in each of these pairs that needs italics added. Then rewrite the passage correctly on the line provided, using underlining to indicate italics.

EXAMPLE (a) My favourite movie is a mystery.
(b) My favourite movie is Citizen Kane.
My favourite movie is Citizen Kane.

1. (a) a book about war and peace
   (b) War and Peace

____

2. (a) the humour of Rick Mercer
   (b) The Rick Mercer Report

____

3. (a) London Free Press
   (b) a London, Ontario, newspaper

____

4. (a) a cruise ship
   (b) The Queen Elizabeth II

____

5. (a) a space ship
   (b) the USS Enterprise

____

6. (a) We are Homo sapiens.
   (b) We are human beings.

____

7. (a) pay particular attention
   (b) nota bene

____

8. (a) Many words have the common root, cycle.
(b) Many words come from the same source.

____

9. (a) Don't tease your pets.
(b) Never tease a hungry crocodile.

____

10. (a) The Orient Express was the setting of a famous mystery novel.
(b) VIA Rail carries passengers across Canada.

____

B: Rewrite these sentences on the lines provided, adding italics (underlining) as needed. If no italics are needed write *correct* on the line.

EXAMPLE How do you pronounce chamois?
How do you pronounce <u>chamois</u>?

1. The word cool has many meanings.

____

2. The new hospital is shaped like the letter H.

____

3. Scientifically the chimpanzee is called Pan troglodytes and the gorilla is Gorilla gorilla.

____

4. You bought us tickets to see Les Misérables? Merci beaucoup.

____

5. The HMS Bounty was a real ship.

____

6. The troubles of its crew are told in the book Mutiny on the Bounty.

____

7. I subscribe to a Regina newspaper.

____

8. Clifford Sifton, a key member of Prime Minister Laurier's cabinet, was the owner of an important newspaper, the Manitoba Free Press.

____

____

9. Sifton encouraged immigration to the Canadian Prairies, which he publicized with the expression "the last, best West."

____

____

10. Years later, the Hollywood movie Rose Marie (1936), with its singing Mounties and maidens, also publicized the Canadian Prairies.

____

Using Abbreviations

EXERCISE 44-3
(44j–k)

A. Rewrite each of these sentences, replacing inappropriate abbreviations with their full forms. If a sentence is correct as given, write *correct* on the line.

EXAMPLE It takes years to become a dr.
It takes years to become a doctor.

1. The Chang bros. are opening a fishing charter co.

2. They have leased a wharf on the W shore of Vancouver Is.

3. At the aquarium we saw giant tortoises that were more than 100 years old.

4. Easter always falls on the Sun. following the 1st full moon in spring—either in Mar. or in Apr.

5. What did you get for Xmas?

6. Everyone ought to know the story of Wm. Lyon Mackenzie King, 10th PM of Canada.

7. He is mentioned in my textbook on the hist. of poli. sci. and econ., and in my other textbook covering WWII.

8. The prof. says the midterm will cover chaps. 1–5.

9. The midterm & final each count 40%.

10. The quarterback picked up 160 yds. in passing in the first 1/2.

11. Some people will do anything for a few $'s.

12. A kilo. equals 2.2 lbs.

13. The counsellor had an MSW degree from UBC.

14. She had put herself through school working as an assist. mgr. in a fast-food rest.

15. Mr. and Mrs. McDonald live on Maple Ave. in Corner Brook, Nfld.

B: Rewrite each of these sentences, replacing inappropriate full forms with standard abbreviations. It may be necessary to slightly rearrange some sentences.

EXAMPLE Canadians celebrate their national day on July first.
Canadians celebrate their national day on July 1st.

1. The bank's loan officer awoke at 2:00 *ante meridiem.*

____

2. He was thinking about the family that had applied for a loan of 30 000 dollars.

____

3. Doctor Jones had given them a letter of reference.

____

4. Bill Smith, a Chartered Accountant, had also sent a letter.

____

5. For collateral, they offered a Spanish doubloon dated *Anno Domini* 1642.

____

6. The doubloon had been in the family since nineteen nineteen.

____

7. Mister and Missus Grossman wanted to use the money to set up a company to make precision measuring devices.

____

8. They already had a contract with the National Aeronautics and Space Administration.

____

9. The banker wanted to give his okay, but loans this big had to be co-authorized by the bank president.

____

10. However, the president had taken her Self-Contained Underwater Breathing Apparatus gear and gone on a vacation.

____

Using Figures

EXERCISE 44-4
(44m–n)

Rewrite each of these sentences, replacing inappropriate figures with words or inappropriate words with figures. If a sentence is correct as given, write *correct* on the line.

EXAMPLE He is six feet four and a half inches.
He is 6' 4 ½ ".

1. There are a hundred and seven women in the first-year class at the law school this year.

   ____

2. Ten years ago there were only 47.

   ____

3. 1/3 the faculty is female now compared with 1/10 then.

   ____

4. Many students share apartments in a building that charges nine hundred dollars for two rooms, $1400 for three rooms, and $1850 for 4 rooms.

   ____

5. The semester begins on September fourteenth.

   ____

6. The entering class will graduate on June first, two thousand and twelve.

   ____

7. Entrance requirements are on pages thirty to thirty-five.

   ____

8. The average law student is expected to drink one point five litres of coffee a day over the next 3 years.

   ____

9. The drop-out rate is about twenty-nine percent.

   ____

10. The law school is located at Fifteen Clark Street.

    ____

Using Hyphens in Numbers

EXERCISE 44-5
(44o)

Formal usage in the humanities requires that numbers, including common fractions, be written in words. Write out each of these numbers, using hyphens as needed.

EXAMPLE 2102 *twenty-one hundred and two*

1. 35 ______________________________
2. ½ ______________________________
3. ⅘ ______________________________
4. 101 ______________________________
5. 1st ______________________________
6. 3457 ______________________________
7. 495 ______________________________

PART SEVEN: WRITING WHEN ENGLISH IS A SECOND LANGUAGE

*45 Multilingual Students Writing Essays in Canadian Colleges and Universities

*46 Handling Sentence-Level Issues in English

47 Singulars and Plurals

48 Articles

49 Word Order

50 Prepositions

51 Gerunds, Infinitives, and Participles

52 Modal Auxiliary Verbs

***Please note**: There are no *Workbook* exercises that correspond to Chapters 45 and 46 of the *Simon & Schuster Handbook for Writers*, Fifth Canadian Edition.

Identifying Nouns

EXERCISE 47-1
(47a)

Divide the following list of words into count and noncount nouns. Give the plural forms of the count nouns. List in all columns any words that can be both count and noncount.

advice	fern	jewellery	paragraph
book	flour	library	physics
calculator	gold	lightning	pollution
chocolate	hair	man	rain
desk	happiness	news	report
earring	homework	novel	storm
essay	honesty	occupation	time
experiment	information	paper	weather

	Noncount	Count	Plural
1.	__________	__________	__________
2.	__________	__________	__________
3.	__________	__________	__________
4.	__________	__________	__________
5.	__________	__________	__________
6.	__________	__________	__________
7.	__________	__________	__________
8.	__________	__________	__________
9.	__________	__________	__________
10.	__________	__________	__________
11.	__________	__________	__________
12.	__________	__________	__________
13.	__________	__________	__________
14.	__________	__________	__________
15.	__________	__________	__________
16.	__________	__________	__________
17.	__________	__________	__________
18.	__________	__________	__________
19.	__________	__________	__________

	Noncount	Count	Plural
20.	___	___	___
21.	___	___	___
22.	___	___	___
23.	___	___	___
24.	___	___	___
25.	___	___	___
26.	___	___	___
27.	___	___	___
28.	___	___	___
29.	___	___	___
30.	___	___	___
31.	___	___	___
32.	___	___	___

Correct Forms

EXERCISE 47-2
(47b-d)

Choose the correct forms of the nouns in parentheses and write them on the lines at the right.

EXAMPLE Some ______________ (hiker) return to ______________ (nature) by walking the Bruce Trail. *hikers* *nature*

1. Hikers with little __________ (money) but much __________ (fortitude) can begin the hike in Niagara Falls and continue to the Bruce Peninsula. ______________ ______________

2. The 720- __________(kilometre) trail extends through many picturesque __________ (town). ______________ ______________

3. The trail passes cultivated __________ (farm) and untamed __________ (wilderness). ______________ ______________

4. The caves and cliffs of the Niagara Escarpment make the Bruce Trail one of the most interesting __________ (trail) in Canada or the United __________ (State). ______________ ______________

5. Few __________ (hiker) have anything but praise for their __________ (experience) on the trail. ______________ ______________

6. Many __________ (youngster) would gladly give up __________ (piano) lessons or __________ (homework) to be climbing wooded __________ (path). ______________ ______________ ______________ ______________

7. The Bruce Trail is one of the nation's __________ (treasure). ______________

EXERCISE 48-1
(48a–c)

In the following blanks write *a, an,* or *the* as needed. If no article is necessary, put a *O* in the blank.

According to some psychologists, _____ young children are actually more violent than teenagers, even though _____ most people assume that teenagers are _____ most violent age group. Further, _____ aggression in young children will almost certainly develop into _____ career of delinquency, if _____ aggression is not spotted and treated early on.

From _____ ancient philosophers, _____ religious thinkers, and _____ earliest Freudian psychologists we have inherited _____ idea that our violent impulses must be recognized and restrained. Freudians put _____ emphasis on _____ sublimation of our wildest impulses by our participation in civilization. In contrast, _____ moral philosophers and theologians advise us to learn _____ virtues of _____ patience, ____ piety, and _____self-control.

_____ team of researchers at _____ University of Montreal who study _____ human aggression insist that _____ evolutionary struggle holds _____ key to _____ problem of _____ violence. They claim that _____ aggressive behaviour is _____ universal human trait left over from _____ ancient struggle to survive. Therefore, these researchers believe that _____ proper question to ask is not how _____ individual becomes violent, but rather, how _____ most people are trained to act peacefully in _____ society.

In _____ most people, _____ rate of violent acts they commit peaks before they reach _____ age of _____ three. _____ research team in Montreal has found that unless _____ damage has occurred to _____ particular area in _____ individual's brain, _____ individual will learn to curb his or her violent behaviour some time around his or her third birthday. _____ adults and _____ other children teach _____ child _____ social and personal costs of acting violently as well as _____ rewards of acting in _____ way that is acceptable to _____ rest of _____ people around them.

Question Form

EXERCISE 49-1

(49a)

Convert the following sentences into questions.

EXAMPLE We should have called first.
Should we have called first?

1. That pizza is enough for all of us.

____

2. Henri understood the lesson.

____

3. You have my lab manual. (two ways)

____

4. Juanita will have finished by the time we return.

____

5. Everyone in the room can see the screen.

____

Order in Adjectives and Adverbs

EXERCISE 49-2
(49b–c)

Rewrite the following sentences using correct word order.

EXAMPLE Our English class took a field final trip to an auction large house.
Our English class took a final field trip to a large auction house.

1. Katrina purchased two Limoges lovely boxes.

____

2. A black leather comfortable chair appealed to Nils.

____

3. He waited to bid on it patiently.

____

4. We left unfortunately before it was auctioned.

____

5. Mario wanted a wooden old table but bought a silver worn spoon.

____

6. Suchen outbid someone for a green round interesting hatbox.

____

7. She was delighted extremely to get it.

____

8. She has admired often such hatboxes.

____

9. The English entire class bought something except Ingrid.

____

10. Because she brought an empty small purse, she bought nothing at all.

____

In, At, On

EXERCISE 50-1
(50b)

In the following blanks, use *in*, *at*, or *on* to show time or place.

EXAMPLE The University of Virginia, located ____________ Charlottesville, was founded by Thomas Jefferson.

The University of Virginia, located ____*in*____ Charlottesville, was founded by Thomas Jefferson.

1. Others wanted to put the new university _____ Staunton or Lexington.
2. _____ 1818, Dalhousie University opened _____ Halifax, Nova Scotia, the same year as Jefferson's.
3. Jefferson designed his university so that students and faculty lived together _____ an "academical village."
4. A rotunda building for classes sits _____ one end of a lawn.
5. _____ both sides of the lawn are sets of student rooms.
6. Faculty members lived _____ pavilions between the sets of student rooms.
7. A similar scheme inspired the design of Ontario's Trent University, whose main campus opened _____ 1966.
8. _____ your next visit to the University of Toronto, you can stand _____ a window _____ the University College Quadrangle and see how that nineteenth-century college was designed with the same idea in mind.
9. _____ his deathbed, Jefferson included founding the university as one of the three accomplishments for which he hoped to be remembered.
10. Today students at the University of Virginia consider it an honour to live _____ the rooms that Jefferson designed.

EXERCISE 50-2
(50c)

A: Fill in each blank with a phrasal verb from the list in this chapter. Use each phrasal verb only once. More than one phrasal verb may be appropriate for some blanks.

EXAMPLE Walid cannot ____________ why it takes so long to register.
Walid cannot *figure out* why it takes so long to register.

1. Ravi will _______________ Walid and explain.
2. First he must _______________ all the forms.
3. He must _______________ all his records to make sure he does not _______________ anything.
4. He must then _______________ the forms at the registrar's office.
5. Should he _______________ the forms without some vital information, the registrar will _______________ him _______________ to get it.
6. Walid will have to _______________ the forms and _______________ what is missing.
7. He must not _______________ any records until he has finished the procedure.

B: Now rewrite the sentences above using as many formal verbs as possible.

1. ____
2. ____
3. ____
4. ____
5. ____
6. ____
7. ____

EXERCISE 51-1

(51a–d)

Complete each sentence with the appropriate gerund, infinitive, or participle form of the verb in parentheses.

EXAMPLE Most students at a university hope _______________(prepare) themselves for a career.

Most students at a university hope _to prepare_ themselves for a career.

1. They are worried about _______________(get) jobs after graduation.

2. They may want _______________ (study) for the pure enjoyment of learning.

3. They may even dream about _______________ (be) philosophers or writers.

4. However, many parents refuse _______________ (support) students who lack a definite career goal.

5. They are happy _______________ (help) their children reach their goals.

6. They resist _______________ (aid) children who lack direction.

7. Yet _______________(read) widely in the liberal arts is one way for students _______________ (know) themselves.

8. Students of the humanities are the first _______________ (see) the value of a liberal education.

9. When they hear their parents _______________ (complain) about wasting money, students try _______________ (explain) their positions.

10. They recommend _______________ (learn) about life before _______________ (train) for a specific job.

Modal Auxiliaries

EXERCISE 52-1

(52a–c)

Fill in the blanks with the correct modal auxiliary forms.

EXAMPLE __________ (present ability) you name a stranger political system than Canada's?

___Can___ (present ability) you name a stranger political system than Canada's?

1. You __________ (present possibility, negative) be aware that Canada's head of state does not live in Canada.
2. We __________ (present advisability, negative) forget, though, that in law, the British monarch is Canada's highest political authority.
3. You __________ (past possibility) heard the prime minister mistakenly being called the head of state.
4. Laws passed in Parliament __________ (present passive necessity) signed, however, by the Queen or her representative, the Governor General.
5. Fortunately, the days when the Governor General __________ (past habit) interfere in government are long past.
6. But as late as 1926, Prime Minister Mackenzie King __________ (past necessity) leave office when instructed by the Governor General.
7. Do you think we __________ (past advisability) changed the Constitution to have the prime minister elected by all voters and not just by voters in one riding?
8. There is no evidence that most Canadians __________ (preference) live under a different political system, however.
9. Still, you __________ (present necessity) admit that it is a strange system.
10. But it is the system that we use, so somebody __________ (past probability) guessed that it would work.

Answer Key

Chapter 1: Thinking Like a Writer

Exercise 1-1: Answers will vary.

1. This statement should emphasize the human catastrophe and urgency of the situation, while detailing specific ways in which your organization can help and how donors can reach you. The tone should be medium level and the vocabulary simple.
2. This letter should seek to minimize the danger, explaining the steps that you would take if an earthquake were to hit. The tone should be informal.
3. This piece should provide colourful description and personal reflections, and, if possible, some analysis. The tone should be between medium and formal.
4. This letter should explain your concerns for your business and its employees, requesting the specific information that will respond to your concerns. (You may wish to indicate also that your evaluation of the reply may lead to further requests for information or for modifications to the design.) Your writing should be calm and practical, and the tone between medium and formal.

Chapter 2: Planning, Shaping, Drafting, and Revising

Exercise 2-1: Answers will vary.

1. celebrity: whether celebrity is given too high a value
2. someone I can count on: the ways in which my sister has helped me
3. travelling alone: safety tips for the young solo traveller
4. fitness: how to design a personal fitness regimen
5. online social sites: how online sites have revolutionized our habits of socializing
6. restaurants: the growing popularity of exotic restaurants
7. the city: attitudes to large cities—danger; alienation; cultural richness
8. my grandparents: the obstacles faced by the author's grandparents in raising their families
9. a personal loss: reaction to the death of a loved one
10. choosing a computer: what is essential and what is an expensive option

Exercise 2-2: Answers will vary.

Exercise 2-3: Answers will vary.

1. Unacceptable. Planned budget cuts will affect university services, housing, and scholarships.
2. Unacceptable. A regular study schedule can improve student grades.
3. Unacceptable. Recent theories suggest three principal causes of contemporary violence.

4. Unacceptable. The Canadian style of hockey is still capable of encouraging skill and artistry.
5. Unacceptable. My first adolescent crush was a painful experience.
6. Unacceptable. Giving brief but complete answers on a job application will make the best impression.
7. Acceptable.
8. Acceptable.
9. Unacceptable. My May visit to Turkey provided an opportunity to learn about history and archaeology.
10. Unacceptable. Victory in the Battle of Vimy Ridge helped give Canadians a sense of of their own nationhood.

Exercise 2-3B: Answers will vary.

1. success: Definitions of success vary from person to person, but I will consider myself successful if I have a well-paying job that I enjoy doing and a happy, healthy family.
2. being a good friend: The hardest thing a good friend has to do is tell the truth even when it might hurt.
3. summer in the city: The heat of summer brings people together because it is too hot to stay inside.
4. laughter: Recent scientific studies indicate that laughter, as well as the positive mental attitude it represents, speeds up recovery from illness.
5. travel safety tips: Young people preparing to travel alone should make an inventory of what they can do without and of what they would need if left in a difficult situation.
6. online social networking sites: Far from being an example of the individual's isolation and domination by technology, online social networking sites expand people's social frontiers and networks of friends.
7. exotic restaurants: Despite what some people think, the popularity of exotic restaurants has little to do with Canadians' attitudes toward multiculturalism.
8. a personal loss: The death of my youngest uncle made me confront issues of life and its purpose that I had never really considered.
9. sacrifice: My grandparents gave up everything they had to come to Canada.
10. shopping: Buying over the Internet is an easy way to beat the Christmas crowds at the malls.

Exercise 2-4:

Thesis Statement: Leaving a roommate for a single apartment can have definite drawbacks.

I. Unsatisfactory furnishings
    A. Appliances
        1. Major
            a. Stove
            b. Refrigerator
            c. Washer
            d. Dryer
        2. Minor
            a. Microwave
            b. Blender
            c. Toaster
            d. Mixer

B. Furniture
    1. Bedroom
        a. Futon
        b. Dresser
    2. Living room
        a. Sofa
        b. Chairs
        c. Tables
    3. Kitchen
        a. Table
        b. Chairs
C. Equipment
    1. For entertainment
    2. For exercise

II. Insufficient finances
    A. Rent
    B. Utilities
        1. ISP
        2. Electricity
        3. Phone
    C. Food
    D. Entertainment

III. Inadequate companionship
    A. Frequent loneliness
    B. Occasional fear

Exercise 2-5: Answers will vary.

Exercise 2-6: Answers will vary.

A: A Brief History of Utensils

Forks, knives, and spoons seem so natural to most of us that it is hard to imagine eating dinner without them. Yet, many people, such as the Chinese, use chopsticks instead, and others use their hands to eat.

Knives are the oldest Western utensils. The first ones were made of stone 1.5 million years ago. They were originally used to cut up animals after a hunt. The same knife was used to butcher game, slice cooked food, and kill enemies. Even later in history, nobles were the only ones who could afford separate knives for different uses. People used all-purpose knives, pointed like today's steak knives. The round-tipped dinner knife is a modern invention. It became popular in seventeenth-century France because hostesses wanted to stop guests from picking their teeth with the points of their dinner knives.

The spoon is also an ancient tool. Wooden spoons twenty thousand years old have been found in Asia; spoons of stone, wood, ivory, and even gold have been found in Egyptian tombs. Spoons were originally used to scoop up foods that were too thick to sip from a bowl.

The fork is a newcomer. Forks did not become widely accepted until the eighteenth century, when the French nobility adopted the fork as a status symbol, and eating with one's hands became unfashionable. At about the same time, individual settings became the rule too. Previously, even rich people had shared plates and glasses at meals, but now the rich demanded individual plates, glasses, forks, spoons, and knives. Today in North America, a full set of utensils is considered a necessity. We forget that as recently as the American Revolution some people considered anyone who used a fork to be a fussy showoff.

B: Thoughts on a Solo Canoe Trip

Last year I had an adventure of the sort that many people never experience in their lives. In a way, however, it was a typical Canadian experience, or at least a part of Canadian folklore. I went on a solo canoe trip to Northern Ontario's Temagami region. It was a journey that had benefits for both body and spirit.

I have been a good canoeist since I was young. Nevertheless, when I told my friends of my intention to do a solo trip, they replied, "Isn't that a dangerous thing you're planning to do?" Admittedly, a solo trip may be dangerous. Still, many other sports and activities—including rock climbing, which has become hugely popular—are dangerous as well. A solo canoe trip need not be a cause for concern, as long as the canoeist is experienced and takes the proper precautions. It is essential to be in good physical condition, of course, and to wear a life jacket in the canoe at all times. The canoeist should come prepared with extra food and warm clothing, and should have learned and be able to apply the techniques of woodcraft and other skills. Once I had met all these conditions, the final preparation was to inform my friends and local people of my route and the expected day of my return.

I chose a route that I knew I could do; a solo trip is no time to show foolish bravado. Then off I went. For six days I was alone beneath the vast sky, paddling hard against the waves and winds of Temagami. All the while, my senses were heightened, for my safety was in my own hands. My eyes, ears, and nose were alert to smells, signs of wild animals, and changes in the weather. I listened to the wind roaring at night. One day I sat out a powerful storm in my tent, perched on the shore of a tiny island. Later that afternoon, I watched with mounting excitement as a strong west wind gradually drove off the clouds and freed me from the storm: I could continue my travels. Every night I crawled into my tent exhausted but pleased with what I had accomplished.

On the last day, I rode the high waves of Ferguson Bay to my final destination, pitching up on the sandy shore with a breath of relief. For my body, the trip had the benefit of giving me exercise in the outdoors. For my spirit, the trip let me feel the deep, meditative calm of being alone with myself and my thoughts. I was reminded how small and vulnerable one single person is, faced with the might of nature. At the same time, I had the satisfaction of depending only on myself and overcoming the challenges that confronted me.

Chapter 3: Writing Paragraphs

Exercise 3-1: Topic Sentence; Irrelevant Sentence

1. 2; 3
2. 1; 4
3. 1; 3; 7
4. 1; 7
5. 1; 7; 9

Exercise 3-2:

1. but; similarly; and
2. however; in the United States; but; in fact
3. and; yet another; because; and also; yet; as well as; further
4. finally; because; or; certainly; unfortunately; actually; so
5. unlike; nor; in fact; and; since its beginnings; in addition to; finally

Exercise 3-3:

1. so; before; them; while; of course; instead; so; for other reasons as well; and; in fact
2. painted/painting; lines; straight; machine/machines; marks; road; truck; one-person/four-person; hot plastic; paint; crew
3. sentence 6: same structure on either side of semicolon highlights contrast; sentence 9: two items in list in same form
4. road or street: it; truck it; crewmembers: they

Exercise 3-4:

1. b, d, a, e, c
2. c, a, d, e, b
3. d, c, e, b, f, a
4. b, a, e, c, d, f

Exercise 3-5: Answers will vary. Here are some likely details:

1. broadening cultural horizons; approach to foreign literatures; insight into structures and peculiarities of English; discipline of memorization
2. numerous options; enticing extras and add-ons; clever ad campaigns; confusing payment plans
3. music; food; vocabulary; art
4. they can develop hand-eye coordination; evidence exists that they help in exercising cognitive skills; interactivity can stimulate imagination
5. based on an old, outdated view; too harsh; discriminatory; don't affect behaviour
6. size; academic ranking; location; sports

Exercise 3-6: Answers will vary.

1. preparing for vacation

   Topic Sentence: A few simple steps can reduce the tension sometimes connected with a major vacation.

   Details:
   1. Begin planning early.
   2. Arrange for time off from work.
   3. Use a travel agent to get the best details.
   4. Get maps and/or booklets about local attractions.
   5. Make a packing list early enough to purchase needed items in advance.
   6. Take enough cash or travellers' cheques.

2. the floor plan of the local video rental store

   Topic Sentence: The floor plan at Jim's Video makes finding the tapes I want easy.

   Details:
   1. movie classics on the left wall
   2. comedies on the right wall
   3. science fiction and horror in the front centre
   4. kids' movies in the rear centre
   5. the counter across the back wall

3. the disadvantages of working while attending school full time

   Topic Sentence: The difficulty with working while attending school full time is that I never have any time for myself.

   Details:
   1. heavy classload
   2. homework and studying for tests
   3. hours at work
   4. required overtime at holidays
   5. family responsibilities

4. why I've chosen my career

   Topic Sentence: I think I would enjoy being a college professor.

   Details:
   1. summers off
   2. opportunity to work with young people
   3. high status
   4. chance to study what interests me

Exercise 3-7: Answers will vary.

1. Topic Sentence: Walking alone at night on campus can be risky.

   Examples:
   a. It's easy to trip on cracked pavement in the dark.
   b. Drunks bother women in front of the Rathskeller.
   c. Two purses were snatched last week.
   d. Someone was robbed at the bus stop a few days ago.

2. Topic Sentence: Peer pressure can be hard to resist.

   Example: My first semester grades were low because I could not say no to all the invitations to go out and party after classes.

Exercise 3-8: Answers will vary.

1. a success story

   Topic Sentence: Sometimes the hardest part about succeeding is just deciding to try.

   Events:
   a. invited to a gathering in Calgary
   b. fearful of driving that far alone
   c. trying to get someone else to go—and drive
   d. studying the map
   e. the ease of the trip itself

2. an odd person in my neighbourhood

   Topic Sentence: The people on my block are worried about Crazy John.

   Details:
   a. dresses shabbily
   b. talks to himself
   c. lives with his elderly parents
   d. can't keep a job
   e. refuses to accept medical help

3. how to study for a test

   Topic Sentence: Studying for a test does not begin the night before the examination.

   Steps:
   a. Read assignments as they are given.
   b. Highlight or take notes.
   c. Answer review questions or work sample problems.
   d. Ask questions in class.
   e. Review in short study sessions.

4. my ideal job

   Topic Sentence: My ideal job would enable me to help other people at the same time that it would allow me to be creative and earn a living wage.

   Qualities:
   a. importance of contributing to my community
   b. helping others take care of themselves
   c. not routine
   d. challenging
   e. money

5. classification: bosses

   Topic Sentence: In my experience, bad bosses fall into a few distinct categories.

   Subgroups:
   a. bullies
   b. socializers
   c. the disorganized
   d. control freaks
   e. climbers

6. my sister and I

   Topic Sentence: No one believes my sister and I are related.

   Points:
   a. looks
   b. choice of friends
   c. career choices
   d. political choices
   e. treatment of others

7. a lie and a forest fire

   Topic Sentence: Sometimes even a small lie can be like a match tossed carelessly into a forest.

   Similarities:
   a. a thoughtless act
   b. may land where it can't be controlled
   c. can spread very quickly
   d. destructive
   e. can hurt the person who began it all

8. why I chose the school I am now attending

   Topic Sentence: Picking a college was not easy, but I finally chose X for several reasons.

   Causes or Effects:
   a. far away enough to live on campus, close enough to visit home on weekends
   b. good Art Department
   c. reasonable tuition
   d. friends going too
   e. near sports arena and theatres

Exercise 3-9: Revised paragraphs will vary. Students should, however, note the following weaknesses.

1. introduction: apologizes; lists topics that will not be discussed

   conclusion: announces what has been done; gives a key definition too late to be of use

2. introduction: lacks thesis or main idea sentence; all specifics, no generalization; has no apparent connection to topic

   conclusion: too abrupt

3. introduction: refers to the title instead of stating thesis; appears to make a circular argument (a logical fallacy)

   conclusion: makes absolute claims

4. introduction: an unadorned thesis statement, not a complete introduction
   conclusion: has no conclusion; this is a body paragraph
5. introduction: announces what will be done
   conclusion: introduces new material

Exercise 3-10: Answers will vary.

Chapter 4: Thinking, Reading, and Writing Critically

Exercise 4-1A:

1. fact
2. fact
3. opinion
4. fact
5. fact
6. opinion
7. fact
8. fact
9. opinion
10. opinion
11. fact
12. opinion
13. fact
14. opinion
15. opinion

Exercise 4-1B:

1. fact
2. opinion
3. opinion
4. fact
5. opinion
6. fact
7. fact
8. fact
9. opinion
10. fact
11. opinion
12. opinion
13. fact
14. opinion

Chapter 5: Writing Arguments

Exercise 5-1: Answers will vary.
Exercise 5-2: Answers will vary.
Exercise 6–1: Answers will vary.
Exercise 6–2: Answers will vary.

Chapter 9: Using Sources and Avoiding Plagiarism

Exercise 9-1A: Answers will vary.

In her book *No Logo*, Naomi Klein writes of the "brand equity mania" of the 1980s, summed up in the purchase of the Kraft brand name for six times the company's worth on paper. A brand name no longer simply added value; it contained enormous value in itself. Klein describes the efforts of corporations to promote something as intangible as a name, "perpetually probing the zeitgeist" to ensure that a brand image "would resonate . . . . with its target market." In the age of branding, she writes, new marketing opportunities were vital, leading manufacturers into "a cultural feeding frenzy."

Exercise 9-1B: Answers will vary.

Exercise 9-1C: Answers will vary.

Exercise 9-2A: Answers will vary.

Branding is different from advertising. Sponsorship, logo licensing, and advertising are tools of branding; the brand, however, is the "core meaning of the modern corporation." Mass-marketing, developed late in the nineteenth century, was not very concerned with brand identities. Rather, it advertised newly invented products—informing people of the products' existence and persuading people that the new products would improve their lives.

Exercise 9-2B: Answers will vary.

Exercise 9-2C: Answers will vary.

Exercise 9-3A: Answers will vary.

Around 1985, management scientists came up with the idea that a successful company sells brands, not products. This concept alone probably accounts for the new importance of multinational corporations in recent years. Traditionally, manufacturers were more concerned with the things they made. Producing goods was the key to economic success: the more you produced, the more wealth you would generate. The factory and the land were the sources of production and hence of economic well-being.

With the 1980s, however, came recession and a re-evaluation of the idea that bigger was necessarily better. Manufacturers with giant facilities—and matching payrolls—began to look like dinosaurs. New companies like Nike and Microsoft were doing things in a different way. They offloaded production, often to overseas contractors, and concentrated on what they claimed was the real job: marketing. The role of the corporation was to produce brand images, not products per se. In demonstrating that marketing is more profitable than production, the modern multinationals have set a new standard. It is the company with the least overhead—and the best-known brand—that will succeed.

Exercise 9-3B: Answers will vary.

Exercise 9-3C: Answers will vary.

Chapter 13: Comparing Disciplines

Exercise 13-1: Answers will vary.

Chapter 14: Writing About the Humanities and Literature

Exercise 14-1: Answers will vary.

Chapter 15: Writing in the Social Sciences and Natural Sciences

Exercise 15-1: Answers will vary.

Chapter 16: Writing Under Pressure

Exercise 16-1: Answers will vary.

Chapter 17: Business and Public Writing

Exercise 17-1: Answers will vary.

Chapter 18: Making Oral Presentations and Using Multimedia

Exercise 18-1: Answers will vary.
Exercise 18-2: Answers will vary.

Chapter 19: Documents and Visual Design

Exercise 19-1: Answers will vary.

Chapter 20: Writing for the Web

Exercise 20-1: Answers will vary.

Chapter 21: Parts of Speech and Sentence Structures

Exercise 21-1:

1. people, e-books
2. books
3. book, appliance
4. book, work
5. file
6. appliances, devices, laptops
7. books
8. dollars, appliances, screens, keyboards
9. time, batteries, books
10. appliances, library, books
11. appliance, books, computer
12. appliances, modems, works, services, lines
13. companies, software, books, computers
14. books, counterparts
15. screens, environment, texts
16. notes, book
17. types, books, form
18. dictionaries, encyclopedias, directories, catalogues, manuals
19. readers, type, book, amount, information
20. reading, people, text
21. paper, technology, interface

Exercise 21-2:

1. their
2. they, her, she
3. they, her, she
4. she
5. that
6. this
7. their, themselves
8. none
9. she, her
10. she, anyone, who
11. what, they
12. whose, them
13. us
14. everyone, this
15. some, one another
16. what, you
17. you, your

Exercise 21-3:

1. can lead
2. recognize
3. has
4. should think
5. may cause
6. discuss
7. might ask
8. is, is
9. take
10. may require
11. might lead
12. tolerate
13. accept
14. do dwell
15. are
16. might learn
17. look
18. be, to assist
19. would do
20. find, enjoy

Exercise 21-4:

1. verb
2. gerund
3. infinitive
4. verb
5. verb
6. past participle
7. verb
8. past participle
9. verb
10. verb
11. infinitive
12. verb
13. present participle
14. present participle
15. verb
16. infinitive
17. verb
18. present participle
19. verb
20. infinitive

Exercise 21-5:

1. acclaimed, television, that
2. popular, brillian, medical
3. brilliant, eccentric, irritable
4. Canadian, his, fictional
5. sly, famous
6. law
7. this, lucrative, risky, comedy
8. His, new
9. another, television
10. dramatic, his, first
11. Crime, legal, evening
12. medical
13. particular, other
14. Methodical, surprising

15. any, intelligent
16. grey, each, piercing
17. unkind, offensive
18. constant, leg
19. Careful, his, wrong
20. intentional

Exercise 21-6:

1. adverb: only
2. adverb: most
3. adverb: most; adverb: easily
4. adverb: typically; conjunctive adverb: however; adverb: mostly
5. adverb: more
6. adverb: extremely; conjunctive adverb: indeed; adverb: often
7. conjunctive adverb: however; adverb: usually ["when humans enter their territory" is an adverb clause]
8. adverbs: not just ["while living in the forest" is an adverb phrase]
9. adverb: also; adverb: quite ["on the ground" is an adverb phrase]
10. adverb: generally; conjunctive adverb: still; adverb: sometimes ["in an upright position"; "much like a human"; and "on all fours" are adverb phrases]
11. ["in fact" and "when standing erect" are adverb phrases]

Exercise 21-7:

	prepositions	objects
1.	in	China
	over	300 million bicycles
	on	the road
2.	[*none* .. "after" is a conjunction here]	
3.	of	foot-powered scooter
	unlike	those that followed
4.	until	the invention
	of	a German baron
	of	the stationary front wheel
5.	for	this bicycle
6.	in	a Scottish workshop
	with	pedals
7.	to	the rear wheels
	by means of	cranks
8.	during	the 1860s
	to	the front wheels
9.	in	England
	in	1879
	with	a chain and sprocket
10.	for	today's bicycle
11.	instead of	a larger front wheel
	in	size
12.	during	the 1880s
	with	compressed air
13.	along with	the derailleur gear
	in	the 1890s

14. of — the bicycle

    to — attempts

Exercise 21-8:

1. when (SC)
2. No conjunctions
3. and (CC)
4. since (SC)
5. Before (SC)
6. while (SC)
7. but (CC)
8. Nor (CC)
9. after (SC)
10. and (CC)
11. yet (CC)
12. As (SC)
13. Although (SC)
14. until (SC)
15. that (SC)

Exercise 21-9:

1. adjective
2. verb
3. preposition
4. noun
5. noun
6. conjunction
7. adverb
8. preposition
9. verb
10. pronoun
11. adjective
12. conjunction
13. adjective
14. preposition
15. verb
16. verb
17. preposition
18. verb
19. verb
20. preposition
21. noun
22. adverb
23. adjective
24. adverb
25. adjective

Exercise 21-10A:

1. Warm air/cannot ...
2. The temperature beneath the ice/is ...
3. This/keeps ...
4. The ice at a figure-skating rink/is ...
5. Ice hockey rinks/have ...
6. The ice/is ...
7. The concrete/contains ...
8. An Olympic-sized rink/has ...
9. A very cold liquid, like the antifreeze in cars/circulates ...
10. The liquid/absorbs ...
11. Machinery/keeps ...
12. More and more people/are ...

Exercise 21-10B:

	subject	verb
1.	toothbrushes	were
2.	people	rubbed
3.	toothbrushes	originated
4.	bristles	came
5.	hogs	grew
6.	Europeans	brushed
7.	toothbrushes	
	sponges	were used
8.	men	
	women	picked

9. stems	were employed
toothpicks	
10. toothpicks	were
11. germs	developed
12. solution	was
13. discovery	led
	made
14. nylon	was
	resisted
15. brushes	were sold
16. they	were
17. tissue	scratched
	bled
18. version	was developed
19. it	cost
20. care	improved
21. dentists	have made
surgeons	
22. toothbrushes	should be used
	should be replaced
23. bristles	are
	can cut

Exercise 21-11:

direct object	indirect object
1. life	~~word~~ world
2. glimpse	friends
3. people	—
4. money	you
5. pride	people
6. trouble	you
7. shock	yourself
8. reason	employer
9. question	yourself
10. people	—
11. updates	friends
12. Facebook	—
13. favour	someone
14. credit	person

Exercise 21-12:

1. SC/N
2. SC/N
3. SC/Adj
4. SC/N
5. OC/Adj
6. OC/Adj
7. OC/Adj
8. OC/Adj
9. SC/N
10. SC/N
11. SC/Adj
12. SC/Adj
13. SC/Adj
14. SC/N
15. OC/N phrase
16. SC/N
17. SC/N
18. SC/N
19. SC/N
20. SC/N phrase
21. OC/Adj
22. SC/Adj
23. OC/Adj

Exercise 21-13A:

1. d. adjective
   e. adverb
2. f. adverb
   g. adjective
3. h. adverb
   i. adjective
4. j. adverb
   k. adjective
5. l. adjective
   m. adverb
6. n. adjective
   o. adverb
7. p. adjective
   q. adverb
8. r. adjective
   s. adverb
9. t. adjective
   u. adverb
10. v. adverb
    w. adverb
    x. adjective

Exercise 21-13B:

1. early: adverb
2. empty: adjective
3. already: adverb
4. new: adjective
5. much: adverb
6. easily: adverb; convenient: adjective
7. luckily: adverb; small: adjective
8. really: adverb; excellent: adjective
9. crystal: adjective; fortunately: adverb
10. finally: adverb; completely: adverb

Exercise 21-14:

1. hockey game
2. match
3. telephone
4. radio transmitter
5. broadcasting studio
6. Maple Leaf Gardens
7. broadcasts
8. shout
9. phrase
10. names
11. the 1950s
12. Hewitt's son
13. Foster Hewitt
14. series

Exercise 21-15A:

1. NP
2. PP
3. VP
4. AP
5. NP
6. VP
7. PP
8. VP
9. VP
10. AP
11. PP
12. PP
13. VP

Exercise 21-15B:

1. part
2. part
3. part
4. part
5. inf
6. part
7. part
8. part
9. inf
10. ger
11. ger
12. ger
13. inf
14. ger
15. ger

Exercise 21-16:

1. which…celebrations
2. which…high
3. when…wheel
4. which…down
5. [*none*]…
6. who…night
7. Although…people
8. as…slowly
9. when…vertigo
10. that…enjoy
11. which… schedule
12. if…it

Exercise 21-17:

1. Since potatoes grown from seed may not inherit the parent plant's characteristics, potatoes are usually grown from the eye of a planted piece of potato.
2. Because potato blossoms look like those of the poisonous nightshade plant, centuries ago Europeans were afraid to eat potatoes.
3. Although tomatoes, tobacco, and eggplant are all relatives of the potato, they do not look alike.
4. The sweet potato is not related to the potato even though its Indian name, *batata*, was mistakenly taken to mean "potato" by its European "discoverers."
5. Most people throw away the potato skin, which is a good source of dietary fibre.
6. While about 25 percent of Canada's potato-farming land is located in Prince Edward Island, this province has only 0.1 percent of Canada's total land area.
7. Would you believe that twelve percent of the U.S. crop is made into potato chips?
8. There are misinformed people who believe that the potato is only a poor person's food.
9. They overlook that potatoes have nourished the people of Europe since the eighteenth century.
10. Nutritious potatoes allowed the population to expand, until 1845, when parts of Europe—especially Ireland—were almost destroyed by a disease that killed the potato crop.
11. Potato chips were created in New England because a hotel chef became angry with a fussy customer.
12. Although no one else had ever complained, the customer sent back his french fries twice, saying they were not crisp enough.
13. The chef, who apparently had a bad temper, decided to teach the man a lesson.
14. He cut the potatoes paper-thin and fried them until they were too crisp to pick up with a fork.
15. Once the customer tasted these potatoes, he was delighted.
16. These "chips" became very popular, so that the chef never got his revenge, but he did get his own restaurant.

Exercise 21-18:

Exercise 7-18:

1. Forgetting is not always permanent. Simple
2. Interference sometimes keeps us from remembering. Simple
3. When this happens, we may not be able to stop thinking about something else even though we know it is wrong. Complex
4. For example, we may not recall a friend's name, and we may even want to call her by someone else's name. Compound
5. Other times, we try hard to remember, but our memories may not work at all. Compound
6. The information seems lost until we receive a clue that helps us remember. Complex
7. Some scientists believe that memories may completely fade away, and then we can never get them back. Compound
8. Recent studies show that storing memory changes the brain tissue. Complex
9. However, no one has shown that these changes can be erased, so the "fading-away" theory of forgetting remains unproven. Compound-Complex
10. Scientists who believe in the interference theory of forgetting identify different kinds of interference. Complex
11. Sometimes learning new material is made difficult by conflicting old material. Simple
12. Confusion between the old material and the new makes it hard to remember either one. Simple
13. Coming upon similar material soon after learning something can also interfere. Simple
14. Scientists have shown this in experiments, but everyday experience can convince us too. Compound
15. Anyone trying to learn two similar languages, such as French and Spanish, at the same time knows the feeling of confusion. Simple

Exercise 21-19A: Answers will vary.

1. Psychoanalysis helps people deal with these forgotten memories, for it works at exploring them consciously.
2. Repression, which is the burying in the unconscious of fearful experiences, can make life difficult.
3. People repress frightening thoughts and experiences, and then they try to go on living normally.
4. When people repress experiences, they avoid having to relive them, so they feel better for a time.
5. Experiments show that people forget bad experiences more quickly than (they forget) good experiences.
6. Repression occurs in the mentally ill, but it also occurs in healthy people.
7. A learning atmosphere where people can relax leads to better memory.
8. Any student knows this, and so does any teacher.
9. Because people are often distracted in stressful situations, they simply do not see everything; therefore, they cannot remember everything.
10. This may explain why accident victims often do not recall details of their experiences.
11. Many people do not remember much from their childhoods, but this does not mean that they are repressing bad memories.
12. They may have been too interested in some events to notice others that were happening at the same time, or maybe their childhoods were simply too boring to remember.

Exercise 21-19B: Answers will vary.

1. Compound: Fast food is not cheap, and it is not especially healthful.
   Complex: Although it is less expensive than other options, fast food is not cheap.
   Compound-Complex: Although it is very popular, fast food is not cheap, nor is it appetizing.
2. Compound: the lecture hall was packed, and a dozen students had to stand at the back.
   Complex: Even though the instructor is a dull lecturer, the lecture hall was packed.
   Compound-Complex: Because she has a reputation as a brilliant speaker, Professor Weiss drew hundreds of students to her introductory course, and the lecture hall was packed .
3. Compound: Read contracts before you sign them, or you could end up in financial trouble.
   Complex: Whenever you purchase goods or services, read contracts before you sign them.
   Compound-Complex: When you rent an apartment, always ask for a written lease, and read contracts before you sign them.
4. Compound: Thai restaurants are increasingly common, so Thai food must be good.
   Complex: Because Thai food is so popular, Thai restaurants are increasingly common.
   Compound-Complex: Even though there is fierce competition in the restaurant business, Thai restaurants are increasingly common, and you can find many in every large Canadian city.

5. Compound: Grocery stores should be open twenty-four hours a day, and so should banks.
   Complex: If staff can be hired, grocery stores should be open twenty-four hours a day.
   Compound-Complex: Because more and more people are working nontraditional schedules, grocery stores should be open twenty-four hours a day, and bus service should be frequent.

Exercise 21-19C: Answers will vary.

1. Because she has a pet snake, she has learned a lot about cold-blooded animals.
2. Whoever has the flu should stay home until the symptoms are gone.
3. Let both sides speak before the union votes on the contract.
4. Even though they paid the electric bill, service was suspended until the cheque cleared.
5. Do you know where the keys are?
6. Electronic devices that fit in your pocket are the best kind.
7. I know who has the prize-winning ticket.
8. Since she learned to drive, she's driven to Moose Jaw and back twice.
9. I can't remember whether the bus stops on that corner.
10. I can understand any complex plaything if it has only one moving part.

Chapter 22: Verbs

Exercise 22-1:

1. rushes
2. ties
3. weighs
4. needs
5. attempts
6. fails
7. starts
8. opens
9. waits
10. occurs
11. reports
12. affects
13. recommends
14. warns
15. posts
16. stops
17. requires
18. knows
19. hears
20. allows
21. remains
22. brakes
23. causes
24. faces
25. practises

Exercise 22-2:

1. started
2. recorded
3. developed
4. used
5. inserted
6. issued, startled
7. perceived
8. jerked, headed
9. employed
10. pulled
11. experimented
12. imagined

Exercise 22-3:

1. woke
2. got, slept
3. froze, stood
4. shook, told
5. threw
6. drove
7. swung
8. drew, came
9. saw, burst
10. thought
11. went, spent
12. got, spoke
13. heard
14. spun, saw
15. sprang
16. shook
17. swept, took
18. clung
19. felt, ate, drank
20. rang, told

Exercise 22-4:

person	present tense	past tense
first	am	was
second	are	were
third	is	was
first	are	were
second	are	were
third	are	were

present participle: being past participle: been

Exercise 22-5:

As Earth's climate warms, the people who live in the far north <u>are</u> looking for ways to cope. Even their housing may <u>be</u> affected. Some houses in Nunavut whose foundations stand on the permafrost have <u>been</u> undermined as the permafrost begins to melt. Buildings today <u>are</u> sinking and are even <u>being</u> torn apart as they tilt and buckle on the softening earth.

Richard Carbonnier, an architect who works for the government of Nunavut, <u>is</u> developing a new kind of house for the far north. His prototype <u>is</u> called the Inuksuk Residence, and its supporters think that it should <u>be</u> adopted widely. It <u>is</u> a strange looking structure, Carbonnier admits, but it <u>is</u> meant <u>to be</u> above all else a practical structure.

Instead of <u>being</u> supported by a regular foundation, the house stands well above the ground on a tripod made of three stilts. Each stilt <u>is</u> able to shift if the earth underneath it moves. Supported by this tripod system, the house will <u>be</u> able to withstand the melting permafrost safely.

Carbonnier always has <u>been</u> eager to borrow those features of the traditional igloo that could make the Inuksuk Residence a practical dwelling for the north. As well, because Carbonnier <u>was</u> concerned from the very start about the environment, he made sure that a number of ecological advances <u>were</u> incorporated in its design.

The prototype house as it can be seen today <u>is</u> a modular building formed from three large cylinders. These <u>are</u> joined together and they all lie flat, so that from the air the whole structure looks like a large Y. If you <u>are</u> ever lucky enough <u>to be</u> flying over Pond Inlet in Nunavut, <u>be</u> sure to look out for Carbonnier's house on the hill overlooking the town.

Exercise 22-6: Answers will vary.

1. are
2. was
3. may
4. do
5. does
6. seem
7. can
8. should
9. will
10. is
11. can
12. would
13. could
14. were
15. can
16. be
17. has
18. have

Exercise 22-7:

1. transitive
2. linking
3. intransitive
4. transitive
5. transitive
6. transitive
7. linking
8. intransitive
9. transitive
10. intransitive
11. transitive
12. linking
13. transitive
14. intransitive
15. transitive
16. linking

Exercise 22-8: Answers will vary.

1. He answered confidently.
   She answered the phone after the third ring.
2. She walked very quietly to the kitchen cabinet.
   Celia walked the dog on the beach early this afternoon.
3. Omar prepares carefully before his exams.
   She prepared her homework for tomorrow's classes.
4. The car drives very well in the snow.
   Sheryl drives her father's car to work every morning.
5. Jeremy paints every weekend.
   John painted the living room with the paint you gave him.

Exercise 22-9A:

	-s form	past tense	past participle	present participle
lie	lies	lay	lain	lying
lay	lays	laid	laid	laying
sit	sits	sat	sat	sitting
set	sets	set	set	setting
rise	rises	rose	risen	rising
raise	raises	raised	raised	raising

Exercise 22-9B:

1. sitting
2. lay, lies
3. raised
4. laying
5. lain
6. sat
7. rose, laid
8. raised
9. set
10. raise

Exercise 22-10:

1. have discovered
2. have been kissing
3. are beginning
4. has been studying
5. has found
6. had been involved
7. are earning
8. had said
9. has been linked; are living
10. have been having
11. has suggested
12. are starting
13. have known
14. have understood
15. have been studying

Exercise 22-11:

1. The Louvre in Paris <u>was</u> not <u>built</u> as an art museum. passive

2. The original Louvre was constructed in the twelfth century as a fortress. passive
3. Francis I began the present building as a residence. active
4. A gallery connecting it with the Tuileries Palace was started by Henry IV and completed by Louis XIV. passive
5. A second gallery, begun by Napoleon, would have enclosed a great square. active
6. However, it was not finished until after his abdication. passive
7. Revolutionaries overthrew the Bastille on July 14, 1789. active
8. Just four years later the art collection of the Louvre was opened to the public. passive
9. The collection can be traced back to Francis I. passive
10. Francis, an ardent collector, invited Leonardo da Vinci to France in 1515. active
11. Leonardo brought the *Mona Lisa* with him from Italy. active
12. Nevertheless, the royal art collection may have been expanded more by ministers than by kings. passive
13. Cardinals Richelieu and Mazarin can take credit for many important acquisitions. active
14. Today the Louvre has a new entrance. active
15. The entrance, a glass pyramid in the courtyard, was designed by I. M. Pei. passive
16. Pei's name can be added to a distinguished list of Louvre architects. passive

Exercise 22-12A: Answers will vary.

1. The French did not build the Louvre in Paris as an art musem.
2. The French constructed the original Louvre as a twelfth-century fortress.
4. Henry IV started a gallery connecting it with the Tuileries Palace, and Louis XIV completed the gallery.
6. However, workers did not finish it until after his abdication.
8. Just four years later authorities opened the art collection of the Louvre to the public.
9. We can trace the collection back to Francis I.
12. Nevertheless, ministers may have expanded the royal art collection more than kings.
15. I. M. Pei designed the glass pyramid entrance in the courtyard.
16. We can add Pei's name to a distinguished list of Louvre architects.

Exercise 22-12B:

1. passive People outside Africa did not know about the ruins until 1868.
2. active
3. passive Acceptable. The building is more important than who built it.
4. passive Acceptable. The unknown builders are less important than the way it was built.
5. passive A nine-metre wall encircles a lower, elliptical building.
6. active
7. passive Acceptable. Emphasis on the sculptures, not the discoverers.
8. active
9. active
10. passive Acceptable. Tools are stressed, not the people who found them.
11. active

Chapter 23: Pronouns: Case and Reference

Exercise 23-1:

	person	subjective case	objective case	possessive case
singular	first	I	me	my/mine
	second	you	you	you/yours
	third	he	him	his
		she	her	her/hers
		it	it	its
plural	first	we	us	our/ours
	second	you	you	your/yours
	third	they	them	their/theirs

Exercise 23-2:

	pronoun	case
1.	me	objective
2.	They	subjective
3.	their	possessive
4.	Your	possessive
	you	objective
5.	its	possessive
	them	objective
6.	their	possessive
7.	we	subjective
8.	I	subjective
	our	possessive
9.	my	possessive
	me	objective
10.	Your	possessive
	his	possessive
11.	me	objective
	me	objective
12.	I	subjective
	you	objective

Exercise 23-3:

1. we, we
2. It
3. us
4. he
5. He, I
6. our
7. he, I, themselves
8. him, himself
9. them, itself
10. their
11. us
12. my
13. himself
14. me, us
15. her
16. her
17. you, you
18. them
19. themselves
20. yours

Exercise 23-4A:

1. he and she: appositives of the composers
2. he: complement of a merry old king
3. ours: appositive of the only furnished attic on the block
4. they: complement of the latest composers
5. my telephone bill: appositive of my last large debt

Exercise 23-4B:

1. she
2. me
3. he
4. him
5. I

Exercise 23-5:

1. who
2. who
3. whoever
4. whom
5. whoever
6. who
7. who
8. who
9. whom
10. who
11. whom
12. whomever
13. who
14. who
15. whom
16. whom

Exercise 23-6:

1. himself
2. him
3. His
4. he
5. he
6. them
7. its
8. itself
9. it
10. him
11. itself
12. their
13. themselves

Exercise 23-7:

1. them
   Unlike most recent Canadian prime ministers, three out of the first five Canadian prime ministers were born in Scotland or England. Most recent Canadian prime ministers were born in Canada.
2. he
   The first Canadian-born prime minister, Sir John Abbott, held office in 1891 and 1892; the last British-born prime minister was John Turner. Turner led the government for a few weeks in 1984.
3. he
   For religious reasons, US president-elect Zachary Taylor refused to take the oath of office on a Sunday, so David Rice Atchison (president of the Senate) was president for a day. Atchison spent the day appointing his temporary cabinet.
4. his
   Correct
5. he
   An American Indian, Charles Curtis, became vice-president when Herbert Hoover was elected president in 1928. Curtis was one-half Kaw.

6. he
   William DeVance King, vice-president under Franklin Pierce, was in Cuba during the election and had to be sworn in by an act of Congress, never bothering to return to Washington. A month later, never having carried out any official duties, King died.
7. their, their
   Correct
8. their, theirs
   Correct
9. she
   The first woman presidential candidate was Victoria Woodhull. Years before Geraldine Ferraro ran for vice president, Woodhull was on the Equal Rights Party ticket—in 1872.
10. She
    The first woman to lead a major party in the Canadian House of Commons was Audrey McLaughlin, and the second was Kim Campbell. Campbell became the first woman prime minister.
11. He, he
    As a child, president-to-be Andrew Johnson was sold as an indentured servant to a tailor. Johnson was supposed to work for seven years, but he ran away.

Exercise 23-8: Answers will vary.

1. A California company called the Space Island Group is planning to recycle one of the shortest-lived components of the space shuttle. The company's plan is ingenious.
2. Engineers at SIG plan to construct dozens of wheel-shaped space stations using empty shuttle fuel tanks. The tanks are eminently suited to the task.
3. A shuttle's fuel tanks are huge. Each one is 8.5 metres in diameter and nearly 50 metres long—approximately the size of a jumbo jet. The shuttle jettisons the tanks just before it reaches orbit, leaving them to burn up and crash into the ocean.
4. Over a hundred of these tanks, known as ETs, have been used and destroyed since the first shuttle launch in 1981. So it is obvious how much hardware has gone to waste.
5. Using ETs to form manned space stations—and developing passenger shuttles to take people to them—was originally NASA's idea. At first, NASA was enthusiastic about this possibility.
6. However, it would have taken too long for NASA to develop and test passenger shuttles, so the idea was dropped.
7. SIG's plan is to build the passenger shuttles and lease them to commercial airlines. SIG believes that this is the fastest way to get ordinary people into space.
8. The space stations will also be leased—at a rate of $10 to $20 per cubic foot per day—to anyone wishing to run a business in space. Businesspeople will simply take the shuttle, transfer to the space station, and set up their offices.
9. While the space stations have a projected life of 30 years, SIG claims that tenants would fully pay for them within 2 to 3 years. This means that the passenger shuttle program could actually operate at a profit.

Exercise 23-9: Answers may vary by using she or he or she in place of he.

Everyone has to be careful when buying on credit. Otherwise, a person may wind up so heavily in debt that it may take years to straighten out his life. Credit cards are easy for a person to get if he is working, and many finance companies are eager to give anyone instalment loans at high interest rates. Once someone is hooked, he may find himself taking out loans to pay his loans. When this happens, he is doomed to being forever in debt.

There are, of course, times when using credit makes sense. If a person has the money (or will have it when the bill comes), a credit card can enable him to shop without carrying cash. Someone may also want to keep a few gasoline credit cards with him in case his car breaks down on the road. Using credit will allow a person to deal with other emergencies (tuition, a broken water heater) when he lacks the cash. He can also use credit to take advantage of sales. However, he needs to recognize the difference between a sale item he needs and one he wants. If he can't do this, he may find himself dealing with collection agents, car repossessors, or even bankruptcy lawyers.

Chapter 24: Agreement

Exercise 24-1A:

1. occupy
2. associates
3. wear
4. refers
5. work
6. consists
7. use
8. bastes
9. cuts
10. reveal

Exercise 24-1B:

1. needs
2. makes
3. are
4. deserve
5. seems
6. are
7. means
8. is
9. becomes
10. are

Exercise 24-1C:

subject	verb	correction
1. Ken, Sara	has visited	have visited
2. places	is	are
they	should see	correct
3. cities	is	correct
that	transmit	correct
4. history	seems	correct
5. more	is	are
6. castles, residences	are	correct
7. gardens	is	are
8. art, architecture	reveals	reveal
9. city	is	correct
10. visitors	comes	come

Exercise 24-1D:

1. is
2. are
3. is
4. have
5. are
6. share
7. is
8. is
9. prefers
10. are

Exercise 24-1E:

1. mystery/continues
2. anyone/sees
3. book/is
4. no one/studies
5. paintings/are
6. decoration/appears
7. pictures/stem
8. birds/wear
9. humour/pervades
10. text/is

Exercise 24-1F:

1. seems
2. show
3. argues
4. look
5. belong
6. makes
7. publish
8. deals
9. gets
10. ask

Exercise 24-1G:

1. knows, dream
2. occur
3. stands
4. gets
5. are, means
6. suggest
7. represent
8. believe
9. spend
10. receive
11. devote
12. form
13. think
14. lacks
15. have
16. claim
17. protect
18. exists, proposes
19. learn
20. combines, are

Exercise 22-2: Answers will vary.

1. Outdoor sports enthusiasts need to rehydrate their bodies regularly.
2. One should not wait to feel dryness in his or her throat before drinking water. [*In one's* throat is also possible.]
3. Rather, anyone engaged in physical exertion should sip fluids regularly as he or she continues with his or her activity.
4. If a family goes on a long hike, it should carry enough water for each of its members.
5. In practical terms, that means that a family should all carry their own water bottles.
6. Neither an adult nor a child can do without his or her water supply on the trail.
7. The Web site of Mountain Equipment Co-op (MEC) informs its members all about these things.
8. Everyone who visits the site can find useful tips for his or her outdoor adventures.
9. To purify water for drinking on the trail, many campers like to boil their water and pour it right into the bottle.
10. This has led many of them to carry their water supply in polycarbonate plastic water bottles.
11. All of the other available plastics melt or lose their shape when filled with boiling liquids.
12. None of the others both holds its shape and resists odours as effectively.
13. In late 2007, however, MEC stores removed all polycarbonate bottles from their shelves.
14. MEC noted on its Web site that one of the compounds used in polycarbonate plastics mimics the hormone estrogen.
15. A liquid or food can have its chemistry altered if the compound leaches out of the plastic.
16. Either one, then, might have unexpected effects on the people who consume it, over time.
17. MEC's Web site referred to a study of these effects that the federal government was conducting under its Chemical Management Plan.
18. Any purchaser wanting to inform himself or herself further on the topic can follow the health and environmental links on the MEC Web site.

Exercise 24-3: Answers will vary.

1. Many people assume that a person who makes a lot of money has <u>his or her</u> happiness guaranteed.
2. However, a person who owns a lot of things is not necessarily as happy as <u>he or she</u> would like to be.
3. An individual who isn't able to buy much beyond life's necessities may not be happy with <u>his or her</u> life either.
4. How do most people define happiness and how can <u>they</u> achieve it?
5. The answer is that everyone has <u>his or her</u> own idea of what makes <u>him or her</u> happy.
6. Therefore, each individual should take time to reflect on what makes <u>him or her</u> happy.
7. One of the oldest and wisest says is "Know yourself." That's the only way to know what makes <u>you</u> happy.
8. It's also important to understand that no matter how much somebody may care for you, <u>he or she</u> is not responsible for your happiness. You are responsible for your own happiness.
9. To be happy, it seems that most people need more than just life's necessities, but <u>they</u> probably don't need nearly as much as <u>they</u> may think.

Chapter 25: Adjectives and Adverbs

Exercise 25-1:

1. adjective
2. adverb
3. adverb
4. adjective
5. adverb
6. adjective
7. adjective
8. adjective
9. adverb
10. adjective
11. adjective
12. adjective
13. adjective
14. adverb
15. adverb
16. adverb
17. adjective
18. adverb
19. adjective
20. adverb

Exercise 25-2:

1. annually
2. available
3. well
4. serious
5. commonly
6. bad
7. delicate
8. dangerous
9. slowly
10. high
11. lengthy
12. ancient
13. chemically
14. recently
15. quickly
16. popular
17. lately
18. regularly
19. quick
20. carefully

Exercise 25-3A:

	comparative	superlative
1.	worse	worst
2.	worse	worst
3.	more forgiving	most forgiving
4.	freer	freest
5.	better	best
6.	more gracefully	most gracefully
7.	handsomer	handsomest
8.	hotter	hottest
9.	littler	littlest
10.	more loudly	most loudly
11.	more	most
12.	more	most
13.	more powerfully	most powerfully
14.	prettier	prettiest
15.	more quickly	most quickly
16.	more	most
17.	more sweetly	most sweetly
18.	more sympathetically	most sympathetically
19.	more talented	most talented
20.	better	best

Exercise 25-3B: Answers will vary.

Exercise 25-4: Answers will vary.

Chapter 26: Sentence Fragments

Exercise 26-1A: Answers will vary.

1. This is a dependent adverb clause.
   When Alyssa arrived at work, she found that there were no parking spaces left.
2. This is a dependent noun clause.
   Laura will accept whichever job offer comes first.
3. There is no subject.
   Every year, my husband joins the bowling league.
4. This is a prepositional phrase.
   There is no room for a CPU on my desk.
5. This lacks a helping verb.
   Fortunately, the tutor is helping my sister.
6. This is a participial phrase.
   Considered the best tennis doubles partner in town, Kofi is constantly receiving calls with offers to play doubles.
7. This is a dependent adjective clause.
   I am researching the short story that I hope to write.
8. This is a noun phrase.
   Biochemistry is my least favourite course this semester.
9. This is either a gerund phrase or a participial phrase.
   Gerund: Visiting with my family in Ireland has taught me all about my family's culture.
   Participial phrase: Visiting with my family in Ireland, I got to meet family members that I have always heard about.
10. This is part of a compound predicate.
    Yasmin likes to read and write short stories.

Exercise 26-1B: Answer will vary.

1. Someone who gets to class on time will not miss any of the lecture. (part of dependent adjective clause)
   Autumn always gets to class on time. (part of the predicate)
2. There lay the manuscript that we thought had been entered in the literary contest. (part of dependent adjective clause)
   The manuscript that we entered in the literary contest will not be returned. (part of dependent adjective clause)
3. I need to buy a textbook for my creative writing class. (infinitive phrase as direct object)
   To buy a textbook is a requirement. (infinitive phrase as subject)
4. When I took the exam, my professor allowed me to stay later. (dependent adverb clause)
   When I took the exam is irrelevant! (noun clause)
5. I never see my friend working to pay for university. (part of the predicate)
   Working to pay for university shouldn't take away too much study time. (gerund phrase as subject)
6. In many of the city's coffee houses, we saw students studying for exams during spring break. (adjective phrase as part of the predicate)
   A small group of students were studying for exams during spring break. (part of the predicate)
7. Administrators, faculty, staff, and students will all get an extra week of summer vacation. (compound subject)
   Everyone on campus, administrators, faculty, staff, and students, will be glad when fall semester begins. (appositive phrase)

8. The power going off suddenly, we hoped and prayed our work on the computers would be saved. (absolute phrase)
   The power going off suddenly is something that has happened too many times when I've been working on my computer. (noun phrase as subject)
9. The retired electrical contractor who attends night classes thought Literature 101 was a superb class. (dependent adjective clause)
   Who attends night classes? (transformed into interrogative sentence)
10. Working in the writing centre is one of the best jobs on campus. (prepositional phrase as part of the subject)
    Students tutored in the writing centre often learn more than they expect to learn. (prepositional phrase as adverb)

Exercise 26-2:

1. Futurist and author Arthur C. Clarke predicted in the 1960s the development of a vast electronic "global library." Surprisingly, he said that it would be in place by the year 2000.
2. In fact, the origins of the Internet can be traced back to 1958. ARPA, the Advanced Research Projects Agency, was set up by the US Department of Defense as an arm of the military.
3. However, before ARPA began supporting networking research seriously, Leonard Kleinrock, a graduate student at the Massachussetts Institute of Technology, had already invented the technology of the Internet. Kleinrock's contribution is known as "packet switching."
4. A method of sending data as short, independent units of information, packet switching was far more efficient than the system that it replaced. This was the traditional circuit-switched method.
5. Packet switching avoided the long periods of "silence" that occur when data is circuit switched and can occupy as much as 99 percent of each transmission. Such delays prevent effective transmission of large files.
6. Packet-switching technology was used in the creation of ARPAnet, which is the network that laid the foundation for the Internet. ARPAnet was inaugurated in 1969.
7. The US military was especially interested in packet switching because it sends messages along a complex network by any route available. Air force planners wanted a way to stay in control if a nuclear war destroyed most communications in the United States.
8. Soon after, in 1972, Ray Tomlinson, a computer engineer involved in the ARPAnet project, invented electronic mail.
9. E-mail was the Internet's first "killer application," a slang term for software that is so useful, it creates a market for new hardware. People bought computers and modems just to have access to the Internet.
10. As academics and researchers in other fields began to use the network, ARPAnet was taken over by NSF. This abbreviation represents the US National Science Foundation.
11. The NSF had created a similar network of its own, called NSFnet, one of the many networks that had begun to introduce improvements in the technology. Among these improvements was the adoption of the transmission protocol known as TCP/IP.
12. In 1989, British scientist Tim Berners-Lee proposed the World Wide Web project. By adopting his HTTP, or Hypertext Transfer Protocol, Web browsers would be able to communicate across the Internet.

13. The Web gives users access to a vast array of documents connected to each other by hyperlinks, which are electronic connections that link related pieces of information.
14. The World Wide Web gained rapid acceptance with the creation in 1992 of a Web browser called Mosaic. This program allowed users to search the Web using "point-and-click" graphics much more easily than with the original system of keyboard-based commands.
15. One of the developers of Mosaic, Marc Andreessen, went on to create Netscape Navigator, which became the first commercially successful Web browser. Its success led to the development of several competing browsers, including many that can be downloaded for free.
16. James Gosling, who studied computer science in Calgary, became known as one of the best programmers in the world. By the early 1990s he sensed the need for a programming language that could integrate every "smart" machine and gadget into the Internet.
17. Gosling's solution was Java, a simple programming language designed to let programmers write applications for nearly any computing device. A major innovation in the new language was the "applet."
18. Applets are mini-programs that are downloaded along with Web pages, which allow the downloading devices to interact and perform new sets of tasks. The resulting interactivity of devices and their software has created the wired world we are just getting to know.

Exercise 26-3: Answers will vary. The following passages are fragments.
A: 1, 2, 5, 7, 9, 10, 12, 13, 14
B: 2, 3, 5, 7, 8, 10, 11, 14, 16, 17, 20, 22, 23, 27

Chapter 27: Comma Splices and Fused Sentences

Exercise 27-1A: Answers will vary. Possible answers are shown below.

1. … grams of salt; without it …
2. … became difficult, so they …
3. … like money; it was a …
4. … are very salty. There's enough salt …
5. …used as seasoning; most of the rest …
6. Although people get some salt …
7. … to crave salt. Now so much salt …

Exercise 27-1B:

1. Salt is a major ingredient in pesticides and herbicides that are used to kill insects and plants.
2. The Romans destroyed the city of Carthage. They ploughed the ground with salt as a symbol of its desolation.
3. Constructive or destructive, salt has many uses; moreover, it is used far more than any other mineral.
4. The Romans knew the value of salt as a commodity; they named a major highway the Via Salaria (Salt Road).
5. The word *salary* comes from the word *salarium*, which meant money used to pay soldiers so they could buy salt.
6. Salt has long been used to preserve food, and the expression "salted away" means to keep for a future time.
7. Salt may become even more important to us than it already is; we may be able to use it to bury radioactive waste.

Exercise 27-1C:

1. … tree. It satisfies …
   … tree; it satisfies …
   … tree, for it satisfies …
   … tree, which satisfies …
2. … ungainly. They …
   … ungainly; they …
   …ungainly, but they …
   Although to most people giraffes appear ungainly, …
3. … giraffes. They …
   … giraffes; they …
   … giraffes, so they …
   Because people have greatly reduced…
4. … fingerprints, Giraffes …
   … fingerprints; giraffes …
   … fingerprints, and giraffes …
   … fingerprints while giraffes …
5. … leopard. Its …
   … leopard; its …
   … leopard, so …
   … leopard so that …

Exercise 27-2: Answers will vary. Possible answers are shown below.

1. The king Jayavarman II introduced into the empire an Indian royal cult. The cult held that the king was related spiritually to one of the Hindu gods; consequently, the king was thought to fill on earth the role the gods had in the universe.
2. Each king was expected to build a stone temple. The temple, or *wat*, was dedicated to a god, usually Shiva or Vishnu. When the king died, the temple became a monument to him as well.
3. Over the centuries the kings erected more than seventy temples within 200 km^2. They added towers and gates, and they created canals and reservoirs for an irrigation system.
4. The irrigation system made it possible for farmers to produce several rice crops a year. Although such abundant harvests supported a highly evolved culture, the irrigation system and the rice production were what we would call labour-intensive.
5. The greatest of the temples is Angkor Wat, which was built by Suryavarman II in the 12th century. Like the other temples, it represents Mount Meru, the home of the Hindu gods. The towers represent Mount Meru's peaks while the walls represent the mountains beyond.
6. The gallery walls are covered with bas-reliefs that depict historical events. They show the king at his court, and they show him engaging in activities that brought glory to his empire.
7. The walls also portray divine images. There are sculptures of *apsarases*, who are attractive women thought to inhabit heaven. There are mythical scenes on the walls as well.

8. One scene shows the Hindu myth of the churning of the Sea of Milk. On one side of the god Vishnu are demons who tug on the end of a long serpent; on the other are heavenly beings who tug on the other end. All the tugging churns the water.
9. Vishnu is the god to whom Angkor Wat is dedicated. In Hindu myth he oversees the churning of the waters. That churning is ultimately a source of immortality.
10. Another temple is the Bayon, which was built by Jayavarman VII around AD 1200. Jayavarman VII was the last of the great kings of Angkor. He built the Bayon in the exact centre of the city.
11. The Bayon resembles a step pyramid. It has steep stairs that lead to terraces near the top. Around its base are many galleries. Its towers are carved with faces that look out in all directions.
12. Because Jayavarman VII was a Buddhist, the representations on Bayon are different from those on earlier temples. Some scholars think they depict a Buddhist deity with whom the king felt closely aligned.
13. To build each temple required thousands of labourers who worked for years. After cutting the stone in far-off quarries, they had to transport it by canal or cart. Some stone may have been brought in on elephants.
14. Once cut, the stones had to be carved and fitted together into lasting edifices. Thus, in addition to requiring labourers, each project needed artisans, architects, and engineers. Each temple was a massive project.
15. After Angkor was conquered by the Thais in the 1400s, it was almost completely abandoned. The local inhabitants did continue to use the temples for worship, however, and a few late Khmer kings tried to restore the city.
16. The Western world did not learn about Angkor until the nineteenth century, when a French explorer published an account of the site. French archaeologists and conservators later worked in the area and restored some of the temples. More recent archaeologists have come from India.
17. Today the Angkor Conservancy has removed many of the temple statues. Some of the statues need repair; all of them need protection from thieves. Unfortunately, traffic in Angkor art has become big business among people with no scruples. There is even a booming business in Angkor fakes.
18. Theft is just one of the problems Angkor faces today. Political upheaval has taken its toll. Although Angkor mostly escaped Cambodia's civil war, some war damage has occurred.
19. More damage has been done by nature, however. Trees choke some of the archways, vines strangle the statues, and monsoons undermine the basic structures.
20. Today many Cambodians do what they can to maintain the temples of Angkor. They clean stones or sweep courtyards or pull weeds. No one pays them; they do it for themselves and their heritage.

Chapter 28: Misplaced and Dangling Modifiers

Exercise 28-1: Answers will vary.

[1]Sailors developed scrimshaw, the art of carving or engraving marine articles, while sailing on long voyages. [2]Because scrimshaw was practised primarily by whalermen, sperm whale teeth were the most popular articles. [3]Baleen, which was also called whalebone, was another popular choice. [4]With whaling voyages taking several years, a sailor needed something to occupy his time. [5]Only imagination or available material limited scrimshaw. [6]All kinds of objects—canes, corset

busks, cribbage boards—were produced by the scrimshander. [7]The sailor used everything from whaling scenes to mermaids to decorate his work. [8]Often a sailor doing scrimshaw drew his own ship. [9]The most frequently depicted ship, the *Charles W. Morgan*, is presently a museum ship at Mystic Seaport. [10]It is easily possible to see it on a visit to Connecticut.

Exercise 28-2A:

1. To paint one's house, one must frequently do it oneself.
2. Almost all homeowners try to paint at one time or another.
3. They usually try to begin on a bedroom.
4. By doing so, they think no one will see it if they botch the job.
5. In no time, most people can learn to paint.
6. Only the uncoordinated should not try it.
7. People that have strong arm muscles have a distinct advantage.
8. Lacking strength, prospective painters can always exercise.
9. Novices need to purchase all supplies, such as brushes, rollers, and drop cloths, carefully.
10. They must bring home paint chips to match exactly the shade desired.
11. It takes nearly as much time to prepare to paint as it does to do the actual job.
12. Painters who think they are done with the last paint stroke are in for a surprise.
13. Painters need to clean their own brushes immediately and put away all equipment.
14. In the long run, they can be proud of their accomplishment.
15. Only then can they enjoy the results of their labour.
16. When all is said and done, painting one's own home can be extremely satisfying.

Exercise 28-2B:

1. Playing the role of a caring and wise father, Richardson told the girls how to handle various situations.
2. To help the girls, Richardson sometimes wrote letters to their suitors.
3. After writing a number of successful letters, Richardson had the idea to write a book of model letters.
4. To prepare the books, Richardson wrote letters as if from adults to sons, daughters, nieces, and nephews.
5. When ready to send advice, a parent copied out a letter and just changed the names.
6. Bought by many, Richardson's book was a success.
7. While working on one letter (. . .), Richardson thought of enough *ideas for a* whole book.
8. By writing a series of letters between a girl and her faraway parents, Richardson hoped to entertain and instruct young readers.
9. Upon finishing *Pamela, or Virtue Rewarded* in 1740, Richardson knew he had invented a new form of literature.
10. After years of development, this form became the novel.
11. Being a nasty person, Horace Walpole wrote a single novel that wasn't very attractive.
12. Correct.
13. Although badly written, it contained the themes, atmosphere, mood, and plots that have filled gothic novels ever since.
14. Featuring gloomy castles filled with dark secrets, gothic movies also entertain people.

Chapter 29: Shifting and Mixed Sentences

Exercise 29-1A: Answers will vary.

The next time you watch a western movie, notice whether it contains any sign language. Some people consider sign language the first universal language. Although few people use it today, it is a Native American language with a lengthy history. One can find some tribal differences, but basic root signs were clear to everyone who tried to interpret them.

Sign language differs from the signage used by hearing-impaired people. For instance, they indicate the forehead to mean *think* while a Sioux pointed to the heart. One also uses extensive facial expression in speaking to someone with a hearing loss while Native Americans maintained a stoic countenance. They believed the signs could speak for themselves. Ideally they made the signs in round, sweeping motions. They tried to make conversation beautiful.

Exercise 29-1B: Answers will vary.

No one knows why sailors wear bell-bottom pants. However, three theories are popular. First, bell-bottom pants fit over boots and keep sea spray and rain from getting in. Second, bell-bottoms can be rolled up over the knees, so they stay dry when a sailor must wade ashore and stay clean when he scrubs the ship's deck. Third, because bell-bottoms are loose, they are easy to take off in the water if a sailor falls overboard. In their training course, sailors are taught another advantage to bell-bottoms. By taking them off and tying the legs at the ends, a sailor who has fallen into the ocean can change his bell-bottom pants into a life preserver.

Exercise 29-1C: Answers will vary.

1. 2. The Aran Isles are situated off the coast of Ireland. They are not far from Galway.
2. 1. Islanders have difficult lives. They must make their living by fishing in a treacherous sea.
3. 2. They use a simple boat called a *curragh* for fishing. They also use it to ferry their market animals to barges.
4. 3. Island houses stand out against the empty landscape. Their walls provide scant protection from a hostile environment.
5. 2. In 1898 John Millington Synge first visited the Aran Isles. He used them as the setting for *Riders to the Sea* and other of his works.
6. 1. Whether people see the Synge play or Ralph Vaughan Williams's operatic version of *Riders to the Sea*, they will feel the harshness of Aran life.
7. 3. The mother Maurya has lost her husband and several sons. They have all drowned at sea.
8. 2. When the body of another son is washed onto the shore, it is identified from the pattern knitted into his sweater.
9. 3. Each Aran knitter develops her own combination of patterns. The patterns not only produce a beautiful sweater, but they have a very practical purpose.
10. 3. The oiled wool protects the fisherman from the sea spray while the intricate patterns offer symbolic protection as well as identification when necessary.

11. 4. When you knit your first Aran Isle sweater, you should learn what the stitches mean. <u>You should not</u> choose a pattern just because it is easy.
12. 2. A cable stitch represents a fisherman's rope; <u>a zigzag stitch depicts winding cliff paths.</u>
13. 3. Bobbles symbolize men in a *curragh* while the basket stitch <u>represents</u> a fisherman's creel and the hope that it will come home full.
14. 3. The tree of life signifies strong sons and family unity. It *is* also a fertility symbol.
15. 5. When someone asks you <u>whether</u> you knitted your Aran Isle yourself, you can proudly say that you did and you also chose the patterns.

Exercise 29-2A: Answers will vary.

1. Carl Fabergé created Easter eggs for the tsars.
2. Because Fabergé was a talented goldsmith, he was able to make exquisite objects.
3. Working for the court of Imperial Russia enabled him to combine craftsmanship and ingenuity.
4. Fabergé pleased his clients by creating unique works of art.
5. He included gems in his creations, but they did not overshadow his workmanship.
6. In adapting enamelling techniques, he achieved a level seldom matched by other artisans.
7. Buyers in Europe expanded his clientele beyond the Russian royal family.
8. Because he had no money worries, he had few restrictions on imagination.
9. Although Fabergé created other examples of the jeweler's art, it is the Imperial Easter eggs for which he is most remembered.
10. The most famous eggs contained surprises inside—a hen, a ship, a coach.
11. One egg opened to reveal a model of a palace.
12. The most ambitious creation represented an egg surrounded by parts of a cathedral.
13. An artist is one who practises an imaginative art.
14. One reason Fabergé is so admired is that he was a true artist.

Exercise 29-2B: Answers will vary. These are possible answers only.

1. The use of cuneiform began <u>in</u> and spread throughout ancient Sumer.
2. This picture language of the Sumerians is thought to be older than <u>that of</u> the Egyptians.
3. Like hieroglyphics, early cuneiform used easily recognizable pictures <u>to</u> represent objects.
4. When scribes began using a wedge-shaped stylus, <u>great</u> changes occurred.
5. The new marks were different <u>from the early pictographs</u>.
6. They had become so stylized <u>that the origin was often unrecognizable</u>.
7. Early Sumerian tablets recorded practical things such <u>as</u> lists of grain in storage.
8. Some tablets were put <u>into</u> clay envelopes that were themselves inscribed.
9. Gradually ordinary people used cuneiform as much as official scribes <u>did.</u>
10. *The Epic of Gilgamesh*, written in Akkadian cuneiform, is older than any <u>other</u> epic.
11. The Code of Hammurabi recorded in cuneiform a more comprehensive set of laws <u>than any previously set down.</u>
12. Correct.

13. Because it was written in three languages, it served the same purpose <u>as the Rosetta Stone.</u>
14. Today we understand cuneiform as much <u>as,</u> if not more than, we understand hieroglyphics.

Exercise 29-2C: Answers will vary.

[1]Wild rice may be the caviar of grains, but it is not really rice. [2]It is, however, truly wild. [3]One reason is that it needs marshy places in order to thrive. [4]Planting it in prepared paddies can produce abundant crops. [5]Nevertheless, most wild rice grows naturally along rivers and lake shores in northern US states and Canada. [6]In certain areas only Native People are allowed to harvest the rice. [7]Connoisseurs think wild rice tastes better than any other grain. [8]It is surely the most expensive of all grains. [9]Some hostesses serve it with Cornish hens exclusively, but the creative cook serves it with many dishes. [10]Try it in quiche or pancakes; your guests will be so pleased that they will ask for more.

Chapter 30: Conciseness

Exercise 30-1:

1. Art Deco took its name from a 1925 Paris exposition.
2. Art Deco used bold and streamlined shapes and experimented with new materials.
3. In the 1920s public fascination with futuristic technology influenced Art Deco.
4. In addition to dominating architecture, the style pervaded glassware, appliances, furniture, and even advertising art.
5. The Marine Building in Vancouver and the Chrysler Building in New York exemplified Art Deco's dynamic style.
6. After the 1929 stock market crash, Art Deco expressed modern ideas and themes less extravagantly.
7. The Art Deco of the Great Depression had restraint and austerity.
8. Architects used rounded corners, glass blocks, and porthole windows.
9. They liked flat roofs.
10. Buildings with plain exteriors often had lavish interiors and furniture to match.

Exercise 30-2:

1. The Romans gave sacrifices to the goddess Maia on the first day of the month named for her.
2. The Celts also celebrated May Day as the midpoint of their year.
3. One of the most important of the May Day celebrations is the Maypole.
4. The Maypole represented rebirth.
5. In Germany a Maypole tree was often stripped of all but the top branches to represent new life.
6. In Sweden floral wreaths were suspended from a crossbar on the pole.
7. The English had a different tradition.
8. Holding streamers attached to the top of the Maypole, villagers danced around it enthusiastically.
9. Because May Day had pagan beginnings, the Puritans disapproved of it.
10. Thus Oliver Cromwell suppressed it after the overthrow of Charles I.

Exercise 30-3:

1. Many new collectors express amazement at the number of stamps to be collected.

2. They get excited about each new stamp they acquire.
3. They hope to make their collections complete.
4. Soon it becomes clear that a complete collection is impossible.
5. Then they may take the pragmatic approach.
6. They confine their collections to one country, continent, or decade.
7. At that point, their collections will again provide great satisfaction.
8. It is a consensus that collecting stamps can be educational.
9. It can teach about history or geography.
10. Nevertheless, a new collector should not become discouraged by trying to collect too much.

Exercise 30-4A: Answers will vary.

In the 1980s the computerized, or digital, animation industry took off. Among the pioneering animation firms were Nelvana, founded in Toronto, and CINAR, founded in Montreal. These firms and others that supplied animated programming for television and films had many hits and won several awards. *Reboot*, the first TV series to be made entirely with computer graphics, came out of Vancouver in the early 1990s. At the same time, Vancouver's Vertigo Technology, Montreal's Softimage, and Toronto's AliasWavefront developed the cutting-edge software that models and animates digital images. These studios brought the Terminator to life—again and again—and put Forrest Gump into historic newsreels. Sheridan College and Algonquin College, both in Ontario, have highly regarded programs in animation. A writer in *Wired* magazine even called Sheridan "the Harvard of animation schools."

Exercise 30-4B: Answers will vary.

Auguste Escoffier was the most famous chef between 1880 and World War I. He was the leader of the culinary world of his day. Until then the best chefs were found in private homes. With Escoffier came an era of fine dining at restaurants to which the nobility and wealthy flocked. After Escoffier joined César Ritz, the luxury hotel owner, they worked together to attract such patrons as the Prince of Wales. Ritz made each guest feel personally welcome. Escoffier added the crowning touch by preparing dishes especially for guests. He created dishes for the prince and for celebrities in the entertainment world. He concocted *consommé favori de Sarah Bernhardt* for the actress. For an opera singer he created *poularde Adelina Patti*. Another singer was fortunate to have more than one dish named for her. When the Australian Nellie Melba sang in *Lohengrin*, Escoffier served *pêches melba*, a combination of poached peaches and vanilla ice cream. To commemorate the swans of *Lohengrin*, he served the dessert in an ice swan. Melba toast was created by Escoffier during one of Melba's periodic diets. Today although many people have not heard of Nellie Melba, they are familiar with melba toast. As a young army chef, Escoffier had to prepare horse meat and even rat meat to feed the troops. Obviously he left those days far behind him when he became the most renowned chef of his day.

Chapter 31: Coordination and Subordination

Exercise 31-1: Answers will vary.

1. Many Canadians made their fortunes as newspaper owners, and others bought newspapers after making their mark in other fields.

2. Reformer George Brown wanted to promote his political ideals, so he founded the *Globe* in 1844.
3. K. C. Irving of New Brunswick founded a huge industrial empire based on oil refining, transportation, and pulp and paper; later he added local newspapers to his holdings.
4. Conrad Black liked to tell how he started his newspaper empire with a small loan, but his wealthy family already had major business investments in other fields.
5. We should not forget other Canadian newspaper tycoons such as the Thomsons and the Beaverbrooks, nor should we ignore lesser-known mavericks like Margaret "Ma" Murray, owner of the *Bridge River-Lillooet News.*
6. The Trudeau government was concerned that newspaper ownership was becoming concentrated in too few hands, so in 1980 it set up a royal commission to study the problem.
7. Tom Kent was named head of the commission, for he had been a newspaper editor and adviser to prime ministers.
8. Kent recommended that the government limit the size of newspaper empires, or soon Canadians would all be reading the same opinions written by employees of a small number of wealthy men.
9. Little was done about the Kent Commission recommendations, and the newspaper empires continued to grow.
10. Kent did not know that his report would be ignored by the Trudeau government, nor could he have guessed that by the 1990s, Conrad Black would own the majority of Canada's daily newspapers.
11. Defenders of big newspaper chains say that size is a good thing, for only wealthy owners can afford the staff and resources to produce the best newspapers.
12. Some people also look back with nostalgia to the legendary days of the strong-willed newspaper boss, and they argue that we can find their counterparts today only among opinionated media tycoons.

Exercise 31-2:

1. A company in Toronto was one of the first ones to install a fragrancing unit in its office ventilation system, in order to control employee behaviour.
2. The company was careful about which fragrances it introduced into the workplace, because some fragrances rev people up, and some calm them down.
3. The scents were designed by Toronto-based Aromasphere, Inc., which created a time-release mechanism to send the scents directly into the work area.
4. Once Bodywise Ltd. in Great Britain received a patent for a fragrance, it began to market its scent, which contains androstenone, an ingredient of male sweat.
5. The scent was adopted by a US debt-collection agency after another agency in Australia reported that chronic debtors who receive scented letters were 17 percent more likely to pay than were those who received unscented letters.
6. Although researchers have recently discovered how much odour can influence behaviour, smell is still the least understood of the five senses.
7. Aromasphere's employees have been asked to keep logs of their moods while they are in the workplace.
8. Researchers have raised many concerns about trying to change human behaviour, for they feel that this kind of tampering may lead to too much control over employees.
9. Smells can have an effect on people who may be completely unaware of what is happening.

10. If employees are forewarned, however, that they will be exposed to mood-altering fragrances, they may protest against the introduction of the scents in the work-place.
11. Even psychiatric wards emit a scent that makes the patients calm.
12. International Flavors and Fragrances of New York, which is the world's largest manufacturer of artificial flavours and aromas, has developed many of the scents commonly used today.
13. It has even created a bagel scent, since bagels lose their aroma when they are kept in plexiglass.
14. There wasn't a true commercial interest in these products until researchers began to understand the anatomy of smell.
15. It turns out that olfactory signals travel to the limbic region of the brain, where hormones of the autonomic nervous system are regulated.

Exercise 31-3: Answers will vary.

1. Surfing the Internet can be very frustrating, but locating specific Web sites has gotten much easier.
   Surfing the Internet can be very frustrating, which is why it intimidates so many people.
2. Vacationing on the beach can be very dangerous, for too few people take the proper precautions to protect themselves from the sun.
   Vacationing on the beach can be very dangerous unless you protect yourself from the harmful rays of the sun.
3. Shovelling snow is wonderful exercise, yet many Canadians move to Florida to escape it.
   Shovelling snow is wonderful exercise, although it is dangerous for people with heart or back conditions.
4. Installing a light fixture can be very easy, but it can be quite difficult for someone with no electrical experience.
   Installing a light fixture can be very easy, provided that the installer is familiar with electrical outlets.
5. Near closing time, the line at the bank can be incredibly long, so it is best to get there earlier in the day.
   Near closing time, the line at the bank can be incredibly long, because many customers wait until the last minute to do their banking.
6. The cost of tuition keeps going up, but the amount of financial aid given to students remains the same.
   The cost of tuition that students have to pay keeps going up.
7. Training a dog can be a challenging task, but it can be done if you bring to the job a lot of patience and love.
   Even if you are a patient and loving owner, training a dog can be a challenging task.
8. Putting together a photo album of a vacation is a great activity, but it is difficult to find the time to do it
   Putting together a photo album of a vacation is a great activity once the vacation itself is over.
9. Cookbooks can be very intimidating to a beginner, for the recipes usually call for unfamiliar ingredients.
   Cookbooks can be very intimidating to a beginner if they use unfamiliar cooking terms and ingredients.

10. Photography is a competitive profession, so you have to be really committed if you want to try to make a living at it.
    Photography is a competitive profession that takes years of practice to master.

Exercise 31-4: Answers will vary.

Senet is a game that was played by ancient Egyptians. Because it was very popular, Egyptians began putting senet boards into tombs as early as 3100 BC. Tomb objects were intended for use in the afterlife, yet they give us a good idea of daily life.

Many senet boards and playing pieces have been found in tombs, where the hot, dry air preserved them well. Tomb paintings frequently show people playing the game while hieroglyphic texts describe it. Because numerous descriptions of the game survive, Egyptologists think it was a national pastime.

Senet was a game for two people who played it on a board marked with thirty squares. Each player had several playing pieces. They probably each had seven, but the number did not matter as long as it was the same for both. Opponents moved by throwing flat sticks that were an early form of dice although sometimes they threw pairs of lamb knuckles instead. Players sat across from each other, and they moved their pieces in a backward S line. The squares represented houses through which they moved.

By the New Kingdom the game began to take on religious overtones. The thirty squares were given individual names, and they were seen as stages on the journey of the soul through the netherworld. When New Kingdom tomb paintings showed the deceased playing senet with an unseen opponent, the object was to win eternal life. The living still played the game, but they played it in anticipation of the supernatural match to come.

Chapter 32: Parallelism

Exercise 32-1:

1. exploration, travel
2. proud, evil
3. he had made plans for a helicopter, he made plans for an underwater ship
4. designed by a British mathematician, built by a Dutch inventor
5. designed in 1578, built in 1620, tested from 1620 to 24
6. on the surface, below the surface
7. boarded the submarine, took a short ride
8. the talk of the town, the focus of scientific investigation
9. When the vessel was to submerge, the bags would fill with water and pull the ship downward; when the vessel was to rise, a twisting rod would force water from the bags and the lightened ship would surface
10. designed, built
11. sneak up on British warships, attach explosives to their hulls
12. launching, steering
13. small four-person ships called "Davids," a full-sized submarine called the *Hunley*
14. providing dependable power, steering to navigate
15. the development of the gasoline engine, the invention of the periscope

Exercise 32-2: Answers will vary.

1. Sometimes after a demanding day at work, it's relaxing to turn on the TV, lie down on the couch, and be entertained.

2. TV shows can be entertaining and informational.
3. Because there are more channels than ever before, channel surfing can be fun or frustrating.
4. Relaxing and interesting are ways some people describe TV viewing.
5. Others describe TV viewing as boring and stupid.
6. Those people claim that finding a good TV show is much more difficult than finding a bad one.
7. But the wonderful range of programs now available means that people of all ages and tastes can find something they want to watch on TV.
8. Like anything else, watching too much TV may cause physical and emotional problems.
9. Just be sure to balance TV viewing with physical activities such as walking or jogging.
10. Also be sure to balance TV viewing with mental activities such as reading or doing a puzzle.
11. It can be upsetting when your favourite TV show is scheduled while you are away from home either working or running errands.
12. However, many people are adept at recording the TV shows they want to watch or can't bear to miss.
13. TV is especially important for people who live in rural areas where live entertainment and sports events are rare.
14. These people can enjoy an evening at the Bell Centre or at Vancouver's Chan Centre for the Performing Arts in the quiet and comfort of their own homes.
15. In spite of what naysayers may think of TV, I would rather have one than not have one.

Chapter 33: Variety and Emphasis

Exercise 33-1: Answers will vary.

1. The first task is choosing a house plan.
2. To choose just the right plan among all the architectural styles and floor plans is difficult.
3. By talking to loan officers at different banks, people can get their finances in order.
4. Most people want to borrow from the bank that gives the lowest interest rate.
5. Every homeowner's dream come true is a contractor who is trustworthy and competent.
6. Once all the permits have been signed by city officials, it's time to begin building the house.
7. The homeowners get a little break as the contractor clears the lot and lays the foundation.
8. Choosing all the materials and colours to use in a new home is exciting and demanding for the homeowners.
9. Before the contractor calls and asks if they have their flooring, counters, cabinets, and paint colours picked out, people who are building a new home should do lots of shopping.
10. Stories people enjoy telling their friends are what went right, what changes they made, and what they would do differently if they could go back in time and build their house again.

Exercise 33-2A: Answers will vary. These are suggestions only.

1. The <u>little</u> children walk to school. (adjective)
   <u>Beause they live so close</u>, the children walk to school. (adverb clause)
   <u>Laughing and shouting</u>, the children walk to school. (participial phrase)
2. The shopkeepers open their stores <u>early</u>. (adverb)
   The shopkeepers, <u>who seem eager to do business</u>, open their stores. (adjective clause)
   <u>Daylight occurring earlier</u>, the shopkeepers open their stores. (absolute phrase)
3. People go shopping <u>in the morning</u>. (prepositional phrase)
   People go <u>grocery</u> shopping. (adjective)
   <u>Happily</u>, people go shopping. (adverb)
4. Delivery trucks are seen <u>holding up traffic</u>. (participial phrase)
   Delivery trucks are seen <u>frequently</u>. (adverb)
   Delivery trucks, <u>which are quite noisy</u>, are seen. (adjective clause)

5. Their cash registers ringing, the coffee shops are crowded. (absolute phrase)
Before 10:00 a.m., the coffee shops are crowded. (prepositional phrase)
The best coffee shops are crowded. (adjective)

Exercise 33-2B: Answers will vary.

1. The big celebration included a loud parade up Main Street.
2. The day being very hot, the crowd was dressed in shorts and thin shirts.
3. The mayor, who was the only one with the power, stopped traffic because he wanted to let the parade go on without interruption.
4. The young astronaut rode comfortably in an open car.
5. Because there was such a fuss, youngsters who had no interest in the space program tried to get autographs.
6. The parade having reached city hall, the mayor gave a long, boring speech.
7. When it was over, everyone cheered because a street fair was about to start.
8. The celebration ended with a fireworks display over the harbour.
9. Walking tiredly, everyone headed home.
10. Once the streets were empty, the street cleaners came out in two garbage trucks.

Exercise 33-3: Answers will vary.

1. With a new emphasis on teamwork and on trust in the workplace, managers hope that the shift in attitude will benefit their businesses.
2. Companies that are trying to make a difference are experimenting with group talks among employees, who discuss issues dealing with workers as individuals and as team members.
3. These talks are very helpful for managers and for the workers who are still with the company and have survived the massive cutbacks, and need a boost in morale.
4. These experimental groups also break down barriers in the workplace that tend to separate one department from another, taking away any feelings of teamwork and cooperation.
5. Teamwork is critical for companies that want to regain competitiveness, and these groups strive to remove obstacles that prevent communication and respect among workers, for teamwork is a necessary step in the right direction.

Chapter 34: Usage Glossary

Exercise 34-1: Answers will vary

Chapter 35: The Impact of Words

Exercise 35-1:

1. informal
2. medium or semiformal
3. formal
4. medium
5. medium or semiformal

Exercise 35-2A:

1. commanded
2. intact
3. overthrown
4. accuracy
5. foul or soiled
6. divided
7. dispersed
8. withheld
9. tall
10. restored
11. immoderate
12. suspend
13. capacity
14. donated
15. guffawed
16. praised
17. rewards
18. impolite
19. secretly
20. skin

Exercise 35-2B Answers will vary.

1. There was danger wherever the private investigator went.
   The skiers were in peril of being buried by the avalanche.
   College students who plagiarize hazard expulsion.
   The game-show contestant decided to risk everything for a chance to win a car.
2. His rich uncle left him $10 000.
   Wealthy people often travel to Europe to shop.
   Can we call a society affluent if all its wealth comes from exploiting oil deposits?
   The opulent mansion contained a private movie theatre and a large indoor pool.
3. The mayor agreed to speak at our meeting.
   Let's talk about where to go on vacation.
   The priest and the rabbi frequently converse about how to get better attendance at services.
   Academic discourse is sometimes confusing to students.
4. The philosophy course required students to think about their most deeply held convictions.
   Rational people reason out their differences without raising their voices.
   Take some time every day to reflect on your actions.
   Scientists speculate on the origins of life.
   The various departments deliberate today about the areas designated for smokers.
5. Having a cold made him irritable.
   Don't disagree with her; she's choleric.
   He's very touchy about his height.
   She always gets cranky if people don't do as she says.
   Ask the boss for an increase later; she's cross about the shipping delay.

Exercise 35-3A:

1. food
   sandwich
   cheese sandwich
   Swiss cheese on rye
2. business
   store
   department store
   The Bay
3. mail
   letter
   bill
   record club charges
4. clothing
   pants
   jeans
   stone-washed jeans
5. land
   islands
   tropical paradise
   Hawaii
6. book
   how-to book
   cookbook
   The Joy of Cooking

7. animal
   carnivore
   cat
   lion

8. entertainment
   television show
   satire
   The Royal Canadian Air Farce

9. art
   painting
   portrait
   The Blue Boy

10. sports
    track
    running
    100-metre dash

Exercise 35-3B:

1. Mustang
2. azaleas
3. sour
4. strode
5. Calgary, Alberta
6. your boyfriend
7. the unification of Italy
8. pigeon
9. accurate
10. the beef smuggler
11. sprained
12. a gold chain
13. grinding
14. difficult
15. considerate of
16. Tom Hanks's latest movie
17. scratched
18. in need of new plumbing and wiring
19. steady, well-paying
20. all her patients who smoke

Exercise 35-4:

1. man
2. edible
3. please
4. address
5. regardless
6. slacks
7. students
8. cars
9. motorcycle
10. dormitories, checked in

Exercise 35-5: Answers may vary.

1. Before I tried skydiving, I thought skydivers were out of their minds.
2. It seemed so bizarre.
3. But now that I've done it, I think it is a great experience.
4. The day of the jump, I was extremely excited.
5. My friends were very concerned on my account, though.
6. But then, they are less adventurous than I am.
7. I was feeling nauseated just before I jumped out of the airplane.
8. But it was phenomenal—I felt exhilarated.
9. It is much more fun than bungee-jumping, which happens far too quickly.
10. Skydiving is an extraordinary activity.

Exercise 35-6: Answers will vary.

Exercise 35-7: Answers will vary.

1. Once I began acting, I felt as though I were living in a fantastic dream.
2. Acting was as easy for me as playing is for a child.
3. I was always able to remember my lines.
4. Sometimes the famous lines I spoke filled me with awe.
5. On stage, I danced with the grace of a gazelle.

6. I sang as so sweetly and clearly that I made the audience cry.
7. I succeeded in getting every part I auditioned for.
8. The teachers, the students, and the students' parents all thought I was a phenomenal actor.
9. Being in a television commercial led to instant fame.
10. I made the product for the commercial seem like the most valuable object in the universe.
11. After that, my agent was so busy she needed a vacation every three months.
12. My schedule became a merry go round of public appearances.
13. During these public appearances, I signed autographs until my hand became as limp as a deflated balloon.
14. I soon learned that being rich and famous doesn't bring inner peace.
15. But my passion for acting continues to expand without bounds like the universe itself.

Exercise 35-8: Answers will vary.

1. The horse seemed to float past us, like a silken banner in the wind.
2. The shack stood off alone in the woods, looking like a pile of sticks.
3. XYZ sound like a dozen monkeys trapped in a garbage can.
4. Grease oozed off the fries onto the paper plate, creating an oil slick worthy of a shipwrecked tanker.
5. At 5:00 a.m. I was awoken by my alarm clock, sounding like the finale at the demolition derby.
6. Professor ABC drives his students like mules.
7. The salesman had a grin like the Cheshire cat's—and like the cat itself, the grin faded away when I said, "I'm not interested."
8. It was so hot that the pigeons were fanning themselves with tattered sheets from last week's newspapers.
9. The library books were so overdue that the records showing they had been charged out were written on parchment.
10. Her voice is so shrill it could shatter plexiglass.

Exercise 35-9A: Answers will vary.

1. After falling off her bicycle, the child bruised her knee.
2. Drivers should fasten their seat belts before starting their cars.
3. Although she was pregnant, she continued to fulfill her responsibilities at home and at work.
4. The city street cleaners are on strike.
5. The dean has asked department heads to confer with him.

Exercise 35-9B: Answers will vary.

Chapter 36: Spelling

Exercise 36-1:

1. bitten
2. framed
3. management
4. foreign
5. dining
6. incredible
7. jumping
8. leisure
9. reluctantly
10. dissatisfied
11. courageous
12. laid
13. trapped
14. used
15. illegible
16. magically
17. permanent
18. proceeds
19. reliable
20. paid

21. believed
22. interaction
23. inventories
24. leaves
25. profitable

Exercise 36-2:

1. oranges
2. kisses
3. strays
4. lives
5. radios
6. pairs
7. speeches
8. flies
9. monkeys
10. pianos
11. mothers-in-law
12. data
13. ice skates
14. themselves
15. echoes
16. halves
17. children
18. women
19. phenomena
20. mice

Exercise 36-3A:

1. motivation
2. guidance
3. noticeable
4. graceful
5. truly
6. accurately
7. mileage
8. argument
9. driving
10. outrageous

Drop the final *e* before a suffix beginning with a vowel, but keep it if the suffix begins with a consonant. (Note that numbers 3, 5, 7, 9, 10 are exceptions.)

Exercise 36-3B:

1. dutiful
2. playing
3. drier
4. supplied
5. noisiest
6. strayed
7. sloppier
8. gravies
9. happiness
10. buying

If the final *y* is preceded by a consonant, change the *y* to *i* before adding a suffix, unless the suffix begins with *i*. If the final *y* is preceded by a vowel, retain the *y*.

Exercise 36-3C:

1. gripping
2. mendable
3. steamed
4. beginner
5. planting
6. stopper
7. poured
8. splitting
9. occurrence
10. reference

If a one-syllable word ends in a consonant preceded by a single vowel, double the final consonant before adding a suffix. With two-syllable words, double the final consonant if the last syllable of the stem is accented. US spelling doubles the final consonant *only* if the last syllable is accented; Canadian spelling doubles the final consonant in many other words as well, such as *travel, travelling; worship, worshipper.*

Exercise 36-4:

1. believe
2. receive
3. neither
4. ceiling
5. foreign
6. field

7. counterfeit
8. weird
9. freight
10. niece

Exercise 36-5: Answers will vary.

1. The show doesn't start for an hour, but the theatre is already crowded.
   I am all ready to begin my vacation.
2. The city is about to celebrate its 300th anniversary.
   It's too late to enroll in any new classes this semester.
3. Overnight delivery costs more than regular mail.
   He finished dinner, then he read the paper.
4. They're my cousins.
   Their flight came in two hours late.
   There is a new shopping centre just down the road.
5. My parents are going to Mexico for their anniversary.
   I have two tickets for the symphony.
   The bridegroom was too nervous to eat breakfast.
6. How many rooms does your apartment have?
   You're going to fail the exam if you don't study.
7. All the students passed the test.
   One should learn from the past but not dwell on it.
8. The library is a quiet place to work.
   My brother is quite a ladies' man.
9. Blood flows through our veins and arteries.
   The pitcher threw the ball past the catcher.
   The police were very thorough in their search for clues.
10. Whose car keys are these?
    I don't know who's going, do you?

Exercise 36-6:

1. you're / to
2. Weather / rain / affect
3. clothes / wear / where
4. Buy / weigh / too / which
5. waste
6. stationery / write / diary
7. country / all ready
8. course / board / plane
9. personnel / assistance
10. aisle / breathe / ascent / descent
11. effect / your
12. whole
13. capital / desert / dominate
14. It's / meet / where
15. human / hear / through / seen / sights
16. presence / there / already
17. counsel / may be
18. ensure
19. alter / fares
20. break / buy / presents
21. piece / advice
22. stationary / quite / bored
23. patience
24. sense / scene
25. passed / conscious / principle

Exercise 36-7:

1. open-heart surgery
2. free-for-all
3. high school
4. pear-shaped
5. birdhouse
6. accident-prone
7. pothole
8. bathing suit
9. breadwinner
10. handmade
11. headache
12. head cold
13. headphone
14. head-to-head
15. headstone
16. free agent
17. freehand
18. free-form
19. free-spoken
20. freestyle

Chapter 37: Periods, Question Marks, and Exclamation Points

Exercise 37-1A:

1. operating?
2. purity.
3. correct
4. 1914.
5. disgusting.
6. blood.
7. green.
8. correct
9. blue-grey.
10. again?
11. does?
12. not!
13. students.

Exercise 37-1B:

Do you know who Theodor Seuss Geisel was? Sure you do. He was Dr. Seuss, the famous author of children's books. After ten years as a successful advertising illustrator and cartoonist, Seuss managed to get his first children's book published. *And to Think That I Saw It on Mulberry Street* was published in 1937 by Vanguard Press. It had been rejected by 27 other publishers. I wonder why. They certainly were foolish! What is your favourite Dr. Seuss book? Mine is *The Cat in the Hat*, published in 1957. Everyone has a favourite. And I do mean *everyone!* His books have been translated into 17 languages, and by 1984 more than a hundred million copies had been sold worldwide. In fact, in 1984 Seuss received a Pulitzer Prize for his years of educating and entertaining children. How fitting! Sadly Dr. Seuss died in 1991. We will all miss him.

Exercise 37-2: Answers will vary.

1. The doctor asked me what was wrong.
2. Please close the door.
3. How much does the piano weigh?
4. Dr. Jones specialized in delivering twins.
5. Oscar Wilde said, "To love oneself is the beginning of a lifelong romance."
6. Wow!
7. Eggs are a good source of protein.
8. Sit down!
9. He asked, "What time does the train reach Montreal?"
10. The shoemaker said that my boots would be ready tomorrow.
11. When I saw my birthday present, all I could say was "Great!"

Chapter 38: Commas

Exercise 38-1A:

1. . . . along, and . . .
2. . . . however, and . . .
3. . . . plasmodium, for . . .
4. . . . correct
5. . . . direction, and . . .
6. . . . colours, but . . .
7. correct
8. correct

9. . . . wood, yet . . .
10. . . . water, so . . .
11. . . . sporangia, and . . .
12. correct
13. . . . sporangia, and . . .
14. . . . ground, or . . .

Exercise 38-1B:

1. Some, however, leave the forest, and they live on cultivated plants.
2. They can cause clubroot of cabbage, or they can create powdery scab of potato.
3. Slime moulds sound disagreeable, yet some are quite attractive.
4. One form produces unappealing stalks, but the stalks are topped with tiny balls.
5. The balls appear to be woven, so they look rather like baskets.
6. The woven balls are really sporangia, and they contain spores for distribution.
7. Another form looks like tiny ghosts, for its white moulds could be small sheeted figures.
8. Serpent slime mould is yellow, and it can look like a miniature snake on top of a decaying log.
9. One would have to work hard to find it in on the Prairies, for it is most common in the tropics.
10. After one learns about slime moulds, they no longer seem disgusting, nor do they even seem disagreeable.

Exercise 38-2A:

1. In fact, it is the largest continuous body of sand in the world.
2. Extending over 650 000 square kilometres, the Rub al-Khali . . .
3. As a point of comparison, Saskatchewan is just slightly larger.
4. Because it is almost completely devoid of rain, the Rub al-Khali . . .
5. Despite the existence of a few scattered shrubs, the desert is largely a sand sea.
6. However, its eastern side develops massive dunes with salt basins.
7. Except for the hardy Bedouins, the Rub al-Khali is uninhabited.
8. Indeed, it is considered one of the most forbidding places on earth.
9. Until Bertram Thomas crossed it in 1931, it was unexplored by outsiders.
10. Even after oil was discovered in Arabia, exploration . . .
11. correct
12. To facilitate exploration, huge sand tires were developed in the 1950s.
13. Shortly thereafter, drilling rigs began operating in the Rub al-Khali.
14. correct
15. As it turns out, the Empty Quarter is not so empty after all.

Exercise 38-2B:

[1]As might be expected, the Rub al-Khali is hot all year round. [2]In contrast, the Gobi Desert is hot in the summer but extremely cold in the winter. [3]Located in China and Mongolia, the Gobi Desert is twice the size of Saskatchewan. [4]Unlike the Rub al-Khali, the Gobi has some permanent settlers. [5]Nevertheless, most of its inhabitants are nomadic. [6]To avoid the subzero winters, the nomads move their herds at the end of summer. [7]When the harsh winters subside, they return to the sparse desert vegetation.

Exercise 38-3A:

1. The vicuna, the smallest member of the camel family, lives in the mountains of Ecuador, Bolivia, and Peru.
2. The guanaco is the wild, humpless ancestor of the llama and the alpaca.
3. The llama stands 1.25 metres tall, is about 1.25 metres long, and is the largest of the South American camels.

4. A llama's coat may be <u>white</u>, <u>brown</u>, <u>black</u>, or <u>shades</u> in between.
5. Indians of the Andes use llamas <u>to carry loads</u>, <u>to bear wool</u>, and <u>to produce meat.</u>
6. Llamas are foraging animals that live on <u>lichens</u>, <u>shrubs</u>, and <u>other available plants</u>.
7. Because they can go without water for weeks, llamas are <u>economical</u>, <u>practical</u> pack animals.
8. The alpaca has a <u>longer</u>, <u>lower</u> body than the llama.
9. It has wool <u>of greater length</u>, <u>of higher quality</u>, and <u>of superior softness</u>.
10. Alpaca wool is <u>straighter</u>, <u>finer</u>, and <u>warmer</u> than sheep's wool.

Exercise 38-3B:

1. I like to spend those holidays with relatives because I like my relatives, I rarely get other chances to see them, and I enjoy their company.
2. My favourite fast foods are hot dogs, hamburgers, and pizza.
3. Swimming, hiking, reading, and sleeping are my preferred vacation activities.
4. My new puppy is a soft, silky cocker spaniel.
5. I found *The Sweet Hereafter* moody, mysterious, and mesmerizing.
6. The groom found rice in his hair, in his ears, and in his shoes.
7. John lifts weights, does pushups, and uses a treadmill.
8. John is developing a sleek, streamlined physique as a result of working out.

Exercise 38-4:

1. correct
2. The dances, both solos and ensembles, express emotion or tell a story.
3. correct
4. A ballet's steps, called its choreography, become standardized over many years of performance.
5. correct
6. The steps, all with French names, combine solos and groups.
7. The *corps de ballet*, the ballet company excluding its star soloists, may dance together or in small ensembles.
8. One soloist may join another for a *pas de deux*, a dance for two.
9. Ensemble members, not just soloists, must be proficient at *pliés* and *arabesques.*
10. correct
11. It is important, therefore, to start lessons early.
12. In Russia, which has some of the most stringent ballet training, students begin at age three.

Exercise 38-5: Answers will vary.

1. My neighbours across the street are kind..
   My neighbours, who have known each other a long time, are kind.
2. They help one another in many ways.
   They help one another, which surprises some people.
3. They are friendly to strangers who approach them.
   They are friendly to strangers, waving or calling hello.
4. The houses and yards on my street are well kept.
   The houses and yards are well kept, which makes the neighbourhood pleasant.
5. Trees that are well maintained line the streets.
   Old maple trees, which were planted more than fifty years ago, line the streets.
6. Many of the neighbourhood families with children have pets.
   Many of the neighbourhood families, who seem to love animals, have pets.
7. The pets that I like best are friendly.
   The pets, mostly cats and small dogs, are friendly.

8. The park that the neighbourhood residents help to maintain is one street away.
   The park, which is the size of ten city blocks, is one street away.
9. The park has a playground that meets all safety requirements.
   The park has a playground, which has swings and slides.
10. The neighbourhood children whose parents let them go out after dinner play in the park.
   The neighbourhood children play in the park, which closes at sundown.

Exercise 38-6:

1. George Sand was most accurate when she said, "Life in common among those people who love each other is the ideal of happiness."
2. "I find that I have painted my life—things happening in my life—without knowing," said the wise Georgia O'Keeffe.
3. "I slept and dreamed that life was beauty," said Ellen Sturgis Hooper. "I woke—and found that life was duty."
4. In passing, a professor said to a student, "Life, dear friend, is short, but sweet."
5. "Life's a tough proposition," declared Wilson Mizner, "and the first hundred years are the hardest."
6. "Life," said Forrest Gump, "is like a box of chocolates: You never know what you're going to get."
7. "That it will never come again is what makes life so sweet," observed Emily Dickinson.
8. "May you live all the days of your life," advised Jonathan Swift.
9. William Cooper was right when he said, "Variety's the spice of life."
10. "Live all you can; it's a mistake not to," said Henry James.

Exercise 38-7:

1. correct (6,000 is also possible)
2. correct
3. The life-sized warriors and horses had been buried for 2200 years.
4. The figures were in a huge tomb near the city of Xian, China.
5. Archaeologists also unearthed almost 10 000 artifacts from the excavation site. (10,000 is also possible)
6. It did not take John Doe, Ph.D., to realize that this was an extraordinary find.
7. Some of the figures were displayed in Quebec City, Quebec, nearly thirty years later.
8. correct
9. correct
10. To get tickets, one could write Musée de la Civilisation, 85 Dalhousie Street, Quebec City, Quebec, G1K 7A6.

Exercise 38-8A:

1. One was the statue of Olympian Zeus, which was covered with precious stones.
2. Unfortunately, it was taken to Constantinople in A.D. 576 and there destroyed by fire.
3. The Hanging Gardens of Babylon, built for Nebuchadnezzar, were considered a wonder.
4. correct
5. To lift water from the Euphrates, slaves had to work in shifts.
6. The Colossus of Rhodes was a huge, impressive statue built to honour the sun god Helios.
7. Constructed near the harbour, it was intended to astonish all who saw it.
8. Another wonder was the lighthouse at Alexandria, Egypt.

9. Because it stood on the island of Pharos, the word *pharos* has come to mean lighthouse.
10. After the death of Mausolus, king of Caria, his widow erected a richly adorned monument to honour him.
11. With sculptures by famous artists, the Mausoleum at Halicarnassus amazed the ancient world.
12. The Temple of Artemis at Ephesus, an important Ionian city, was also considered a wonder.
13. It was burned, rebuilt, and burned again.
14. Some wonders, such as the Colossus and the Mausoleum, were destroyed by earthquakes.
15. Of the seven works that astounded the ancients, only the pyramids of Egypt survive.

Exercise 38-8B:

[1]St. Andrews, Scotland, is an old city. [2]Named for a Christian saint, the city was once an object of devout pilgrimage. [3]Its cathedral, the largest in Scotland, is now a ruin. [4]It was destroyed in 1559 by followers of the reformer John Knox. [5]All the revered, carefully preserved relics of St. Andrew disappeared. [6]Although the castle of St. Andrews also lies in ruins, it preserves two fascinating remnants of medieval history. [7]One is a bottle-shaped dungeon, and the other is a countermine. [8]When attackers tried to mine under castle walls, defenders tried to intercept the tunnel with a countermine. [9]Interestingly, one can actually enter both mine and countermine. [10]The University of St. Andrews, which is the oldest university in Scotland, was established in 1412. [11]From all parts of the globe, students come to study there. [12]Nevertheless, most people who think of St. Andrews associate it with golf. [13]Even golf at St. Andrews is old, the first reference dating to January 25, 1552. [14]The famous Old Course is only one of four courses from which the avid golfer may choose. [15]St. Andrews is still an object of pilgrimage, but today's pilgrims come with drivers, wedges, and putters.

Exercise 38-9:

[1]Originally a slightly offbeat country singer, k.d. lang has continued to push the boundaries. [2]Kathryn Dawn Lang, born in 1961 in Consort, Alberta, made her mark by bringing a punk sensibility to the interpretation of the songs of the U.S. country star Patsy Cline. [3]After joining with fiddler, guitarist, and composer Ben Mink in 1985, lang began to show her full range of tonality and emotion. [4]Since then, the two of them, and especially lang, have won several major recording awards. [5]A brave public figure, lang was not afraid to reveal her sexual orientation when most gay performers were still keeping their sexuality a secret. [6]Further, she did not hesitate to proclaim her vegetarianism in Alberta's ranching country. [7]Following her surprising collaboration with aging jazz singer Tony Bennett, lang took yet another direction. [8]In summer 2004, she released an album of Canadian folk and popular music standards, *Hymns of the 49th Parallel.* [9]This intensely personal project allowed lang to reveal new depths in her vocal style and even in the meaning of the songs, which include well-known pieces by Leonard Cohen, Joni Mitchell, Neil Young, Jane Siberry, and others.

Exercise 38-10:

Money, in terms of its value, is really a matter of trust and confidence in the government. By definition, money is anything that a society accepts as having value. With such a broad definition, it is not surprising that money has, throughout history, taken on some forms that were both creative and unique. Precious stones, fish hooks, nails, livestock, throwing knives, and axe-heads are just a few examples of money that is equivalent to ours today. In a successful society, money must serve three basic functions: It must serve as a store of wealth, a medium of exchange, and a unit against which items are valued. Forms of money must be portable, easy to store, durable, and relatively hard to acquire. Successful forms of money, like gold and silver, have all these properties. However, trust is also necessary in a society, such as ours, that uses paper money. Although the paper itself is of little value, we trust that a bill is worth the number printed on the front of it.

Chapter 39: Semicolons

Exercise 39-1A:

1. The sclera is the outer cover of the eye; it helps . . .
2. The choroid is just inside the sclera; it keeps . . .
3. The pupil is the opening in the eye; this is where . . .
4. The cornea is the clear cover of the pupil; therefore . . .
5. The pupil is opened or closed by muscles in the iris; in fact, in bright light the iris closes to decrease the amount of light entering; in low light . . .
6. correct
7. The retina contains cells, cones, and rods, which are outgrowths of the brain; when light . . .
8. The optic nerve connects the eye to the brain; thus . . .
9. Cone cells give us colour vision; they . . .
10. Rods are sensitive to low light; they . . .

Exercise 39-1B: Semicolons appear in the following lines.

line 1	Hearing is based on sound waves; these are . . .
lines 2–3	ripples on water; like ripples . . .
line 5	Pitch is the number of wave vibrations per second; it . . .
lines 6–7	waves; this is called . . .
line 9	130 decibels is painful; however, people . . .
line 10	Timbre is hard to describe in everyday language; in physics terms . . .
line 15	as too many unrelated frequencies vibrating together; nevertheless . . .

Exercise 39-2:

1. Colourblindness is inherited; it appears . . .
2. The most common colourblindness is the inability to tell red from green; but more . . .
3. Different colours, the result of differences in light wavelengths, create a spectrum; the spectrum . . .
4. People who are severely red-green colourblind cannot "see" any colours at that end of the spectrum; that is, they cannot . . .
5. Colourblindness varies from person to person; people . . .
6. Some people have no cone cells (the cells that send signals about colour to the brain), so they . . .
7. They have achromatism, a rare condition.
8. Such people can see only black, white, and greys; what . . .
9. However, their problem is much more serious than this; they also have . . .
10. The part of the eye that usually receives images is the fovea, which contains the cone cells; achromatics' . . .

11. To compensate, they look at objects off centre, to pick . . .
12. It is possible to be colourblind and not know it; how . . .
13. There are several tests for colourblindness; most involve seeing (or not seeing) a number or word written on a background of a complementary colour, for example . . .

Chapter 40: Colons

Exercise 40-1:

1. People believe that Napoleon was short, but he was average height: 5'6".
2. . . . US males; three favourite freetime activities are as follows: eating . . .
3. correct
4. . . . these are the most common street names in Canada: Queen . . .
5. . . . *Burrowing: The Adventures of a Bookworm.*
6. The train, 20 minutes late, was due at 6:40.
7. . . . what we were fearing: "I forgot . . ."
8. . . . remember one thing: Be alert!
9. The nineteenth century was a bad time for Turkey: It lost . . .
10. . . . those that do include the following: polar bears . . .

Exercise 40-2: Answers will vary.

1. *Parallel Lives: Five Victorian Marriages*
2. My favourite classes are as follows: English, Drama, and History.
3. Here is some advice about what to do when you go on a job interview: Don't be afraid to tell what you can do, but don't brag needlessly.
4. The star players on the X are these: a, b, c, and d.
5. The University of British Columbia has a large campus bordered by public streets, and most notably by a nature preserve and an arm of the Pacific Ocean: the University Endowment Lands and the Strait of Georgia.

Chapter 41: Apostrophes

Exercise 41-1:

	singular possessive	plural possessive
1.	sheep's	sheep's
2.	pony's	ponies'
3.	turkey's	turkeys'
4.	lion's	lions'
5.	mouse's	mice's
6.	her	their
7.	gorilla's	gorillas'
8.	goose's	geese's
9.	gnu's	gnus'
10.	ox's	oxen's
11.	your	your
	singular possessive	plural possessive
12.	buffalo's	buffalos'
13.	zebra's	zebras'
14.	ibex's	ibexes'

15. fly's	flies'
16. my	our
17. giraffe's	giraffes'
18. dodo's	dodos'
19. zoo's	zoos'
20. zoo keeper's	zoo keepers'
21. his	their
22. farm's	farms'
23. farmer's	farmers'
24. ranch's	ranches'
25. its	their

Exercise 41-2:

1. a day's work
2. a dollar's worth
3. a horse's hooves
4. the horses' hooves
5. nobody's business
6. the lion's share
7. the cat's meow
8. the bodybuilder's weights
9. the neighbour's mail
10. the neighbours' mail
11. the boss's laptop (the boss' laptop is also acceptable)
12. my sister-in-law's anniversary

Exercise 41-3:

1. aren't
2. won't
3. let's
4. he'd
5. wasn't
6. you'd
7. didn't
8. I'll
9. what's
10. I'm
11. isn't
12. wouldn't
13. can't
14. doesn't
15. I've
16. you're
17. there's
18. we'd
19. weren't
20. they're
21. it's
22. we've
23. she'll
24. we're
25. don't

Exercise 41-4:

1. Poe's
2. correct
3. author's
4. Dupin's
5. didn't
6. public's, hero's
7. weren't
8. '66
9. correct
10. Collins's
11. book's, wasn't
12. *The Moonstone's*, public's
13. Collins's
14. one's
15. It's
16. Doyle's
17. Holmes's
18. People's
19. Holmes's
20. readers'
21. Holmes's
22. couldn't

Chapter 42: Quotation Marks

Exercise 42-1:

1. According to Chesterfield, "Advice is seldom welcome."
2. "If you are looking for trouble, offer some good advice," says Herbert V. Prochnow.
3. Marie Dressler was right: "No vice is so bad as advice."
4. Someone once remarked, "How we do admire the wisdom of those who come to us for advice!"
5. "Free advice," it has been noted, "is the kind that costs you nothing unless you act upon it."
6. correct
7. "I sometimes give myself admirable advice," said Lady Mary Wortley Montagu, "but I am incapable of taking it."
8. Says Tom Masson, "'Be yourself!' is the worst advice you can give to some people."
9. The Beatles' song "With a Little Help from My Friends" contains some good advice.
10. correct
11. My uncle advised me, "The next time you are depressed, read Lewis Carroll's poem 'Jabberwocky.'"
12. Do you recall the Beach Boys' words: "Be true to your school"?
13. correct
14. However, comedian Phyllis Diller suggests, "Never go to bed mad. Stay up and fight."
15. Rachel Carson advised, "The discipline of the writer is to learn to be still and listen to what his subject has to tell him."
16. correct

Exercise 42-2: Answers may vary slightly.

1. She said, "The committee has received an anonymous donation."
2. "The donation is $5000," she said.
3. "The big problem," she concluded, "is deciding how to spend the money to help the community."
4. The treasurer suggested, "Let's use the money to repair town hall."
5. Someone shouted, "That's stupid!"
6. After much discussion, the committee agreed and the minutes read, "The money will be used to make the library handicapped-accessible."

Exercise 42-3: Answers will vary.

Chapter 43: Other Punctuation Marks

Exercise 43-1: Answers may vary slightly.

1. Niagara Falls is not the tallest waterfall in Canada—Della Falls, British Columbia, is.
2. The next tallest waterfalls are (2) Takakkaw Falls, British Columbia, (3) Hunley Falls, British Columbia, and (4) Panther Falls, Alberta.
3. Niagara Falls is relatively low—it stands about one-seventh the height of Della Falls.
4. Greenland (the largest island in the world) was given . . .
5. The name was a masterstroke of publicity—convincing . . .
6. Let's go to Québec for Carniv—Oops! . . .
7. The most expensive part of a trip—the airfare—can be reduced . . .

8. . . . "the winner must appear to claim his/her prize in person."
9. "Broadway [my favourite street] is a . . .
10. "Too often travel . . . merely lengthens the conversation,". . . (Note that you have the option of enclosing the ellipsis in brackets, according to MLA style.)
11. Northern Ontraio [sic] has . . .
12. . . . he/she will always want to return.
13. I can only say one thing about camping—I hate it.
14. We leave as soon as—Have you seen the bug spray?—we finish packing.
15. "Let's take Highway 69 across—" "Are you crazy?"
16. Finding an inexpensive hotel/motel isn't always easy.
17. Motels (named for a combination of *motorist* and *hotel*) . . .
18. When travelling, always remember to (a) leave a schedule with friends, (b) carry as little cash as possible, and (c) use the hotel safe for valuables.

Exercise 43-2A: Answers will vary.

The cheetah is the fastest animal on earth. It can accelerate from 1.6 kilometres an hour to 65 kilometres an hour in under two seconds, briefly reaching speeds of up to 110 kilometres an hour. Its stride may, during these bursts of speed, be as much as 7 metres. To help it run at these speeds, the cheetah is built unlike any of the other large cats: powerful heart; oversized liver; long, thin leg bones; relatively small teeth; and a muscular tail used for balance. Unlike other cats, it cannot pull in its claws. They are blunted by constant contact with the earth, and so are of little use in the hunt. The cheetah, instead, makes use of a strong dewclaw on the inside of its front legs to grab and hold down prey.

Exercise 43-2B: Answers will vary.

Have you ever built an inukshuk? If you have, you may be among the countless people to have borrowed this ancient Inuit symbol, using it for some purpose of your own. Corporations, government agencies, and Vancouver's Olympic Committee have used it. A communications network that, when it was founded, actually excluded the home of the inukshuk—Nunavut and the Northwest Territories—from its reach calls itself Inukshuk. Drivers on country highways encounter hundreds of these simple constructions, stones (flat ones are normally used) that are piled up to resemble a human form with arms extended. Sometimes, these appear to be an eco-friendly alternative to roadside graffiti in southern Canada. For the people of the far north, however, the inukshuk's purpose is a practical one: to serve as a landmark for travellers and hunters on the featureless tundra. Traditionally, it can also do the following things: mark hunting and fishing spots; indicate navigable channels and waterways; and simply proclaim one's presence on the land. The CBC's Historica Minutes (named after the educational foundation that provides the funding for these 60-second TV and radio spots) include a vignette about an injured mountie in the 1930s. The scene is the far north; the mountie is being cared for by a group of Inuit. He puzzles over the thing they build out of boulders as they prepare to move on to a new encampment. A boy explains: "Now the people will know we were here."

Exercise 43-3:

1. sleep/less
2. slend•der/ize
3. ref•er/ee
4. phlegm
5. pal/ate
6. mus•cle-/bound
7. in•de/cent
8. Hol•ly/wood
9. ex•pi•ra/tion
10. echo
11. cuck•oo
12. cough

13. butte
14. av•o/ca•do
15. av•oir/du•pois or av•oir•du/pois
16. loose
17. cat/tail
18. en•rol
19. grouch
20. pro/gress•ing
21. sleeve
22. sap/suck•er
23. Pol•y/ne•sia
24. pal/ace
25. non/res•i•dent
26. in/crease
27. how/ev•er
28. ges/tic•u•late, ges•tic/u•late, or ges•tic•u/late
29. e•merge
30. cu•bic
31. col•our/less
32. care/tak•er
33. but•ter/milk
34. a•wait
35. ant/ac•id
36. moth•er-/in-•law or moth•er-•in/law
37. trous/seau
38. midg•et
39. con•trol/ling
40. far/ther

Chapter 44: Capitals, Italics, Abbreviations, and Numbers

Exercise 44-1A:

1. Prime Minister Laurier
2. God's love
3. the Board of Broadcast Governors
4. a meeting on Friday
5. my Aunt Clara
6. when I graduate
7. the Musical Ride
8. Mother Teresa
9. dinner at the Steak Palace
10. English 202
11. across Main Street
12. the Edmonton Oilers
13. the Group of Seven
14. a town in the West
15. a college in British Columbia
16. "The Gift of the Magi"
17. learning French
18. Victoria Township Medical Centre
19. the moon and Venus shining in the sky
20. the St. Lawrence River

Exercise 44-1B:

1. The spring semester starts in February.
2. They live ten kilometres north of Elm Street.
3. The hotel has 450 rooms.
4. Green, the ambassador, had a meeting with Foreign Minister Ramirez.
5. I want to visit Lake Louise to go skiing.
6. The Bible is full of great adventures.
7. They plan to open an Italian restaurant downtown.
8. The New Democratic Party believes in the democratic system.
9. correct

10. Springfield High School has a large PTA.
11. Texans will always remember the Alamo.
12. Travelling around the cape of Good Hope is dangerous.
13. Rembrandt's "Aristotle Contemplating the Bust of Homer" is one of his best known paintings.
14. The Manitoba Theatre Centre is in Winnipeg.
15. Tickets to the Grey Cup were not available at the stadium.

Exercise 44-2A:

1. b. War and Peace
2. b. The Rick Mercer Report
3. a. London Free Press
4. b. The Queen Elizabeth II
5. b. The USS Enterprise
6. a. We are Homo sapiens.
7. b. nota bene
8. a. Many words have the common root, cycle.
9. b. Never tease a hungry crocodile.
10. a. The Orient Express was the setting of a famous mystery novel.

Exercise 44-2B:

1. The word cool has many meanings.
2. The new hospital is shaped like the letter H.
3. Scientifically, the chimpanzee is called Pan troglodytes and the gorilla is Gorilla gorilla.
4. You bought us tickets to see Les Misérables? Merci beaucoup.
5. The HMS Bounty was a real ship.
6. The troubles of its crew are told in the book Mutiny on the Bounty.
7. correct
8. Clifford Sifton, a key member of Prime Minister Laurier's cabinet, was the owner of an important newspaper, the Manitoba Free Press.
9. correct
10. Years later, the Hollywood movie Rose Marie (1936), with its singing Mounties and maidens, also publicized the Canadian Prairies.

Exercise 44-3A:

1. The Chang brothers are opening a fishing charter company.
2. They have leased a wharf on the western shore of Vancouver Island.
3. At the aquarium we saw giant tortoises that were more than 100 years old.
4. Easter always falls on the Sunday following the first full moon in spring—either in March or in April.
5. What did you get for Christmas?
6. Everyone ought to know the story of William Lyon MacKenzie King, tenth prime minister of Canada.
7. He is mentioned in my textbook on the history of political science and economy, and in my other textbook covering World War II.
8. The professor says the midterm will cover chapters 1 through 5.
9. The midterm and the final each count 40 percent.
10. The quarterback picked up 160 yards in passing in the first half.
11. Some people will do anything for a few dollars.
12. A kilogram equals 2.2 pounds.

13. The counsellor had an MSW (or Master of Social Work) degree from the University of British Columbia.
14. She had put herself through school working as an assistant manager in a fast food restaurant.
15. Mr. and Mrs. McDonald live on Maple Avenue in Corner Brook, Newfoundland.

Exercise 44-3B:

1. 2:00 A.M. *or* 2:00 a.m.
2. $30 000
3. Dr. Jones
4. Bill Smith, CA,
5. A.D. 1642
6. 1919
7. Mr. and Mrs. Grossman
8. NASA
9. correct *or* his OK
10. SCUBA gear

Exercise 44-4:

1. There are 107 women . . .
2. Ten years ago there were only forty-seven. (Note: A case could be made for "47," as this is a precise discussion involving numerous figures.)
3. One-third of the faculty is female now compared with one-tenth then.
4. ... $900 for two rooms, $1400 for three rooms, and $1850 for four rooms.
5. correct *or* . . . September 14.
6. . . . June 1, 2012.
7. correct
8. . . . to drink one-and-a-half litres of coffee a day over the next three years. (Note: "1.5 litres" is also correct.)
9. correct *or* . . . 29 percent.
10. correct *or* . . . 15 Clark Street.

Exercise 44-5:

1. thirty-five
2. one-half
3. four-fifths
4. one hundred one (*or* one hundred and one)
5. first
6. three thousand four hundred fifty-seven (*or* three thousand four hundred and fifty-seven)
7. four hundred ninety-five (*or* four hundred and ninety-five)

Chapter 47: Singulars and Plurals

Exercise 47-1:

	Noncount	Count	Plural
1.	advice	——	——
2.	——	book	books
3.	——	calculator	calculators
4.	chocolate	chocolate	chocolates
5.	——	desk	desks
6.	——	earring	earrings
7.	——	essay	essays
8.	——	experiment	experiments
9.	——	fern	ferns
10.	flour	——	——
11.	gold	——	——
12.	hair	hair	hair
13.	happiness	——	——
14.	homework	——	——
15.	honesty	——	——
16.	information	——	——
17.	jewellery	——	——
18.	——	library	libraries
19.	lightning	——	——
20.	——	man	men
21.	news	——	——
22.	——	novel	novels
23.	——	occupation	occupations
24.	paper	paper	papers
25.	——	paragraph	paragraphs
26.	physics	——	——
27.	pollution	——	——
28.	rain	rain	rains
29.	——	report	reports
30.	——	storm	storms
31.	time	time	times
32.	weather	——	——

Exercise 47-2:

1. Hikers with little money but much fortitude can begin the hike in Niagara Falls and continue to the Bruce Peninsula.
2. The 720-kilometre trail goes through many picturesque towns.
3. The trail passes cultivated farms and untamed wilderness.
4. The caves and cliffs of the Niagara Escarpment make the Bruce Trail one of the most interesting trails in Canada or the United States.
5. Few hikers have anything but praise for their experiences on the trail.
6. Many youngsters would gladly give up piano lessons or homework to be climbing wooded paths.
7. The Bruce Trail is one of the nation's treasures.

Chapter 48: Articles

Exercise 48-1:

According to some psychologists, 0 young children are actually more violent than teenagers, even though 0 most people assume that teenagers are the most violent age group. Further, 0 aggression in young children will almost certainly develop into a career of delinquency, if the aggression is not spotted and treated early on.

From 0 ancient philosophers, 0 religious thinkers, and the earliest Freudian psychologists we have inherited the idea that our violent impulses must be recognized and restrained. Freudians put the emphasis on the sublimation of our wildest impulses by our participation in civilization. In contrast, 0 moral philosophers and theologians advise us to learn the virtues of 0 patience, 0 piety, and 0 self-control.

A team of researchers at the University of Montreal who study 0 human aggression insist that the evolutionary struggle holds the key to the problem of 0 violence. They claim that 0 aggressive behaviour is a universal human trait left over from the ancient struggle to survive. Therefore, these researchers believe that the proper question to ask is not how an individual becomes violent, but rather, how 0 most people are trained to act peacefully in 0 society.

In 0 most people, the rate of violent acts they commit peaks before they reach the age of 0 three. A research team in Montreal has found that unless 0 damage has occurred to a particular area in an individual's brain, the individual will learn to curb his or her violent behaviour some time around his or her third birthday. 0 Adults and 0 other children teach the child the social and personal costs of acting violently as well as the rewards of acting in a way that is acceptable to the rest of the people around the child.

Chapter 49: Word Order

Exercise 49-1:

1. Is that pizza enough for all of us?
2. Did Henri understand the lesson?
3. Do you have my lab manual?/Have you my lab manual?
4. Will Juanita have finished by the time we return?
5. Can everyone in the room see the screen?

Exercise 49-2:

1. Katrina purchased two lovely Limoges boxes.
2. A comfortable black leather chair appealed to Nils.
3. He patiently waited to bid on it.
4. Unfortunately, we left before it was auctioned.
5. Mario wanted an old wooden table but bought a worn silver spoon.
6. Suchen outbid someone for an interesting round green hatbox.
7. She was extremely delighted to get it.
8. She has often admired such hatboxes.
9. The entire English class bought something except Ingrid. *Or*, The entire English class except Ingrid bought something.
10. Because she brought a small empty purse, she bought nothing at all.

Chapter 50: Prepositions

Exercise 50-1:

1. Others wanted to put the new university in Staunton or Lexington.
2. In 1818, Dalhousie University opened in Halifax, Nova Scotia, the same year as Jefferson's.
3. Jefferson designed his university so that students and faculty lived together in an "academical village."
4. A rotunda building for classes sits at one end of a lawn.
5. On both sides of the lawn are sets of student rooms.
6. Faculty members lived in pavilions between the sets of student rooms.
7. A similar scheme inspired the design of Ontario's Trent University, whose main campus opened in 1966.
8. On your next visit to the University of Toronto, you can stand at a window in the University College Quadrangle and see how that nineteenth-century college was designed with the same idea in mind.
9. On his deathbed, Jefferson included founding the university as one of the three accomplishments for which he hoped to be remembered.
10. Today students at the University of Virginia consider it an honour to live in the rooms that Jefferson designed.

Exercise 50-2A: Answers will vary.

1. Ravi will speak to Walid and explain.

2. First he must fill out all the forms.
3. He must go over all his records to make sure he does not leave out anything.
4. He must then drop off the forms at the registrar's office.
5. Should he hand in the forms without some vital information, the registrar will call him back to get it.
6. Walid will have to look over the forms and find out what is missing.
7. He must not throw away any records until he has finished the procedure.

Exercise 50-2B: Answers will vary.

1. Ravi will speak to Walid and explain.
2. First he must complete all the forms.
3. He must review all his records to make sure he does not omit anything.
4. He must then leave the forms at the registrar's office.
5. Should he submit the forms without some vital information, the registrar will call him back to get it.
6. Walid will have to examine the forms and discover what is missing.
7. He must not discard any records until he has finished the procedure.

Chapter 51: Gerunds, Infinitives, and Participles

Exercise 51-1:

1. They are worried about getting jobs after graduation.
2. They may want to study for the pure enjoyment of learning.
3. They may even dream about being philosophers or writers.
4. However, many parents refuse to support students who lack a definite career goal.
5. They are happy to help their children reach their goals.
6. They resist aiding children who lack direction.
7. Yet reading widely in the liberal arts is one way for students to know themselves.
8. Students of the humanities are the first to see the value of a liberal education.
9. When they hear their parents complain about wasting money, students try to explain their position.
10. They recommend learning about life before training for a specific job.

Chapter 52: Modal Auxiliary Verbs

Exercise 52-1:

1. You may not (present possibility, negative) be aware that Canada's head of state does not live in Canada.
2. We should not (present advisability, negative) forget, though, that in law, the British monarch is Canada's highest political authority.
3. You might have (past possibility) heard the prime minister mistakenly being called the head of state.
4. Laws passed in Parliament must be (present passive necessity) signed, however, by the Queen or her representative, the Governor General.
5. Fortunately, the days when the Governor General used to [or would] (past habit) interfere in government are long past.
6. But as late as 1926, Prime Minister Mackenzie King had to (necessity) leave office when instructed by the Governor General.
7. Do you think we should have (past advisability) changed the Constitution to have the prime minister elected by all voters and not just by voters in one riding?
8. There is no evidence that most Canadians would rather (preference) live under a different political system, however.
9. Still, you have to [or must] (present necessity) admit that it is a strange system.
10. But it is the system that we use, so somebody must have (past probability) guessed that it would work.

NOTES

NOTES